薪
一
传

Keep
the Fire Going

薪一传

Keep the Fire Going

宋子刚

Song Zi Gang

老字号里的药膳传人

Inheritor of a Time-honored Chinese Dietary Therapy Brand

北京市商务局　编

中国轻工业出版社

图书在版编目（CIP）数据

老字号里的药膳传人——宋子刚 / 北京市商务局编. —北京：中国轻工业出版社，2022.1
ISBN 978-7-5184-3737-5

Ⅰ. ①老… Ⅱ. ①北… Ⅲ. ①宋子刚－传记 Ⅳ. ①K825.38

中国版本图书馆CIP数据核字（2021）第229240号

责任编辑：张 弘 谢 兢 责任终审：张乃柬 整体设计：锋尚设计
策划编辑：张 弘 责任校对：宋绿叶 责任监印：张京华

出版发行：中国轻工业出版社（北京东长安街6号，邮编：100740）
印 刷：鸿博昊天科技有限公司
经 销：各地新华书店
版 次：2022年1月第1版第1次印刷
开 本：889×1194 1/16 印张：12
字 数：200千字
书 号：ISBN 978-7-5184-3737-5 定价：280.00元
邮购电话：010-65241695
发行电话：010-85119835 传真：85113293
网 址：http://www.chlip.com.cn
Email：club@chlip.com.cn
如发现图书残缺请与我社邮购联系调换
210889S1X101ZBW

编委会

Editorial Committee

宋子刚个人照

Song Zigang

宋子刚与他的“胶旗”。“熬胶跟炒菜不一样。熬胶需要耐心等待胶慢慢地熬出‘挂旗’，人往往一站就是几小时。‘挂旗’是胶熬好了的标准，熬大了煳，熬小了挂不了旗。”宋子刚解释道。

Song Zigang is making his “gelatin flag”. “Making gelatin is not the same as cooking a stir-fry. It requires patience to wait for the animal hides to slowly become gooey enough, which often takes hours. The ‘flag’ is the measure of well-made gelatin. If the hides are overheated, they will be burnt. If they are underheated, they aren’t gooey enough to make a flag.” Song Zigang explained.

序言

2020年，时疫肆虐。直到秋天，北京的紧张气氛才有所缓和。在这个特殊的时期，我们认识了宋子刚先生，也就是本书的主角。这个时候见面总是免不了聊起疫情，宋先生说他刚给几所医院捐了六吨阿胶、鹿胶，这个数字把我们惊了一跳，最初的访谈就从这里很自然地开始了。宋先生的身份很多元，用他自己的话讲，“是个能说会练的真把式，上得了课堂，下得了厨房，还能做企业管理”。他是一个大厨，更是一位成功的企业家，他所创办的金丰餐饮是当今团餐领域的翘楚，给137家部委单位食堂服务，还为2008年奥运会提供过国际水准的团餐。他恢复的大通饭庄则是目前北京唯一一个以药膳、养生菜为主打菜品的老字号。

药膳是用药材和食材相配制作而成的美食，我国古已有之。早在西周时期，注重食材搭配，按节气调味，用食疗辅助治疗的理念就已经形成，甚至还有负责药膳制作的专职官员——“食医”。经过几千年的发展，现在的药膳炮制综合了中医学、营养学和烹饪学的知识，是一门专业技艺，非系统学习而不能。因此，我们很好奇宋先生的从业经历。通过聊天得知，宋先生的祖上长期从事医药服务行业，绝活是熬胶。在山东德州的运河边上，宋家的药铺和饭铺曾经并足而立，这边儿用驴皮熬胶，剩下来的骨头和肉就配合药材做成炖菜，放在那边儿卖。这种经营模式被后人从山东搬到北京，就有了前门外，以牛羊肉铜锅著称的小吃铺。

从家族继承得来的制药本领，再加上自己的厨师技艺，宋子刚将滋补性的胶药融入日常饮食，创制了大量药膳。并且，他所做的药膳不止供于王谢堂前，还通过团餐、食堂这种平易近人的方式惠及大众。随着了解的深入，我们不禁想问，他到底是如何通晓川、鲁、粤等几大菜系，甚至包括西餐的多种技法呢？他又是如何从厨师变成企业家的呢？他为什么执着地想要恢复家里的老字号呢？

我们带着这些问题和宋先生进行了4次长谈，除了正式访谈之外，我们还受邀参与了几次洽谈生意的饭局。在接触过程中，我们留意到他待人接物没有丝毫“大老板”的架子，并很爽朗地主动讲起：“我就是服务员出身的！”他先是把这归因于曾祖所传下来的家风[1]，又强

1 因为服务出众，宋先生的曾祖父宋相如在1956年被评为全国先进生产者代表。

Preamble

In 2020, the pandemic of COVID-19 ran rampant. It was not until the fall that tensions in Beijing eased. At this particular time, we met Mr. Song Zigang, the protagonist of this book. It's unavoidable to talk about the pandemic when we met at this time. Mr. Song said he had just donated six tons of deerskin gelatin and donkey-hide gelatin to several hospitals, a figure that surprised us, and from there, our interview began quite naturally. Mr. Song has many identities. He is, in his own words, "a true master who can talk the talk and walk the walk. He can take on apprentices, work in the kitchen, and manage a business." He is a chef and a successful entrepreneur. His company, Jinfeng Group, is a leading event caterer today, serving 137 ministries and commissions under the State Council. The company once catered for the 2008 Olympic Games. He revived Datong Restaurant, which is currently the only time-honored brand in Beijing specializing in Chinese dietary therapies and recuperative cuisine.

Chinese dietary therapies, which include a combination of herbs and ingredients, have been used in China since ancient times. As early as the Western Zhou Dynasty, the philosophy of focusing on the combination of ingredients, flavoring according to seasonality, and using dietary therapies to complement treatment has already taken shape. For example, there were even full-time officials responsible for preparing dietary therapies, known as "food doctors" or dietitians. After thousands of years of development, the preparation of dietary therapies now incorporates the knowledge of traditional Chinese medicine, nutrition and gastronomy. It's a discipline that cannot be mastered without systematic study. Therefore, we are curious about Mr. Song's journey in the industry. During the conversation, we learned that Mr. Song's ancestors had long been engaged in the pharmaceutical industry, specializing in making gelatin. Along the canal in Dezhou, Shandong Province, the Songs' pharmacy and restaurant used to stand side by side. The pharmacy made gelatin from donkey hides, and the restaurant made medicinal stews with the remaining bones and meat. This business model was replicated in Beijing by their descendants from Shandong. Hence the restaurant outside Zhengyangmen, known for its copper pot dishes of beef and mutton.

With the pharmaceutical skills inherited from his family and his own skills as a chef, Song Zigang has created many dietary therapies by incorporating nutritional gelatin into everyday dishes. Moreover, his dietary therapies are not only for the gentry, but also for the grassroots population in group meals and eateries. As we learned more about him, we couldn't help but wonder how exactly he came to be versed in different cuisine from Sichuan, Shandong and Guangdong, and even a variety of techniques of Western cuisine. How did he go from being a chef to an entrepreneur? Why was he obsessed with reviving the time-honored brand of his family?

With these questions in mind, we had four long conversations with Mr. Song. In addition to the formal interviews, we were invited to several business dinners. As we got to know him, we noticed that he wasn't "bossy" in any way. For example, he recalled, "I used to be a waiter!" He first attributed the way he conducts himself to the family tradition passed down by his great-grandfather[1], and emphasized that it was his military experience that offered him a wealth of learning opportunities. From hospitality, to culinary arts, to business management, he is a "man made

1 Because of the outstanding service, Mr. Song's great-grandfather Song Xiangru was named the National Representative of Advanced Producers in 1956.

调是服役经历使他获得了大量的学习机会，从服务到厨艺，再到企业管理，他是一个“被部队成就的人”。虽然祖上并没有给他多少言传身教，但家庭遗留下来的行事风格使得他在工作、创业之时，也像药匠们一样专注、用心。这种认真为他带来了丰厚的回报。2008年奥运会之后，他的公司开始向全业态转型，饭庄、团餐、物流公司、厨师学校、工厂基地……形成了一个完满的闭合链条。讲起“药食同源”，他的眼睛灼灼发亮，谈到未来发展，他更是雄心勃勃：“我要把中国食品通过工业化生产带到国外去，宣传药膳文化。”

这是一部为成功企业家所做的访谈，但不同于目前坊间类似题材的口述、传记类文章那样失于细节、千篇一律。我们不仅记录了宋先生的人生经历，还对他家族的历史进行了追溯，试图通过这种细致、系统的叙述来保留一种珍贵并且真实的个体经验。改革开放四十余年，在这一大潮中，成功者虽然很多，但和前赴后继的总体人数相比就显得少之又少。宋先生虽然祖上颇有家学，但无奈同族经过历史的淘洗，到他这一代，仍需要从底层赤手空拳地闯事业，即使入伍给了他很多机会，但曾经当过兵的人又何其之多！为什么只有他成功了呢？[1]

经过我们与宋先生不断地接触与访问，这样几个答案呼之欲出。宋先生是家中老来独子，承继了祖辈的荣光、父辈的殷切期望，在他前进的道路上，始终有着榜样和催促的声音，这赋予他的努力一种使命感，正因如此，他永远是充满着干劲儿。此外，宋先生的创业开始于中国改革的第三个十年，又是2003年“非典”一役之后，北京市开始投入到筹备2008年奥运会的建设之中[2]，私营经济的“春天”再次来到[3]，他的“下海”可谓适逢其时。还必须要说的是：他的个人特质也是成功路上不可或缺的重要因素。他在自己的本行上留心看、用心学，始终保持着旺盛的求知欲。并且，他没有傲气，讲话总是带着谦语，交往中给人赤诚之感，这对他从事餐饮、服务行业无疑是种助力。

宋先生独特的经历给了这本书独特的意义。首先，它留下了一种“匠人精神”“服务精神”隔代传承的记录；其次，它提供了一个顺时应势，在大潮中抓住机遇的案例；最后，或

---

1 在我们过去所做过的口述项目里，一位被访者就曾对军人转业时面临的抉择有番辛辣评论，到底是回到地方当个“小国之星”，还是在北京芸芸人海之中做项事业，这并不是个简单的决定（见定宜庄、苏柏玉：《“文物人”与“人文物”——常人春、常寿春兄弟口述》，北京出版集团2020年版，第417页）。

2 2003年8月16日，北京最后一批“非典型性肺炎”合并症病人康复出院，9月，北京市首届奥林匹克文化节举行。11月召开的中央经济工作会议上明确指出，2004年经济工作的一个重点就是“不失时机深化经济体制改革，向私营经济放宽市场”（参见当代北京编辑部编《当代北京大事记（2003—2013年）》，当代中国出版社2014年第1版，第20页）。东风已来，宋先生又在“非典”时期积累下了口碑与经验，在此时选择“下海”，可谓顺应天时地利人和。

3 改革时期地区政策的调整会给市场形势带来影响，这里所讲的“再次”，意在强调对比和变化。以北京城南大红门一带以服装加工、经营为业发展起来的“浙江村”为例，其人员在1995年被大量清理。但在2006年，丰台区“十一五”规划纲要提出要将此地建设成“四大经济板块”之一和“北京市第六大商圈”，这又给个体经营带来了新的发展商机。

by the army". Although his ancestors did not teach him much by example, the style of conduct inherited from his family taught him to be as focused and attentive as a pharmacist when working and starting his own business. Such conscientiousness has paid off handsomely for him. After the 2008 Olympics, his company began to branch out into other business sectors. His restaurant, event catering, logistics company, chef school and factory base formed a complete closed-off chain. His eyes would sparkle when he talked about "the homology of medication and diet". When discussing his plan for the future, he was even more ambitious: "I want to take Chinese food abroad through industrialized production and promote the culture of Chinese dietary therapy."

These are interviews of a successful entrepreneur. But unlike dictations, biographies and articles on similar topics, these are detail-oriented and unique. We have not only documented Mr. Song's life stories, but also retrospectively traced his family's history in an attempt to preserve a precious and authentic experience of an individual through this meticulous and systematic account. Over the past forty years of Reform and Opening-up, there have been many achievers riding the wave, but they are merely a small part of those who ventured ahead. He was born into a knowledgeable family, who were long gone in the vicissitudes of time. By the time he came of age, he had to start from scratch. Undoubtedly, his military experience has opened doors for him. Of all the veterans, why was he the only one who made it? [1]

Through our interviews with Mr. Song, the answers become clear. As the only son of his old parents, Mr. Song was expected to carry on the glory of his forefathers. In his upbringing, he always had role models to look up to, which gave him a sense of mission. For this reason, he has never been more motivated. He started his own business in the third decade since China launched the Reform and Opening-up. After the SARS outbreak in 2003, Beijing initiated the construction for the 2008 Olympic Games[2], bringing another prime opportunity for the development of the private enterprise[3]. His timing of starting a business couldn't be more perfect. It's worth mentioning that his personality traits are an essential and vital contributor to success. He has always been a keen learner in his own line of work. He has no arrogance. When he talks, he always has a sense of modesty and sincerity, which definitely helped him in the catering and hospitality industry.

Mr. Song's unique experience gives the book meaning beyond comparison. Firstly, it's an account of craftsmanship and service spirit that skipped a generation in Song's family. Secondly, it provides an example of jumping on the bandwagon and seizing the opportunity. Finally, and perhaps more revealingly, it suggests how we can play to our strengths and take a different path of development. Mr. Song repeatedly talked about one of his family's

---

1 In the oral project we have done in the past, an interviewee once had the pungent comment on the choice faced by the military personnel when they retired from the army. To return to be a "small country star" in the local area or to make a career in the midst of Beijing is not a simple decision to make (See Ding Yizhuang and Su Baiyu, *"Heritage Man" and "Human Cultural Relics"- Dictation of Chang Renchun and Chang Shouchun*, Beijing Publishing Group, 2020, Page 417).

2 On August 16, 2003, the last group of SARS patients in Beijing were discharged from hospital after their recovery. In September, the first Beijing Olympic Culture Festival was held. At the Central Economic Working Conference held in November, it was clearly pointed out that one of the key points of economic work in 2004 was to "lose no opportunity in deepening the reform of the economic system and liberalizing the market to the private sector "(See *Chronicle of Events in Contemporary Beijing (2003-2013)*, Contemporary China Publishing House, 2014 (1st Edition, Page 20). Faced with the opportunity, with the accumulated word of mouth and experience during "SARS", Mr. Song chose to "venture into business", which can be said to follow the trend.

3 The adjustment of regional policies during the reform period would have an impact on the market situation. The words "once again" here are intended to emphasize contrast and change. Take "Zhejiang Village", which developed from garment processing and management in Great Red Gate in the south of Beijing, as an example, its personnel were cleaned up in a large number in 1995. However, in 2006, Fengtai District's "11th Five-Year Plan" outline proposed to build this area into "one of the four economic plates" and "Beijing's sixth largest business area", which brought new development opportunities to the individual business again.

许也是更有启示性的，它提示我们如何发挥自身长处，走出一条别开生面的发展之路。宋先生反复在访谈中讲起他家的一条家训：“尊古不泥古，创新不失宗”，配合他的故事来看，更能体会出其中的深意。

我们将这些访谈的内容编成了六个部分：第一章记述了宋氏一族和大通药铺、大通饭庄的早年历史；第二章回顾了宋先生在部队学习各种知识、研发菜品的生活；第三章着眼于他创业之初的日子；第四章谈药膳和老字号的发展；第五章请宋先生总结了自己在企业管理、发展方面的心得，以及对未来的展望；第六章介绍了宋先生研发的几道经典菜品的制作方法。此外，为便于读者参考，还制作了宋先生的个人年表附于书后。

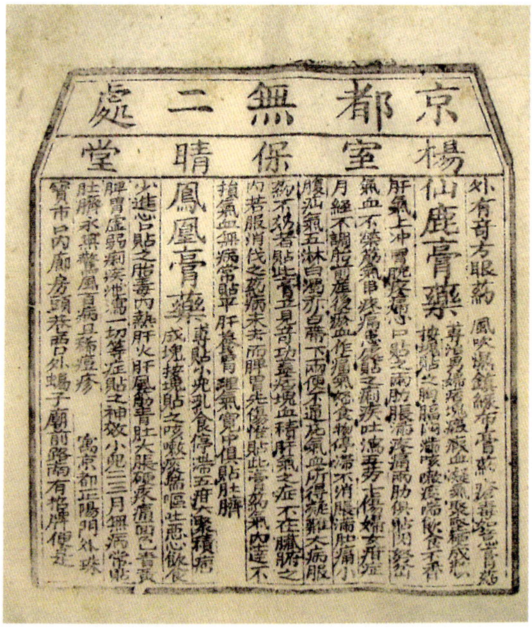

宋氏胶药门前世宋杨室（字保睛），首创仙鹿膏与凤凰膏，经宋氏历代门人传承，其医方记录在清宫脉案中

Song Yangshi (courtesy name: Baojing), the former generation of the Song Family's Gelatin Medicine Sect, pioneered Xianlu Ointment and Fenghuang Ointment, which were inherited by the disciples of the Song Family through the ages, and their prescriptions were recorded in the Imperial Palace Medical Records of the Qing Dynasty

宋子刚恢复并经营故宫“御膳房”多年，他主理的24节气宫廷养生宴席（鹿全席、出征壮行宴、凯旋庆功宴、状元及第宴等）受到中外食客的好评

Song Zigang has restored and operated the “Yu shan Restaurant” of the Forbidden City for many years. His 24 solar terms palace health banquets (deer full feast, expedition banquet, triumphal celebration banquet, champion and first banquet, etc.) have been well received by Chinese and foreign diners

mottoes in the interview: "Respect the past without rigidly adhering to it, innovate without losing the tradition". When viewed in the context of his story, one can better appreciate the profound meaning of it.

We have arranged these interviews into six parts: Chapter 1 recounts the early history of the Song family and the Datong Pharmacy and the Datong Restaurant; Chapter 2 traces Mr. Song's life in the army learning diverse knowledge and developing recipes; Chapter 3 looks at the beginning of his business; Chapter 4 talks about the development of Chinese dietary therapy and time-honored brands; Chapter 5 summarizes Mr. Song's experience in business management and development, and his vision of the future; Chapter 6 introduces some classic dishes developed by Mr. Song. In addition, a personal chronology of Mr. Song has been created and attached at the end of the book for readers' reference.

国家卫生部原副部长陈啸宏（中）、世界中餐业联合会食药养生委员会主席邵刚（左一）与宋子刚合影留念。陈啸宏副部长为大通御德堂题写牌匾

Group photo of Chen Xiaohong (middle), former Vice Minister of the Ministry of Health, and Shao Gang (first from left), Chairman of the Food and Drug Health Committee of the World Federation of Chinese Catering Industry, and Song Zigang. Vice Minister Chen Xiaohong wrote a plaque for Datong Yu De Tang

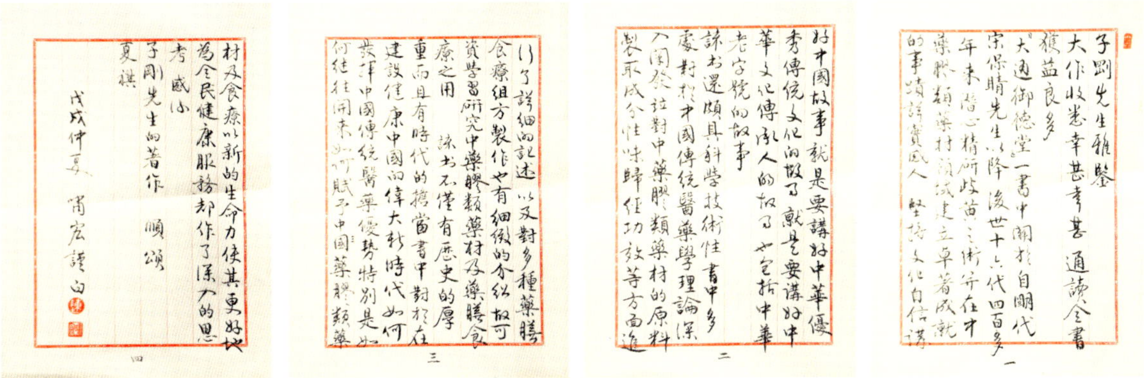

国家卫生部原副部长陈啸宏为宋氏胶药门《中国鹿胶》题序

Preface to *The Songs' School of Medicinal Gelatin* by Chen Xiaohong, former vice minister of the Ministry of Health

目录

Contents

宋氏先祖所创保晴堂在京经营久泰药栈、御德堂，其所制作的“御厨膳茶”专供皇室使用。包括“御”字牌宫廷银针茶、宫廷梅片贡茶、宫廷普洱茶膏、宫廷人参茶膏、宫廷桂花茶膏、宫廷龙井芽茶、宫廷永安砖茶

Baoqing Tang, created by the ancestors of the Song family, operates Jiutai medicine store and Yude Tang in Beijing. The “imperial kitchen meal tea” produced by it is exclusively used by the royal family. Including Court Yinye tea, Court Meipian tea, Court Pu’er, Court Ginseng tea, Court Osmanthus tea, Court Longjing green tea, Court Yongan brick tea

第一章

Chapter 1

祖上与传承

Ancestors and Heritage

【访谈者按】 2020年10月21日，我们在北海仿膳饭庄与宋先生初次见面。席间闲聊时间虽然不长，但已使我们对宋家的曲折经历产生了很大兴趣。宋先生的曾祖父宋相如曾经在同仁堂任“查柜”[1]，有口述资料特别提到，当“查柜”有三个基本条件：熟悉医药业务，有管理知识，还得被资本家看得起[2]，用现在的话说，就是“复合型人才”。他们内外兼顾，德高望重，其他职工见面要尊称一声“老先生”，也是很多民众心中可以信赖的坐堂大夫。同仁堂还有一种特别的生产方式，叫作“一角活”，即每人仅需负责一项工作，做精、做专，以此来提高生产效率，保证产品质量。我国的中医药有八种主要剂型：丸、散、膏、丹、酒、露、汤、锭。宋氏家族的不同支脉就是各自负责不同的活计，有的做丹，有的做丸，有的做散，而宋子刚这一脉，专做膏方中的胶类[3]。

宋先生是父母的老来子，三岁就随着家族远徙塞北苦寒之地，全家靠父亲在煤矿下井维生。一次意外事故导致父亲骨折，在物资、医生急缺的环境下，是祖上传下来的医药技艺让父亲恢复了行走能力。从此，宋家治红伤的名头在当地越传越响，方圆几百里的人都来寻医问药。宋先生就在这种耳濡目染的环境下长大，但他的父母早年并没有和子女讲述家族的历史，他是在12岁返乡探亲时，才开始对老家有了认识。机缘使他无法从事祖祖辈辈传承下来的医药行业，却给了他充分的条件来发展由药铺衍生出来的老字号饭铺。由于相隔时间太远，宋先生对祖上和家族的记忆很模糊，但即使一知半解，他对家风和信念的传承却是始终如一的，这也对他后来的事业发展起到了很大作用。这部分访谈提供了宋家的早年历史，我们对宋先生的最初了解也是由此开始的。

---

1 “查柜”是同仁堂特有的一个职位，他们主要负责监看售药、查问账房、考核人事、接洽生意，以及进买药材等。

2 参考定宜庄、张海燕、邢新欣：《个人叙述中的同仁堂历史》序言，北京出版社2014年版。

3 胶在成药中主要起两个作用，一是辅助复合药材成型，二是滋补，例如阿胶养血滋阴，鹿胶温肾助阳。

[Interviewer's Note] We first met with Mr. Song at the Beihai Fangshan Restaurant on October 21, 2020. Despite the short casual conversation during the meal, we were intrigued by the many ups and downs that the Songs had gone through. Mr. Song's great-grandfather, Song Xiangru, used to work as a "*chagui*"[1] (store manager) at Tong Ren Tang. According to verbal accounts, being a "*chagui*" required three essentials: familiarity with the business of medicine, knowledge of management, and the appreciation of entrepreneurs.[2] In modern parlance, a "*chagui*" is a versatile talent. They were well-balanced and well-respected. Other employees respectfully addressed them as "old masters" For many people, they were trustworthy resident doctors. Tong Ren Tang had a special system for the division of labor known as "*yijuehuo*". That is, each employee was responsible for only one task so as to improve production efficiency and ensure product quality. There are eight main dosage forms of traditional Chinese medicine: pill, powder, ointment, pellet, liquor, dew, decoction and tablet. The clans of the Songs specialized in different kinds of products. Some made pills, some pellets and some powders, while Song Zigang's family specialized in making gelatin, a type of ointment.[3]

Song was born into the family when his parents were old. At the age of three, he moved with his family to the remote north of the country. The entire family relied on his father's work in a coal mine to survive. An accident left Song's father with a fracture. In a time when supplies and doctors were scarce, it was the medicinal skills passed down from his ancestors that restored his father's ability to walk. From then on, the Songs became a local legend for treating injuries, and people from the surrounding areas came to them to seek medical care. Although raised and nurtured in such a positive environment, Mr. Song wasn't aware of his family's history until he returned to visit his family at the age of 12. Fate prevented him from practicing medicine, which had been practiced by his ancestors for generations. However, he was well-positioned to establish a restaurant derived from the time-honored pharmacy. Because of the great lapse of time, Mr. Song's memories of his ancestors and his family are hazy. But even though he knows vaguely about his family, he has consistently carried on the family traditions and beliefs, which have contributed much to his career later on. These part of interviews talks about the early history of the Songs, from which we first learned about Mr. Song.

1 "chagui" (store manager) was a special position at Tong Ren Tang, mainly responsible for supervising sales of drugs, checking the account room, personnel assessment, contact business, and purchase of medicinal materials.

2 Refer to Ding Yizhuang, Zhang Haiyan, Xing Xinxin: *The History of Tong Ren Tang in Personal Narratives*, Beijing Publishing House, 2014.

3 Gelatin mainly plays two roles in the patent medicine. One is to assist the compound medicine to shape and the other is to nourish. For example, donkey-hide gelatin nourishes blood and yin, deerskin gelatin warms the kidney and nourishes yang.

宋氏胶药门

云程：你们家生产什么中药？

宋子刚（以下简称“宋”）：我们家做胶属于世袭制。没出五服的子弟里，专门熬胶的人不能做丹，做丹的人不能做丸，做丸的人不能做散。

杨原（以下简称“杨”）：所以您这一家只能做胶是吗？

宋：对，我和我父亲、我爷爷都只能做这个。要是都做，叔叔大爷不就打架了吗？我父亲原先老跟我说我们家药店在台基厂那儿，挨着太医院。但是现在台基厂那儿都拆了，咱也不知道到底在哪儿。

杨：太医院就在天安门广场东，确实是挨着台基厂。

宋：我是服务员出身，曾是人民大会堂的特三级服务员。我们部队所在单位大裁军解散后，我本想回家熬家药，但因为没有资质，做不了。

杨：您父母都会看病？

宋：我们家熬膏药治红伤——比如胳膊腿折了、砸坏了这些外伤——属于独一方。小时候，方圆七八百里都认识我爸妈。我妈还替小孩、妇女和不孕不育者看病，比如男同志不育或者女同志不孕，她就用补益医方给他们补气血，调理身体。男同志吃鹿角胶、女同志吃阿胶，这是我们家的两个拳头产品，特别好使，成功率应该有70%~80%。打仗或者是干力气活的，就吃牛胶、羊胶和龟胶。还有鱼鳔胶，就是花胶，调理脾胃还补肾，治胃病特别好使。山西的醋胶，这个很少有人知道，心血管病可以用它扩张血管，起清道夫的作用。茶胶是茶熬出来的膏，现在一般人都说不喝浓茶，实际上，过去大部分人喝的都是浓茶，尤其在内蒙古地区。树胶，比如，桦树皮会在夏天的时候裂开，树胶顺着树皮往外淌，可以治糖尿病、高血压。还有鹿胶、桃胶、羊胶、蜂胶、黑骨胶（就是黑色的食材集中在一起熬出来的胶）、龟胶、牛胶、枣胶、鳖甲胶……我们恢复了一些方子、创新了一些方子，蜜柚胶清肺就是我们新创制的方子。我就是做胶，再用胶类制菜，因此跟其他餐饮有很大的区别。以前宫廷里的胶都是单一配方，没有复合配方，我们家的所有东西也都是单一配方，拿出来一个就能起到很强的滋补作用。

The Songs' School of Medicinal Gelatin

Yun Cheng: What kind of traditional Chinese medicine do you make?

Song Zigang (hereinafter referred to as "Song"): We make gelatin in a hereditary system. Among the descendants within five generations, those who specialize in making gelatin are not allowed to make pellets, those who make pellet are not allowed to produce pills, and those who make pills are not allowed to make powders.

Yang Yuan ("Yang"): so your family are only allowed to make gelatin, right?

Song: Yes, my father, my grandfather and I can only make gelatin. If we make anything else, the system will be disrupted. My father used to tell me that our pharmacy was located on Taijichang Street, next to the Imperial Academy of Medicine. But now everything has been demolished, so we don't know exactly where it is.

Yang: The Imperial Academy of Medicine is just east of Tiananmen Square, and indeed next to Taijichang.

Song: I started out as a waiter, I was a special third-class waiter in the Great Hall of the People. After our unit was disbanded, I wanted to go home and make medicine. But because of the lack of medical qualifications, I can't do that.

Yang: Your parents know medicine?

Song: We brew poultices for treating injuries, such as broken arms and legs, of which the recipes are exclusive to our family. When I was a kid, my parents were well known throughout the area. My mother also diagnosed pediatric diseases, gynecological diseases, and fertility issues. For example, she prescribed medical remedies to tonify the *qi* (a vital force believed to form part of any living entity in traditional Chinese medicine) and blood of men and women who were infertile. Antler gelatin for men and donkey-hide gelatin for women are two of our most sought-after products, which are particularly effective in improving pregnancy, with a success rate of 70%~80%. For soldiers and laborers, we recommend bovine-hide gelatin, sheepskin gelatin and tortoise-shell gelatin. And isinglass, also known as *huajiao*, which is obtained from the dried swim bladders of fish, is particularly effective in treating gastric diseases, and also tonifies the kidneys. Vinegar gelatin, which comes from Shanxi, is known to few. It can be used to treat cardiovascular diseases. It can dilate blood vessels, dubbed the "scavenger in the blood vessels." We also have tea gelatin, which comes from brewed tea. Although we don't drink strong tea anymore, most of our ancestors did, especially in Inner Mongolia. We also have gum, a viscous secretion of trees. For example, the bark of birch trees in summer would crack open and gum would trickle out of it, which can be used to treat diabetes and hypertension. We also have deerskin gelatin, peach gum, sheepskin gelatin, propolis and "black bone gelatin," which is literally black. We also have tortoise-shell gelatin, bovine-hide gelatin, silver berry gum, turtle-shell gelatin and so forth. We've recreated some of the old formulas and innovated some of the new formulas. For example, the honey pomelo pectin is a lung cleanser, and this is our newly created formula. We are quite different from other caterers and our products are not the same, such as pastry and other dishes. In the past, the imperial palace created single-ingredient formulas rather than compound formulas. So did we. Any of our products is an effective tonic.

杨：您家的胶是属于滋补类的？

宋：对，我们家的药不是治疗类，而是补益和长寿类。[1]讲究未病先治，要是等有病了再吃，就来不及了。

苏柏玉（以下简称“苏”）：胶和膏是什么关系？之间有什么区别呢？

宋：凝聚成块的、纯的叫胶，膏则在胶的基础上添加了其他原料。我父亲曾在扎赉诺尔下矿时被砸断了脚和胳膊，伤筋动骨在家休养了很长时间。母亲就上山采旱三七——负责结骨，再去集上买马鹿和龟，买回来后，在家将这些原料熬成膏药，贴在父亲腿伤的地方。后来我才知道，那会儿父母熬的就是现在所说的龟鹿二仙膏，鹿胶加上酒、旱三七、鸡蛋清，再用鹿皮糊上、鹿筋捆上。一个月左右，父亲就能下地了，母亲继续拿酒天天帮他揉搓腿和胳膊，两个多月后就慢慢好了。从那以后，谁家摔断了胳膊、腿都会来找我们家治。就是回山东老家，也有很多人找我妈看病。

杨：你们家熬药的时候用高度酒，而不用黄酒吗？

宋：那时候不像现在交通发达，山里面哪儿有黄酒？只有我妈酿的高度酒、杂粮酒。我姥姥、姥爷，包括大舅都在山东开烧锅、酿白酒，后来我们家出事，我姥姥家也跟着一起受连累，全家搬到了辽宁昌图开酒坊。直到现在我大舅和我哥哥还在那儿开酒坊，我大舅专门负责烧酒。黄酒和白酒也是药，关键时候酒能起到很好的消毒、消炎、提神的作用。过去部队打仗，没有药消毒，都是用酒。现在我们生产的养生酒，一般都是用五年、八年的花雕黄酒，不用现做的、勾兑的黄酒。

杨：您现在使用陈酿黄酒，过去家里使用白酒，到底哪种更好呢？

宋：肯定是黄酒更好，度数太高的酒不能做药，再说喝起来都是酒味也不行。但过去为了给自己治病没有办法。我妈自己做的酒，最高度数能达到68度。我爸病好后，一口酒都不碰，就是因为我妈一天两遍地用酒捋我爸，他被熏着了。

苏：您母亲怎么知道能用酒帮助您父亲治疗？

宋：我父亲告诉她的。我特别敬佩母亲，她有一个绝活，一般人都做不

---

1 补益类医方有八珍糕、八仙糕、定升糕、定胜糕、状元糕、千叟糕、保元固本膏、龟鹿二仙膏、平肝清热代茶饮、噙化三宝（鹿胶、人参、灵芝）、扶元和中膏、加减扶元和中膏、扶元益阴膏、加减扶元益阴膏。长寿类医方有凤凰膏、仙鹿膏、益寿膏、益寿膏又方、延年益寿膏、培元益寿膏、菊花延龄膏、太乙紫金锭、玫瑰纯露、鹿角盘散、全鹿膏（宋子刚注）。

Yang: The gelatin you make is mostly tonic?

Song: Yes, they aren't therapeutic, but tonic and good for longevity. [1]Traditional Chinese medicine puts a premium on "zhiweibing," which means preemptive treatment of diseases. It believes that if we start the therapy after one falls ill, it's already too late.

Su Boyu (hereinafter referred to as "Su"): What is the relationship between gelatin and ointment? What are their differences?

Song: Gelatin is pure and coalesced into lumps, and ointment is made by adding other ingredients to the gelatin. My father broke his foot and arm when mining in Zhalainuo'er, and spent a long time at home recuperating. My mother picked "*hansanqi*" (Panax pseudoginseng Wall. var. notoginseng) in the mountains, which helps to strengthen the bones, and then bought red deer and tortoises from the market, which she made into a poultice at home and applied to my father's injured leg. Later I learned that what she made is now known as "Guilu Erxian Ointment". It's made from deerskin gelatin plus liquor, *hansanqi* and egg white. To treat an injury, the ointment should pasted on deer skin and then strapped on with deer tendons. After a month or so, my father was able to walk. My mother then rubbed his arm and leg with liquor every day. It took more than two months for him to recover. From then on, anyone who broke an arm or leg would come to us for treatment. Back home in Shandong, more people sought medical advice from my mother.

Yang: When making medicine, did they use spirit (strong drink) instead of *huangjiu* (yellow wine)?

Song: Transportation back then was not as developed as it is now. There was no *huangjiu* in the mountains. My mother made spirits and mixed-grain spirit herself. My grandma, grandpa and my mother's eldest brother all worked in Shandong brewing *baijiu* (a colorless liquor). Then a mishap befell my family and my grandma's family was implicated. So, they moved to Changtu, Liaoning, and opened a distillery. To this day my mother's eldest brother and his son still run the distillery there, with the former specializing in distilling. *Huangjiu* and *baijiu* have excellent effects of disinfection, anti-inflammation and refreshment when medicine is unavailable. In the past when soldiers had no medicine to disinfect their wounds, they used liquor. We now usually produce recuperative liquor with five- or eight-year-old *huangjiu*, instead of the ready-made, flavored one.

Yang: Which is better, the aged *huangjiu* you use now or the *baijiu* your familia used to keep at home?

Song: *Huangjiu* is better for sure. Those of extremely high alcohol content cannot be used as medicine because of their pungent smell. But in the past, we had no better options. The alcohol content of the liquor my mother made herself can be up to 68%. After my dad recovered, he wouldn't take a sip of liquor. It's because my mom rubbed his injury twice a day with liquor, and he was smothered by the smell.

Su: How did your mother know that she could use liquor to treat your father's injury?

Song: My father told her. I couldn't help but respect my mother for reaching down into the fire

1 Eight-Dainty Cakes, Eight Immortals Cake, Promotion Cake, Victory Cake, Scholar Cake, Thousand Old Cake, Gelatin Ointment, Guilu Erxian Ointment, Pinggan Qingre Clearing Heat Tea, Qinhua Sanbao (deerskin gelatin, ginseng, ganoderma), Fuyuan Hezhong Ointment, Jiajian Fuyuan Hezhong Ointment, Fuyuan Yiyin Ointment and Jiajian Fuyuan Yiyin Ointment are tonic. Fenghuang Ointment, Xianlu Ointment, Yishou Ointment, Yishou youfang Ointment, Yannian Yishou Ointment, Peiyuan Yishou Ointment, Chrysanthemum Yanling Ointment, Taiyi Zijin Tablet, Rose Dew, Deer Horn Powder and Deer Ointment are good for longevity (Note by Song Zigang).

到。手下到火里，把酒抓上来。我试过很多次，都抓不上来。我们家治红伤，先在铜洗脸盆里倒三四两高度酒，拿火点着后，我妈就用手把酒抓上来开始给人搓，直到酒搓没了，再拿膏药一贴。因为有些受伤的地方会肿起来个大包，必须用酒搓开。有的人疼得嗷嗷直叫，但过后就好了。

杨：您之前说过家里的医术不传给女性。

宋：不传。但因为父亲病了，如果不让母亲治，就只能等死，在这种情况下他才把医术传给了母亲。另外，父亲比较内向，不愿意说话，母亲则不一样。所以平时都是母亲看病，父亲制药。

苏：您的父母教过您怎么看病吗？

宋：没有刻意教过。那时候农村的房子就只有一个大通铺，晚上睡觉的时候弄个木板往中间一摞，姐姐她们睡一边，我和父母睡另一边，等到了早上就把木板收起来，放在房梁上。因此来了病人，我也没地方去，只能在旁边坐着看、坐着听，我就是这样一点一点地学习父母的医术。很早的时候，我就知道我们家做驴肉、驴胶不是熬，而是蒸，蒸不存在熬煳的问题。我们那的冬天特别冷，11月就下雪。我们就用木头烧起大火，一边取暖，一边蒸胶。驴皮、鹿皮拿来之后，切好放在盆里，上锅一蒸就是多少天，蒸完后皮全化开了，都是纯的胶。然后我妈再拿木锤子捣碎，分装成一小袋，悬挂在房梁上。我们住在山底下，出门就是林子，当时还用木耳、蘑菇、黄芪、党参熬胶，但这些做的比较少，主要还是鹿胶、阿胶。醋胶是晒出来的，我现在也还做。

杨：您家里是怎么用胶入菜的呢？

宋：我们家自己常用的方子是用胶熬粥。[1]以前条件不好，舍不得这么吃。后来条件好了，我姐做饭的时候就会往里搁点母亲用木锤子捣碎的胶，现在已经形成了习惯。在我小时候，父母也会用胶入菜替病人调理。曾经有两口子吵架生气后，觉得身上没劲来找我妈，我妈就让他们在我们家住两天，用萝卜和胶一起炖成菜给他们吃，吃几天就好了。我妈有自己的理论：生气得先用萝卜顺气，再用胶补上。后来我们家有一款菜特别受欢迎——在所有菜中排第五位——叫牛胶萝卜，萝卜通气、牛胶强筋骨，而且炖得烂糊糊，老少皆宜。在给养老院的配餐中就有这道，特别受老同志欢迎，运动员也特别喜欢。我妈还用捣碎后的萝卜籽、韭菜籽和鹿胶、阿胶混合，治疗不孕不育。

1 粥是药膳的一个重要组成部分。明《本草纲目》中记载药粥62方，《普济方》中有180方，清代曹慈山所著《养生随笔》，专收适合脾胃虚弱的老年人食用的药粥100方。

and taking up the liquor with her bare hands. It's mission impossible for ordinary people. I have tried many times to do the same but all of my attempts have failed. To treat injuries, we first pour three to four *liang* (150g~200g) of strong alcohol in a copper washbasin, and light it up. Then my mother will take up the liquor with her bare hands and start rubbing it on the injuries. When the liquor is all gone, she will apply a plaster. For some people, their injured spots will swell up and must be rubbed with liquor to subside. Some of them will wail in pain, but they will be all better afterwards.

Yang: You said earlier that your family doesn't impart medical skills to women.

Song: No, we don't. But my father was injured and he could only face death if my mother wasn't allowed to treat him. Therefore, he passed on his medical skills to my mother. In addition, my father was an introverted man of few words, whereas my mother was the opposite. Usually my mother treated the patients and my father made the medicines.

Su: Did your parents teach you how to treat patients?

Song: No special teaching. At that time, we only had a large bunk in the house. When it's bedtime, we put a board in the middle. My sisters slept on one side while my parents and I slept on the other side. In the morning, we put the board away on the beam. When my parents treated patients, I had no place to go, so I sat and watched them. In this way, I learned little by little. When I was very young, I already learned that we made donkey-hide gelatin by steaming instead of boiling them, steaming wouldn't have the problem of getting them burnt. It was so cold in winter in the countryside that it would snow in November. We would make a blazing fire with firewood to keep ourselves warm while steaming the animal hides. We cut up the donkey hides and deer skin, put them in a pot and steamed them for a few days. After the steaming, they all dissolved and became gelatin. Then my mother pounded it with a wooden hammer and hung it from the beams in small bags. We lived at the foot of the mountains, surrounded by woods. At that time, we also made a few gelatin from fungus, mushroom, Astragalus membranaceus and Codonopsis pilosula. But we mostly made deerskin gelatin and donkey-hide gelatin. We made vinegar gelatin by drying vinegar in the sun, and I still do it now.

Yang: How do your familiar cook with gelatin?

Song: A common recipe in our family is making gruel with gelatin. [1]We used to be poor and couldn't afford to do so. As our life got better, my elder sister would add a bit of the gelatin that my mom made into the dishes, now it has become a habit. When I was a child, my parents would also cook with gelatin to take care of patients. Once a couple felt strengthless and weak after they fought with each other. My mother had them living in our house and fed them with stewed turnips and gelatin. After a few days, they got better. My mother's theory was that to treat anger, we should first regulate the *qi* with turnips and nourish the body with gelatin. Later on, one of our dishes became exceptionally popular, ranking fifth among all the dishes, which is called the Turnip Stew with Bovine-hide Gelatin. Turnip helps regulate the qi and bovine-hide gelatin strengthens the muscles and bones. Moreover, the stew is so mushy that both the young and the old can enjoy it. This dish is included in the meals we serve in nursing homes and is particularly popular with the elderly. Also athletes are particularly fond of it. My mother also mixes mashed turnip seeds and leek seeds with deerskin gelatin and donkey-hide gelatin to treat infertility.

1 Gruel is an important part of Chinese dietary therapy. In the *Compendium of Materia Medica* of the Ming Dynasty, 62 recipes of medicinal gruel were recorded, 180 recipes were recorded in Prescriptions for Universal Relief, and 100 recipes of medicinal gruel suitable for the elderly with weak spleen and stomach were collected in the Essay on Health by Cao Cishan in the Qing Dynasty.

杨：其实各种物质都能产生胶。

宋：对，比如说银耳、木耳熬化了，可以做素胶。制药的时候，要把原料融合在一起，就放素胶来修合，相当于身体里的黏合剂、修复剂。鹿，上品六兽之首。鹿胶的第一个作用就是补益身体、强筋健骨；第二个就是补肾、温肾、壮阳，男女皆宜。后来我父亲半身不遂，就是吃鹿胶的药养好的，不仅又能走了，80多岁还能上齐齐哈尔赶集，60多里地，你不让去都不行，他们要去集市上买药材。但是我家搬到富拉尔基后，改烧煤，就没有了熬胶的条件，再加上他们年纪大了，也干不了熬胶的活儿。父亲常说要是年轻的时候不干力气活儿，他应该能活一百岁。

苏：大家族叔辈兄弟有的做膏、有的做丸、有的做散……您对具体哪一支做什么有了解吗？

宋：有两支做散和做丸的去了台湾省，还有一拨做药酒的在贵州，但是对不上号，也找不着人。我太爷爷宋相如行三，我爷爷有九个孩子，我父亲应该是最小的，父亲比母亲大了10岁。我是家里的老来子，上面有五个姐姐。母亲在57岁的时候生了我，通常女人到了这个年纪很难怀孕生子，我妈能生下我跟胶离不开关系。我妈80多岁的时候，没有一个人说她像80多岁。

苏：您父亲跟您说过他的学艺经历吗？

宋：父亲对北京特别熟，他年轻的时候就跟着我祖父往返于山东和北京。那会儿我们家在台基厂有个九泰药栈，在山东老家熬好了胶，就送到那儿分货。我们家的胶是给皇上吃的。

杨：您之前说在同仁堂坐堂的老大夫是谁呢？

宋：我太爷爷从宫里太医院出来后，就在同仁堂坐堂。[1]我父亲后来也想让我当医生，他不让我做饭，觉得做饭是不务正业。我跟他思想不同，认为做食品比做药还好。药食同源，能把餐饮做好、把药膳做好、把大通饭庄做好，就能把这一套传承下来。

苏：您父亲从小对您管教很严格？

宋：我父亲是个讲究人，讲究高低之分，非常注重礼数。我从小就在这种环境中长大，家里虽然穷，穿的衣服不大好，但父母都特别干净。

---

1 关于宋子刚的太爷爷宋相如，其早年经历没有多少文字见载，家庭内部口传下来的记忆也因父辈的忌讳心理，加之时间久远，模糊而不可考。《个人叙述中的同仁堂历史》中，同仁堂的老职工贾荫生说宋相如原来在南京，是乐笃周带到北京来的（第121页），也为一说。

Yang: In fact, many things can be made into gelatin or gum.

Song: Yes. For example, snow fungus and black wood ear can be simmered and made into vegetarian gum. To fuse the ingredients together when making medicine, we often use vegetarian gum. It's equivalent to an adhesive and repair agent in our body. In traditional Chinese culture, deer is considered the most important of the six beasts—elk, deer, bear, water deer, boar and rabbit. Deerskin gelatin is known for tonifying the body, strengthening the muscles and bones, tonifying the kidneys, and strengthening the yang, making it suitable for both men and women. My father was in poor health and partially paralyzed. It was deerskin gelatin that made him able to walk again. My parents still went to the market in Qiqihar in their 80s, which is over 30km away. I couldn't stop them from going because they wanted to buy herbs there. After my family moved to Hulan Ergi District, where coal was used for cooking, we had no more facilities for making gelatin. In addition, my parents were too old to work. My father used to said that if he hadn't been working hard when he was young, he would have lived to be 100 years old.

Su: Some of your uncles in the extended family make ointments, some make pills, some make powders ... Do you have any knowledge of which clan makes what?

Song: There are two clans making powders and pills went to Taiwan Province, and another clan making medicinal wine was in Guizhou. However, I couldn't match the clan to the specialty, and I couldn't find anyone. My great-grandfather Song Xiangru was the third oldest. My grandfather had nine children, and my father must have been the youngest, and he was 10 years older than my mother. I was born when my parents were old, with five elder sisters. My mother gave birth to me at the age of 57. Usually women cannot have children at such an age. It's the gelatin that worked wonder for my mother. When my mother was in her 80s, no one said she looked like it.

Su: Did your father ever talk about his experience of studying medicine?

Song: My father was particularly familiar with Beijing. When he was young, he followed my grandfather around and they traveled back and forth between Shandong and Beijing. At that time, our family had a Jiutai pharmacy in Taijichang. When our family finished making gelatin, we delivered it there for distribution. Our family's gelatin was for the emperors.

Yang: Who was the doctor that you said was resident at Tong Ren Tang?

Song: After my great-grandfather retired from the Imperial Academy of Medicine, he worked at Tong Ren Tang.[1] Later, my father also wanted me to practice medicine and wouldn't let me cook, thinking that it was not a proper job. I held a different view from his, believing that making food is better than making medicine. Medicine and food come from the same source. If we manage to cater well, improve the Chinese dietary therapy, and keep Datong Restaurant running well, we will be able to carry on the legacy.

Su: Your father was very strict with you since childhood?

Song: My father was a man of honor. I was raised in an environment where he was extremely conscious of manners. Although we were poor and dressed modestly, our parents were exceptionally neat.

---

1 As for Song's great-grandfather, Song Xiangru, his early experiences were not recorded in many words, and the memories passed down by mouth in the family were not examined because of the taboo psychology of the parents and the long time. In *The History of Tong Ren Tang in Personal Narratives*, Jia Yinsheng, an old worker at Tong Ren Tang, said that Song Xiangru once lived in Nanjing and was brought to Beijing by Le Duzhou (page 121).

我们家的老字号

宋：在德州武城和故城中间有一条运河，水流特别宽阔，形成了一条通达的水道。最早的时候，我们的药铺和饭铺就在这条运河边上。制作阿胶需要杀驴，驴皮拿去熬胶，剩下的肉和骨头等杂碎就拿到饭铺，用带把儿的小铜锅（形状类似现在的砂锅）熬成牛杂、羊杂，再到市集上跟人换东西。我们把换来的白菜、萝卜、豆腐搁到肉里炖，这就叫铜锅宴。铜锅火上来得特别快，铜锅炖肉的味道跟普通锅炖的不一样。当时的山东巡抚孙宝琦还给我们家题了“大通饭铺”的招牌，现在我对铜锅宴进行了恢复。

杨：您家大通饭铺有药膳的传统吗？

宋：大通饭铺拥有悠久的药膳传统。头一天晚上杀完驴后，我们用八珍料（八种药材配制的料）提前把肉腌制好。第二天，洗干净骨头下锅里煮，汤熬到一半的时候，撇掉上面的浮沫，把腌制好的肉放进去，一起煮两个小时左右。一般早上三点开始煮，煮到五六点钟，赶集的人就来了，这时候再往里放入提前洗好、腌制好的驴内脏（肠、肝、心等）接着煮。煮熟后把汤捞到另外一个锅里，放上萝卜、白菜、豆腐再一起炖会儿。客人来了就给切点肉、切点肝、切点肠搁碗里头，旁边有汤，再配上黑蜜枣、黑酱菜，还有白饽饽、白馒头。这就是“三黑三白”这道菜的起源。我们家的老汤保存了很多年，每次杀完驴直接把棒骨放里面，循环使用。

杨：这是你们家的传统做法吗？

宋：这是从清朝传承下来的烹饪方式，逐渐形成了我们家族独特的饮食文化。我们家清朝的时候就开始在山东养驴熬胶，做好后再送去北京的药栈卖。后来我们家族一支负责熬牛胶、羊胶的分支，发现北京的牛比较多，就根据山东武城县驴肉铜锅的模式，在北京复制出牛肉铜锅、羊肉铜锅。

苏：您父亲经营过这个饭铺吗？

宋：我爷爷经营过山东的饭铺，叔叔经营过北京的饭铺，而父亲主要负责熬胶。我父母还做过跑棚，就是在红白喜事上做饭。我的炒鸡蛋就是跟父亲学的，他把跑棚拿回来的鸡蛋放到大锅里和葱花一起翻炒，我在旁边帮忙烧火，他一边炒一边告诉我怎么做才更好吃。我母亲则会炸油条（类似现在的炸糕），

Time-honored Brand of Our Family

Song: Between Wucheng and Gucheng in Dezhou there is a canal, which flows particularly far and wide, creating an accessible waterway. In the very beginning, our pharmacy and restaurant were located along the canal. Making donkey-hide gelatin requires the slaughter of donkeys to obtain the hides. The remaining variety meats and bones were taken to the restaurant to be boiled in small copper pots (similar in shape to the modern casserole), and then traded for something at the market. We stewed the exchanged cabbage, radish and tofu in the meat, which is called a copper pot feast. Copper pots heat up especially fast. The stews that we made in it quite different from those made in ordinary pots. Sun Baoqi, the then grand coordinator of Shandong, inscribed the signboard "Datong Dinning House" for our family, and now I have renewed the copper pot feast.

Yang: Is making dietary therapy a tradition of Datong Dinning House?

Song: Yes, it's a time-honored tradition. For example, on the first night, after slaughtering a donkey, we marinated the meat in advance with eight kinds of ingredients (herbs). The next day, we washed the bones and cooked them in a pot. When the soup was half boiled, we skimmed off the froth on top and put the marinated meat in and cooked it together for about two hours. The cooking usually started at three o'clock in the morning and at five or six o'clock, when the fair-goers gathered, we then added the donkey offal (intestines, liver, heart, etc.) that had been washed and marinated in advance and continued to cook them. Once we finished the cooking, we put the soup into another pot and added turnips, cabbage and *tofu* and stewed them together for a while. For customers, we cut up meat, liver and intestines and put them in a bowl. We then served the soup, accompanied by black candied dates, black pickled vegetables, white pastry and white steamed buns. Hence the origin of the "three black and three white" dishes. Our soup stock has been stored for many years. After slaughtering the donkeys, we put the bones directly into it, and the stock was used repeatedly.

Yang: Is this a tradition in your family?

Song: This is a way of production passed down in my family from the Qing Dynasty, which has developed into a culinary style. Our family started to rear donkeys and make gelatin in Shandong during the Qing Dynasty, and then transported them to Beijing for sale. Later on, another clan of our family making bovine-hide gelatin and sheepskin gelatin found that beef was abundant in Beijing, so started to sell copper pots of beef and sheep in Beijing according to the way of donkey meat pot in Wucheng County, Shandong Province.

Su: Did your father run this restaurant?

Song: My grandfather ran a restaurant in Shandong, my uncle owned another one in Beijing, and my father is mainly responsible for making gelatin. My parents also used to cater for weddings and funerals. I learned how to scramble eggs from my father. My father would put the eggs from the wedding and funerals into a large pot with chopped scallions, I helped with the fire while he cooked and showed me how to make it tasty. My mother would deep-fry dough sticks, which are similar to the fried cakes of today. They are particularly delicious when filled with bean paste and honey.

里面搁上豆馅儿和蜂蜜，特别好吃；用红糖和麻子油炸糖裹儿，就是现在的糖油饼；用阿胶做阿胶枣。我们家的饭铺是当时镇上唯一的饭铺，省领导吃过后觉得不错，认为不能叫饭铺，就改名叫饭庄了。但当时的菜品远不如现在丰富，卖的都是跟驴有关的东西，驴头、驴肉、驴腱子、驴板肠……搁药材酱成熟食，叫八珍驴肉。

后来我对铜锅宴进行了恢复与改革，撤掉了一些我认为在制作过程中没必要添加的药材。比如八珍驴肉放了八样东西，但牛肉就只放三四样。因为我在国际饭店学过西餐，接触、了解了不同的东西。方子永远都在变化，以适应不同时代的不同人群。直到今天，顾客对我们的菜肴评价很高的重要原因就在于：我在调整的过程中，针对不同的原料，采用了不同的调料，这跟我父亲之前的"一成不变"不同。这也与我们家的家训"尊古不泥古，创新不失宗"相合。

苏：您记忆中是什么时候第一次听说家里的故事？

宋：12岁。我记得特别清楚，当时要分家，我跟父母坐了四天半的车回到武城县和故城县交界的山东老家。之前我对老家一点印象都没有，那次回去一看，老家是个四进院带园子的大院。跟父母去上坟，祖坟里有五六个坟头，父亲烧纸，得拿纸往坟上面搁。后来叔叔、大爷来讨论分家，我就在桌上听着。有时候分不均，大爷、叔叔还有姑姑会为镇上的生意而争吵，我就是从那时候开始知道我们家的饭铺和药铺。我们在山东本地的家族很庞大，记得我结婚的时候一共来了300多人，我根本认不全，母亲就在旁边给我介绍这些人是谁。

苏：您家现在还有亲戚做这些事吗？

宋：他们后来有的去了新疆种地，有的去了山区，干的都跟医药没有关系，就我一个人还在做这个。最开始父母也不跟我说家族的事情，后来我开始做药膳，跟家族的过去重新建立起了联系，他们觉得我能继承家业才告诉我这些事情。

杨：您父亲的手艺就一直搁着了？

宋：我父亲过去在河东卖油条，姑姑在河西卖。叔伯去世前，把这套东西全写下来传给了儿子，他儿子靠炸油条供出了两个大学生。我父亲自认为有文化，可以靠脑子记住，就没有写下来。半身不遂后，虽然他的身体机能得到了恢复，但脑子还是受到了影响，说话慢，记忆也不行，就把家里的手艺都忘了。等我条件慢慢好起来，那会儿我爸都80多岁了，才开始跟我讲家族的历史，父母总跟我说咱家的东西你可别忘记了。记得有一年回家过年，父亲一直

Deep-fried sweet balls, which are sweetened cakes made with brown sugar and sesame oil. She also would make dates with donkey-hide gelatin. At that time, their business was the only restaurant in town. Later, the provincial leadership tried their dishes and thought they were great, so my parent expanded their business and renamed it as a restaurant. But back then there was no such a wide variety of dishes as now. All of them were things of donkeys only, such as donkey head, donkey meat, donkey tendon, and donkey intestine. With herbs they were marinated into deli, called the Eight Dainties of Donkey Meat.

I later restored and reformed the copper pot feast by removing some herbs that I thought were unnecessary to put in the process of seasoning donkey or mutton. For example, the Eight Dainties of Donkey Meat has eight ingredients, but the beef only has three or four. This was because I had studied Western food in international restaurants and was exposed to different materials. The recipes are always changing to suit different times and different people. An important reason why our customers rate our dishes highly today is that I use a variety of seasonings for different ingredients in the process of adjustment, unlike my father's principle of "one size fits all". This was also in line with our family motto, "Respect the past without rigidly adhering to it, innovate without losing the tradition."

Su: When was the first time you can recall hearing about the stories of your family?

Song: When I was12 years old. I remember it particularly well. When our big family had to split up, I rode for four and a half days in a car with my parents back home in Shandong, right at the border of Wucheng and Gucheng counties. I had no memory of my hometown before. That time I went to my hometown and saw that there was a house with four courtyards. I visited the graveyard with my parents. There were five or six graves in our ancestral grave, and my father burned ancestor money on the top of a grave. Later, when my uncles came to discuss about dividing up family property and living apart, I listened at the table. There have been squabbles in the process, and my father's brothers and sisters would dispute over their businesses in the town. That's when I first learned about our family's restaurant and pharmacy. We're a humongous family in Shandong. I remember when I got married more than 300 people turned up and I couldn't recognize them all, my mother introduced them to me.

Su: Do your relatives still engage in the business?

Song: Some went to Xinjiang to farm their land, some went into the mountains. They all switched to other jobs, and I'm the only one still doing this. In the beginning my parents didn't mention anything about our family. It was until I reconnected with my family's past and opened a restaurant that they told me. They though I could carry on my family's legacy.

Yang: Has your father's craft been lost?

Song: My father used to sell fried dough sticks on the east side of the river, and my aunt sold them on the west side of the river. Before he died, my uncle passed on the craft of making dough sticks to his son, who managed to raise two kids until they graduated from college. My father didn't write it down because he thought he was educated enough to remember it. Later on he was partially paralyzed. Although he recovered physically, his brain was still somewhat affected. He stumbled over his words and forgot all that. As our livelihoods improved, my father started to tell me the history of our family when he was in his 80s, my parents would always remind me not to forget my family's legacy. I remember one year I went home for the Chinese New Year, my father kept talking to me until the middle of the night. I told him I had to go to bed because it's too late and I was in a daze. I later regretted it because my father died the next year. My father once asked me whether

拉着我讲到下半夜，我困得迷迷糊糊，什么都记不住，就去睡觉了。后来我很后悔，因为第二年父亲就去世了。父亲还曾经让我去同仁堂寻找认识我们家族的人和我们家族的东西，但他其实是想让我去同仁堂找一份工作。等我去的时候，人家说我们家的东西都已经捐给了同仁堂，不能再要回去，而且他们也没办法让我在同仁堂工作。虽然没办法给我任何承诺，但他们对我还是特别客气，因为同仁堂里很多人都是我太爷爷的徒孙，只是有些人愿意承认，有些人不愿意，像金世元就尊我太爷爷为师祖。

杨：您是通过什么部门跟金世元取得了联系？还是您早就认识他？

宋：金世元是享受国务院政府特殊津贴的专家，也是国医、国药双大师，既会看病，又会做药，一般人见不到，是同仁堂的领导帮我们牵的线。第一次去他们家的时候，他就跟我说："过来，咱俩盘盘道。"他担心我的身份是假的，想同我聊一聊家族根源。当时的国药集团党委书记邵钢陪我一块去的，我说那就盘盘吧。金世元问宋相如住在北京什么地儿？我答在北京海淀。他一听就说："嗯，这个靠谱。"又问我鹿胶熬的是什么胶？我答一个黄毛胶，一个青毛胶。黄毛胶就是梅花鹿，青毛胶就是马鹿。他接着问在哪儿能弄到？我答大兴安岭和新疆伊犁，这两个地方的原材料最好。听到这儿他就相信我真的是宋家传人。金世元告诉我黑龙江四医堂有当年最好的梅花鹿鹿胶。后来我俩越聊越投机，他问我都会熬哪些胶？我就跟他讲鹿胶、阿胶、素胶、龟胶、桃胶、仙霞胶……他觉得很惊讶，我竟然还知道仙霞胶。我说我们家是胶药门的，父亲经常给我讲这些东西，但是有的我会做，有的我不会做，我想重振家族的胶药。他又问我为什么来找他？我说您是同仁堂里最清楚我们家历史的人，是我们家族的见证者。金世元告诉我当时他也只能仰视我太爷爷，没办法跟我太爷爷学习。因为那会儿同仁堂还施行等级划分的学徒制，他年纪太小，不能跟着我太爷爷学习。但他希望我能把胶发扬光大，因为现在会做胶的人已经很少了，同仁堂里会的人很少，全国就更少了。金世元觉得我想把胶做成食品的想法很好，这样受众面更广。过去普通老百姓吃不到胶，现在做成食品，能更好地发挥胶的补益身体、强筋健骨、修复软组织等功效。所以他给我写了幅字："国宝补品之冠，皇家御牌鹿胶"。

in Tong Ren Tang there were people who knew about our family and whether Tong Ren Tang still had anything from our family, but he actually wanted me to find a job in Tong Ren Tang. When I visit Tong Ren Tang, they said all the things from our family had been donated to Tong Ren Tang. It's impossible to get them back. Also, I couldn't get a job there. Although they couldn't promise me anything, they treated me kindly. Many employees there are once apprentices of my great grandfather, which some of them acknowledged, and some of them didn't. For example, Jin Shiyuan called my great grandfather the "grandmaster."

Yang: Did you get in touch with Jin Shiyuan through any authority? Or did you know each other a long time ago?

Song: Jin Shiyuan is an expert enjoying the government special allowance of the State Council, and also the nationwide renowned TCM master well versed in treating patients and making medicines. He never meets with anyone ordinary. It was the leadership of Tong Ren Tang who introduced me to him. The first time I went to his house, he said to me, "Come and let's talk about our roots." He wanted to talk to me about my roots and was afraid that my identity wasn't real. Shao Gang, the then secretary of the CPC Committee of Sinopharm, went to Jin's home with me, so I agreed to Jin's request. Jin asked me where Song Xiangru lived in Beijing. I said in Haidian. He was satisfied with my answer. And then he asked what kinds of deerskin gelatin there were. I replied there were *huangmao* gelatin and *qingmao* gelatin. *Huangmao* means the skin of sika deer and *qingmao* means that of red deer. He then asked where to get them. I replied that one is the Daxinganling region and the other is Yili Kazakh Autonomous Prefecture in Xinjiang. These two places offered the best raw materials. Hearing this he was convinced that I was really a family member of the Songs. Jin Shiyuan told me that the Four pharmacies in Heilongjiang produced the best gelatin made from the skin of sika deer. The more we talked, the more we got to know each other. He asked me what kind of gelatin I could make. I said that I could make deerskin gelatin, donkey-hide gelatin, vegetarian gum, tortoise-shell gelatin, peach gum, *xianxia* gelatin, etc. He seemed surprised that I knew about *xianxia* gelatin. I said that I came from a family making medicinal gelatin and gum for generations and my father has taught me how to make them. However, I could only make some of them and I wanted to restore the past glories of medicinal gelatin and gum. He then asked why I came to visit him. I replied that he was the person who knew the best about our family in Tong Ren Tang and he bore witness to the history of our family. Jin said that back then he could admire my great grandfather from afar and couldn't become one of his apprentices. At that time, because of the apprenticeship in Tong Ren Tang that divided apprentices into different classes, Jin was too young to be my great grandfather's apprentice. However, he had hoped to carry on the legacy of medicinal gelatin and gum. Only few people today can make them in Tong Ren Tang and China. Jin thought my idea of making medicinal gelatin and gum into food was great, which would introduce them to more people. In the past, the common people had no access to such "luxury". As gelatin and gum are made into food, we can bring into play their efficacy of nourish the body, strengthening bones and muscles, repairing soft tissue and tonifying the kidneys. Jin then inscribed "Deerskin gelatin—gem of Chinese tonic once used by the imperial court" for me.

1915 年，御德堂御牌贡鹿胶获巴拿马万国博览会金奖

In 1915, Yu De Tang Imperial Deerskin Gelatin won the Gold Medal of the Panama-Pacific International Exposition

宋子刚与金世元

Song Zigang and Jin Shiyuan

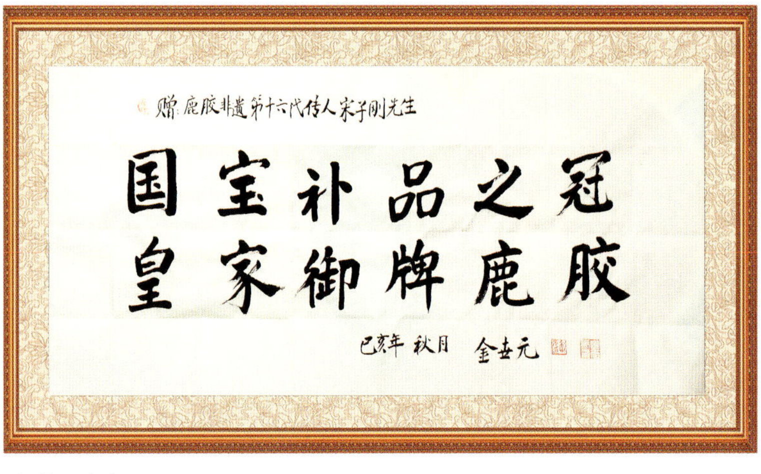

金世元为宋子刚题词

Inscription for Song Zigang by Jin Shiyuan

宋子刚父母宋泽清（右）、王桂兰（左）

Song Zigang's parents Song Zeqing (righe) and Wang Guilan (left)

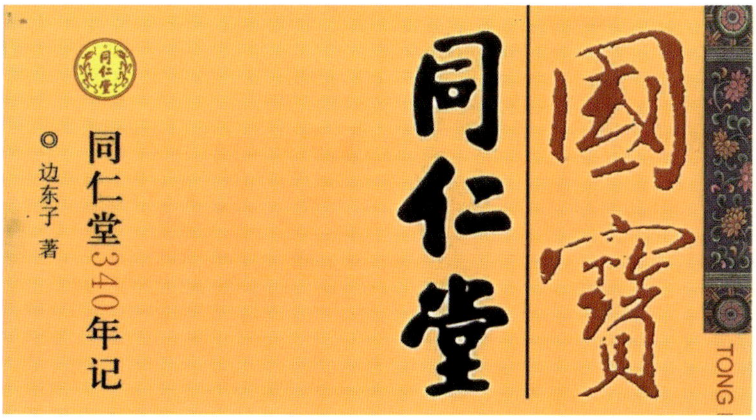

店里的领导还告诉老人说："老宋同志曾经是 1956年出席全国先进生产者代表大会的代表呢，北京市一共只有十七名代表。不简单啊！此外，他还是1957年的北京市劳动模范，光荣啊！"

老人听了连连鼓励自己的女儿，在同仁堂好好干，也要争当劳动模范。他还感叹说，怪不得不认识同仁堂了，同仁堂变化太大了。

新时代的劳动模范，同仁堂药店的"老查柜"宋相如在接待顾客（1962）

摘自人民日报出版社出版的《国宝同仁堂》

Excerpted from "The National Treasure—Tong Ren Tang" published by *People's Daily press*

宋相如（一排居中）在同仁堂的合影

Song Xiangru (center a row) is Group photo in Tongrentang

宋相如在接待顾客

Song Xiangru was receiving customers

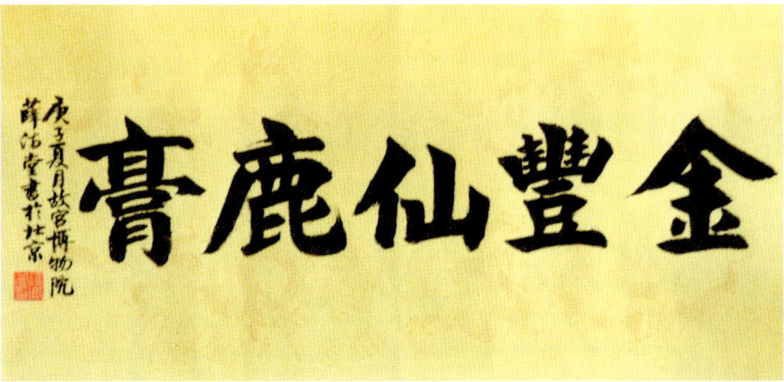

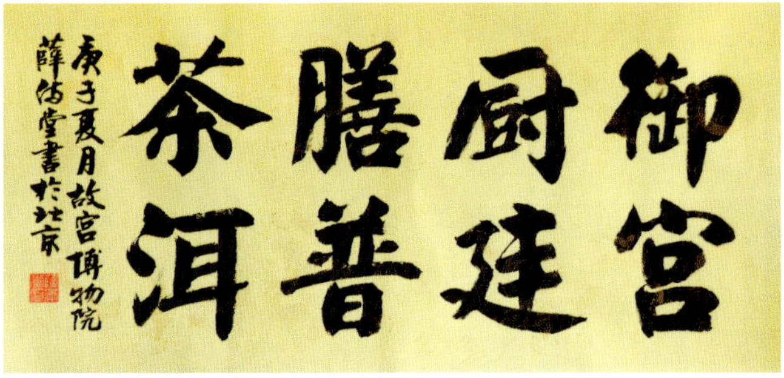

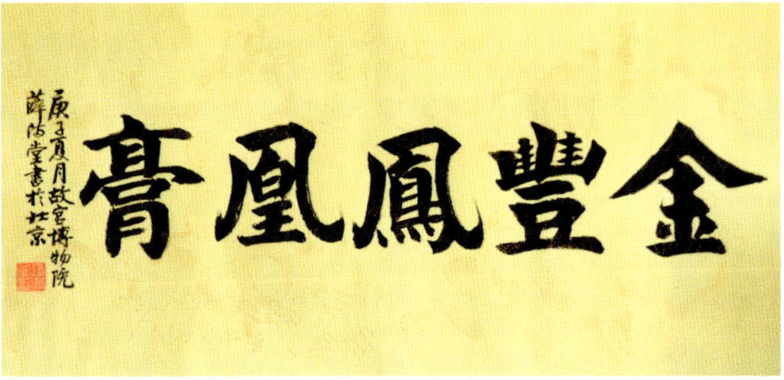

宋子刚在故宫“御膳房”主理时，著名书法家、画家、雕刻家薛满堂题写了“金丰仙鹿膏”“金丰凤凰膏”“宫廷普洱”

When Song Zigang was running the “Yushan Restaurant” in the Forbidden City, Xue Mantang, a famous calligrapher, painter and sculptor wrote inscriptions for “Jinfeng Xianlu Ointment” “Jinfeng Fenghuang Ointment” “Court Pu’er”

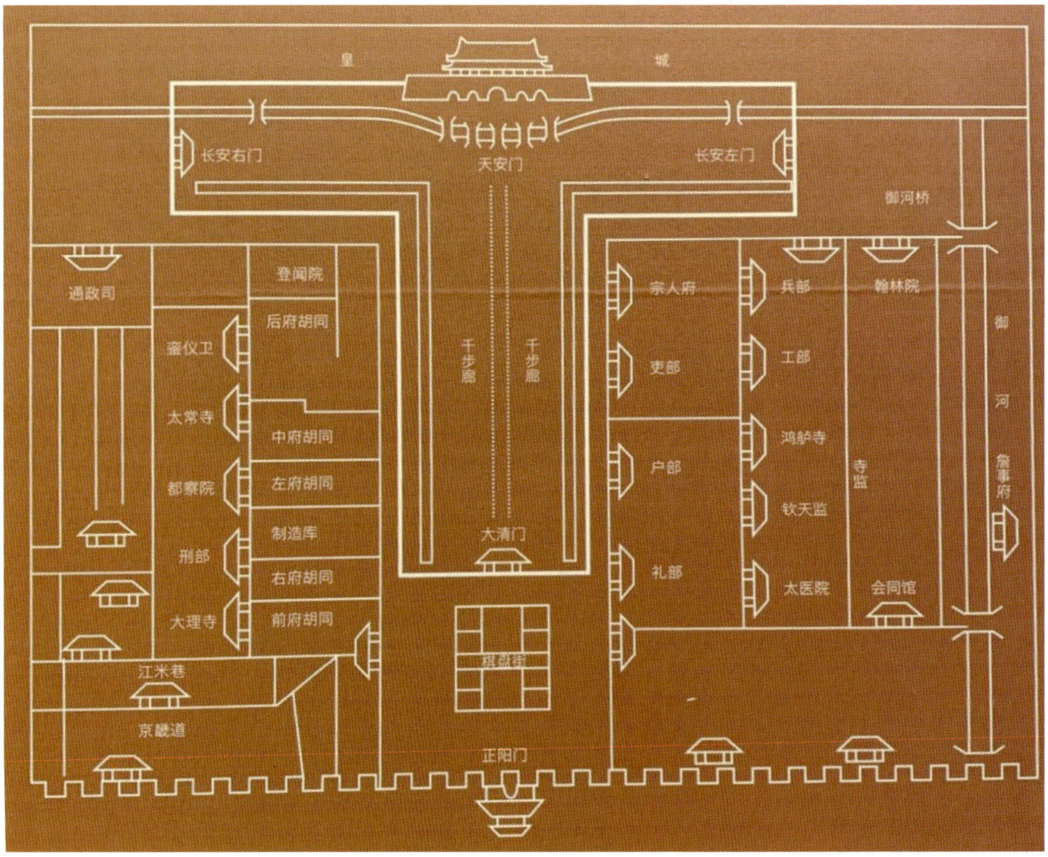

清朝时期五府六部示意图[1]

The Five Chief Military Commissions and Six Ministries during the Qing Dynasty[1]

---

1 杨原摄于首都博物馆“探秘北京中轴线”展览。
“Exploring the Central Axis of Beijing”, shot by Yang Yuan, at the exhibition at the Capital Museum.

第二章

Chapter 2

现代厨师的养成

The Making of a Modern Chef

【访谈者按】宋先生在16岁时入伍当兵。即使年龄尚幼，他已经显现出了一些成功所必需的个人品性：认真负责、求知欲旺盛、好学肯干。他在前线获得首长的赏识，被调到北京做警卫员。相比于侦察兵，这种岗位的隐性要求更高，但能接触到的东西、可以学习的机会也更多。宋先生很快就被提拔成了干部，还被送到大专院校攻读学位，但他没有像一般人那样安于现状，而是主动地要求学习更多知识。除了系统掌握食品加工、旅游烹饪、营养配餐等专业知识，他还在工作之余留心地看、认真地钻研人民大会堂、北京饭店、宽沟招待所、钓鱼台国宾馆各个顶级餐饮单位的菜式和服务。他的闲暇时间主要用来实践新学的菜肴，并将自家传下来的胺药和不同菜系的手法、味型相结合，炮制、创造、调整和试验各种药膳。这些勤学苦练的日日夜夜，可以说是他后来事业能够迅速成功的基石。这部分访谈主要是宋先生对他青少年时期的记忆，也包含了他对自己烹调知识来源的总结和对各种菜系的认识。[1]

走上烹饪之路

宋：我的一生中，餐饮可以分为三个阶段。从1984年到1998年是起步阶段。我最早接触到餐饮是在1984年，那会儿我在部队边看边学习做菜，也是从那时开始，把我们家里的东西一点一点地进行恢复、应用。

苏：您为什么去当兵？

宋：1967年，我3岁的时候跟随父母从山东德州武城县宋塘庄下放到了扎赉诺尔。1979年，国家征了两次兵，明确规定要在山东、河北、四川、湖南、江西、湖北等地进行大面积征兵。村里按花名册画钩，那时候没有电话，就跟我们发电报说你们家孩子要去当兵。我父母听后乐坏了，带着我坐了四天火车才到德州，一下车我就直接被武装部接管了。

1 需要特别加以说明的是：我们为了更好地体现这些内容对宋先生研发药膳的影响，没有严格地按照目前通认的菜系对章节内容进行编排，而是采取了他本人对不同菜的分类方式，这种编排考虑也是出于本书重在追溯被访者的学艺之路。中国目前通认的主要菜系有八种，即鲁菜、川菜、粤菜、苏菜、闽菜、浙菜、湘菜、徽菜。但本书中所讲到的“国宴菜”包含了其中多种菜系，“宫廷菜”则不被这八种菜系所收录。

[Interviewer's Note] Mr. Song enlisted in the military when he was 16 years old. Even at a young age, he already demonstrated some of the personal characteristics necessary for success: conscientiousness, intellectual curiosity, and willingness to learn. He was appreciated by a senior officer at the battlefront and was transferred to Beijing as a security officer. Compared to scouts, such positions are more implicitly demanding. But they also offer significantly greater access to things and opportunities to learn. Mr. Song was soon promoted to the position of cadre and was also sent to a junior college to pursue a degree. Instead of being content with the status quo, he took the initiative and sought to learn more. In addition to systematically acquiring professional knowledge of food processing, catering for tourists and nutrition, he also attentively studied the dishes and services of various top catering establishments such as the Great Hall of the People, Beijing Hotel, Kuangou Guesthouse and Diaoyutai Guesthouse after work. He spent most of his free time working on his newly learned dishes and concocting, creating, adapting and experimenting with various medicinal dishes by combining the medicinal gelatin and gun handed down from his family with the techniques of different cooking styles. These days and nights of diligent study and training were arguably the cornerstones of his subsequent rapid career success. These part of interviews focus on Mr. Song's memories of his teenage years, but also encompass the summaries of the sources of his culinary knowledge and his knowledge of different cooking styles. [1]

Embarking on a Journey of Culinary Excellence

Song: My experience with culinary arts in my life can be divided into three phases. From 1984 to 1998 was the initial stage of catering in my life. I was first exposed to catering in 1984, learning as I watched in the army. It was also from that time that I restored and applied what we did at home little by little.

Su: Why did you join the army?

Song: In 1967, when I was 3 years old, I moved down from Songtangzhuang, Wucheng County, Shandong Province to Zhalainuo'er District with my parents. In 1979, China drafted soldiers twice, specifying that large-scale conscription to the front was to be carried out in Shandong, Hebei, Sichuan, Hunan, Jiangxi and Hubei. In our village, we selected candidates according to a roster. In those days, there were no telephones, so they telegraphed us that your children were going to be soldiers. My parents were so happy to hear this that they took me on a four-day train ride to Dezhou.

1 It should be noted that, in order to better reflect the influence of these contents on Mr. Song's research and development of medicinal dishes, we have not arranged the contents of the chapters strictly according to the currently recognized cuisines. Instead, we adopted his own classification of different dishes, and this arrangement is also due to the book's focus on tracing the path of the interviewee's learning skills. At present, there are eight main cuisines recognized in China, namely Shandong cuisine, Sichuan cuisine, Guangdong cuisine, Jiangsu cuisine, Fujian cuisine, Zhejiang cuisine, Hunan cuisine and Anhui cuisine. The "state banquet cuisine" mentioned in this book includes a variety of cuisines, and the "palace cuisine" is not included in the eight cuisines.

1980年1月，我在云南马关待了七个月。后来因为所在部队集体立了三等功，我得以在前线加入了中国共产党。当时装备部部长去视察时，我正好在指挥部，他觉得这小孩挺好，就把我带到了北京。到北京后，我被分到了位于京西宾馆的经营局，在那儿待了不到三天，又把我派到了红安招待所，钓鱼台国宾馆我也待过挺长时间。部队在全国有八大接待处——棒棰岛、秦皇岛、庐山、五指山……都是部队疗养的地方，我们就是在这些地方工作，经营五星级酒店，要不我哪能学到这么多东西？

苏：您在红安招待所主要做什么呢？

宋：在首长家做了一段时间的工务员[1]。那时候我还不会做饭，后来才慢慢学的。

杨：什么机缘让您接触到了做饭？

宋：应该是在1987年或1988年，我调到北京提干后，开始接触烹饪。我在景山后边儿待了7年，专门负责首长的饮食保障。首长每个月的饮食计划都得提前上报，报完后我们根据计划给他采购食材、安排制作的厨师。我们还经常去人民大会堂、四川饭店给首长安排宴会。当时有两位厨师叫王锡田和陈松如，经常来我们这儿做川菜，我就是跟他们学的服务和做菜。还有康辉、侯瑞轩、熊四智、彭铭泉、张文海、王旭东，他们分别是钓鱼台国宾馆、人民大会堂、北京饭店、成都同仁堂药膳馆、四川烹饪学校、四川烹饪杂志社的川菜、粤菜、鲁菜、国宴菜、药膳大厨和专家。我经常跟他们接触，就学会了这些，最后我还考了人民大会堂的特三级服务员。

杨：等于您在部队期间一直跟着厨师在学做菜？

宋：厨师到我们这儿做饭，我和他们有了工作接触，也就有了学习的机会。按理说康辉他们做饭的时候，是不让别人进厨房的，但我身穿军装，负责首长的饮食保障工作，首长不管去哪儿吃饭，都需要我们先品尝，“看着”他们就是我的任务，除此之外，还得对菜品、食材、如何烹制等进行详细的询问。

苏：这些大师是怎么教您做菜的呢？

宋：我们不会在炒菜的时候交谈，炒菜的时候我就在旁边看着，一个环节都不落下！我是侦察兵出身，对每个环节的观察和别人不一样。比如：有一次首长想吃油条，我到单位的时候，厨师已经和好了面准备炸油条了，我一看觉

1 这里的工务员是俗语，实际工作的性质类似于警卫员，不少回忆性的文章里，这两个称谓经常混用，都是指给首长提供保障服务的士兵。

As soon as I got off the train, I went straight to the ministry of armed forces.

From January 1980, I spent seven months in Maguan, Yunnan. Later, my unit was collectively awarded the third-class merit, and I joined the CPC at the front. I happened to be in the command when the Minister of the Equipment visited. He found me to be quite a nice kid and brought me to Beijing. After arriving in Beijing, I was assigned to the operation bureau, which was located at the Jingxi Hotel. After staying there for less than three days, I was sent to the Hongan Guesthouse, and I spent quite a long time at the Diaoyutai Guesthouse. There are eight major receptions for our troops nationwide, including Bangchui Island, Qinhuangdao, Lushan, Wuzhishan... These are the places where we are responsible for the convalescence of our soldiers, so we also operated five-star hotels. How else could I have learned so much?

Su: What did you mainly do at the Hongan Guesthouse?

Song: I worked as a clerk in a senior officer's house for a while. [1]I didn't know how to cook at that time, so I learned to do it gradually.

Yang: What inspired you to get into cooking?

Song: I think it was in 1987 or 1988, after I was transferred to Beijing for promotion, that I started to be exposed to cooking. I spent seven years in Jingshan, specializing in catering for a senior officer. His monthly diet was announced in advance, according to which we procured ingredients and appointed chefs for him. We also often went to the Great Hall of the People and the Sichuan Hotel to schedule meals at events for the senior officer. At that time, there were two chefs named Wang Xitian and Chen Songru, who often came to cook Sichuan cuisine, so I learned to prepare meals and cook from them. There were also chefs of Diaoyutai Guesthouse, the Great Hall of the People, Beijing Hotel, Chengdu Tong Ren Tang Medicinal Restaurant, Sichuan Culinary School, Sichuan Cuisine making Sichuan cuisine, Cantonese cuisine, Shandong cuisine, state banquet cuisine, medicinal diet, etc., such as Kang Hui, Hou Ruixuan, Xiong Siji, Peng Mingquan, Zhang Wenhai and Wang Xudong. I learned all this from working with them, and I ended up becoming a Special Class III attendant at the Great Hall of the People.

Yang: So you learned how to cook from chefs during your time in the army?

Song: The chefs came to cook with us, giving the opportunity to learn from them. Usually, they didn't let others into the kitchen when they were cooking. But I was in uniform and was responsible the senior's dietary safety, so keeping an eye on them was my task. No matter where the senior officer went for dinner, we needed to taste the food first and had to make detailed inquiries about the dishes, ingredients, and how they were prepared.

Su: How did they teach you about cooking?

Song: We never talked while making dishes. I watched and learned while they're cooking without missing one step! I started out as a scout, and I observed each part of the process differently than others. For example, on one occasion, the senior director wanted to have fried dough sticks and the chef already prepared the dough by the time I arrived at the unit, I must report to the senior officer. What if the chef had put something in the dough? The senior then instructed me to watch the chef when he's making the dough. So, at four or five o'clock in the afternoon on the day when

1 Clerk is folk adage. The nature of a clerk is guardsmen. In many memorable articles, the two terms are often used interchangeably, referring to the soldiers who provide security services to the senior officer.

得不对，就赶紧回去跟领导汇报——厨师提前把面和好了，我没有看到和面的过程，万一和面的时候往里面搁了东西呢？领导就指示我看着他们和面。这样头天下午四五点钟，厨师和面的时候我就先过去看着。所以首长吃饭，我必须提前两三天过去打前站。保障首长安全是接待处的重点任务，每个细节都必须掌握，不细心不行。我就是这样学会的做菜。

所有接待处的人都明白这一套流程，但只有我愿意去学、愿意去炒。但我不能在人民大会堂炒，只能回我们单位炒。这样我从人民大会堂回来就给平时给首长做饭的老同志、老战士做菜，做完后也得到了领导的肯定和表扬。领导越说好，我就越有干劲，也就越喜欢做菜。

苏：学了这么多菜系，哪一个菜系对您的药膳开发影响最大？

宋：鲁菜、粤菜、川菜、淮扬菜对我影响很深，其中又属鲁菜的影响最大。因为鲁菜中“烧”的烹调方法跟我们做药膳相同，可以说鲁菜是药膳的首要基础。第二个基础是粤菜。我跟康辉学了很多吊汤，也就是熬汤的方法。粤菜中的汤跟鲁菜的汤很不一样，康辉熬的汤比较鲜，领导特别愿意吃。他讲究先上汤、粥，然后再上菜，这也跟别人不一样。还有几个首长是湖北、四川、江西人，他们爱喝瓦罐汤，这也对我的药膳造成了一些影响。第三个影响较大的是跟陈松如学的川菜。粤菜和鲁菜都是咸鲜口，但川菜是辣口，且味型特别多，大概得有一百多种类型，其中我们药膳常用的有十来种。另外，我还跟侯瑞轩学习“精致”，他做的淮扬菜偏清淡、细致。彭铭泉做的药膳没有药味，这也对我后来的药膳影响很大。人民大会堂总厨师长王锡田的菜肴美学，还有他做的大型宴会和团餐，对我日后的团餐管理影响很深。烹饪教授汪荣、熊四智、杨铭铎给我的烹饪理论、营养配餐奠定了坚实的基础。宫廷名师潘喜发、金喜升，则对我的宫廷药膳及宫廷礼仪帮助很大。

跟随康辉学习的粤菜煲汤、国宴接待对我的药膳生涯起了一定作用，康辉去世时我还写了一篇祭文，内容如下：

缅怀恩师康辉——弟子大通御德堂第十六代传人、金丰餐饮宋子刚。

惊闻吾师康辉先生于2020年1月27日仙逝，悲痛疾首，三拜叩首！

尊师康辉曾为毛主席主厨，北京饭店厨师长，俗称“五虎上将”之粤菜泰斗。

康门师训：“先立品，再学艺”，影响了我一生，在此，勉励诸君。

1982年，我在钓鱼台国宾馆跟康辉老师学习粤菜。恩师平易近人、技艺精

he was making the dough, I had to go over there and watched him. Whenever the senior officer had his meals, I had to go there two or three days in advance to keep an eye on the chefs. Ensuring the safety of the senior officer is a key task of the reception office, and every detail must be supervised with great care. This was how I learned to cook.

All the reception staff understood the process, but I was the only one willing to learn. I wasn't allowed to cook at the Great Hall of the People, so I had to practice at our unit. I came back from the Great Hall of the People to cook for the elderly comrades and soldiers who usually prepared meals for the senior officer, and I also received recognition and praise from the leadership. The more praise I received from the leadership, the more motivated I became, and the more I enjoyed cooking.

Su: Having studied so many different cooking styles, which one has had the most influence on your development of Chinese dietary therapy?

Song: Shandong cuisine, Cantonese cuisine, Sichuan cuisine, and Huaiyang cuisine have had a profound influence on me. I was most inspired by Shandong cuisine. Because the cooking method of "roasting" in Shandong cuisine is the same as the way we make dietary therapy, it is fair to say that Shandong cuisine is the primary basis of dietary therapy. The secondary cornerstone is Cantonese cuisine. I learned a lot from Kang Hui about how to make refined broth. The soup in Cantonese cuisine is very different from the soup in Shandong cuisine. The soup Kang Hui made was much tastier, and the leadership was particularly pleased with his soup. He preached serving soup and congee first, and then serving dishes, which was also different from what others did. There are also a few senior officers from Hubei, Sichuan and Jiangxi who loved clay pot soup. It also had some influence on me. The third major influence is the Sichuan cuisine that I learned from Chen Songru. Both Cantonese and Shandong cuisine are salty and fresh. However, Sichuan cuisine is characterized by its spiciness, and there are more than a hundred types of flavors, of which about ten or so are commonly used in my dietary therapy. In addition, I learned how to refined dishes from Hou Ruixuan, whose Huaiyang cuisine was light and delicate. Pang Mingquan's dietary dishes have no medicinal flavor, which also influenced mine later on. The culinary aesthetics of Wang Xitian, the then chief chef of the Great Hall of the People, and how he catered large-scale events, had profound influence on my management of catering later on. Culinary professors Wang Rong, Xiong Sizhi and Yang Mingduo helped prepare me for the theory of gastronomy and dietetic nutrition. The famous palace chefs, Pan Xifa and Jin Xisheng, helped me a lot with palace medicinal dishes and court etiquette.

Learning Cantonese soup-making and state banquet receptions from Kang Hui contributed to my culinary career, and I wrote a eulogy when he passed away, which reads as follows.

In Memory of My Mentor Kang Hui, by Song Zigang, the 16th-Generation Heir to Datong Yude Pharmacy and Jinfeng Restaurant.

I was shocked to hear that my mentor, Mr. Kang Hui, passed away on January 27, 2020. In grief I kowtowed to him thrice!

My mentor, Mr. Kang Hui, was once the chief chef of Chairman Mao and the head chef of Beijing Hotel. He was dubbed the guru of Cantonese cuisine among the "Five Renowned Chinese Chefs".

His motto, "Develop your moral virtues before learning", has inspired me throughout my life. Now, I would like to motivate you with this motto.

From 1982, I studied Cantonese cuisine from Mr. Kang Hui at the Diaoyutai Guesthouse. He is an affable, skillful and versatile chef skilled in French, Sichuan and Shanghai cuisine in addition to

湛、涉猎广泛，除粤菜外，尤擅法餐、川菜、上海本帮菜等烹饪技艺。遇国家重大活动，恩师必被请去人民大会堂主理国宴。

1984年，恩师推荐我去国际饭店学习法餐，使我的烹饪技艺上升到了一个新的高度，您的谆谆教诲仍回响在我耳旁，记忆犹新。

当时，恩师与我的两位老师——北京饭店的黄子云、徐海元，常到我们单位米粮胡同五号和官园儿童中心来献艺。

我向恩师康辉学习的粤菜有：雄鸡破晓、核桃酪、狮头鹅掌鲍花菇、烤比目鱼、明炉烤乳猪、蜜汁叉烧、西餐果味虾球、田园酱等，至今受益匪浅。

1998年7月，我转业时，在人民大会堂广东厅宴请恩师康辉和另外两位恩师——人民大会堂总厨师长王锡田、钓鱼台厨师长侯瑞轩，向三位老师告别。我亲自给三老做菜：阿胶海参、三黑三白、沙葱盐焗鸡、海水豆腐、盘式雕刻——龙马精神。席间，喝了两瓶茅台酒厂酱红瓶人民大会堂特供茅台酒，大家敞开心扉，畅谈国内外烹饪趣事，记忆颇深，使我久久不愿离开……

记得1998年中秋节，我到您家东城区霞公府15号，为您做了一桌饭菜，得到了恩师的亲自指点。当时，您还请了钓鱼台国宾馆厨师长侯瑞轩、北京饭店的叶焕林、罗国荣与周恩来总理的专职理发师朱殿华一起聚餐。我主理的宫廷药膳：八珍糕、阿胶月饼、鹿胶海参、龟胶鱼肚、桃胶雪蛤、大通鹿胶茅台酒、宫廷普洱，得到了您的高度赞扬。

当时，恩师勉励我说："宋子刚，你是个有文化的人，你的老师汪荣教授是我的好朋友。很少有厨师在黑龙江商学院学习过，硕士研究生毕业的就更少，作为祖传御德堂'胶药门'宫廷药膳的继承人，有机会你一定要将其发扬光大……"

那时，您还说："我今年退休也要回老家广东顺德开学校，以便发挥余热，老有所为。"

2019年，我出资捐助北京商委和北京烹饪协会《薪火相传——烹饪名家》系列画册出版时，还建议云程会长为康辉老师编辑出版专属画册，以求将恩师的精湛烹饪技艺发扬光大！

今闻一代烹饪宗师、粤菜泰斗，恩师康辉先生驾鹤西去，吾悲怆地深感惋惜。愿老师一路走好！弟子大通御德堂第十六代传人、金丰餐饮宋子刚将秉承康门师训："先立品，再学艺"，为中国药膳奉献力量！

Cantonese cuisine. Whenever there was a major state event, he would be asked to cater at the Great Hall of the People.

In 1984, he recommended me to study French cuisine at an international restaurant, which brought my culinary skills to the next level. Your teaching still echoes in my ears and my mind.

At that time, my mentor and my other two teachers, Huang Ziyun and Xu Haiyuan from Beijing Hotel, often came to our unit at No.5 Miliang Hutong and Guanyuan Children's Center to cook.

The Cantonese dishes I learned from my mentor—Rooster Crowing at the Break of Dawn, Walnut Cheese, Lion-Head Geese's Feet and Braised Mushrooms in Abalone Sauce, Grilled Halibut, Roasted Suckling Pig, Barbecued Pork in Honey Sauce, Fruity Shrimp Balls, and Ranch Dressing, have contributed to my success to this day.

In July 1998 when I retired from military service, I entertained my mentor Kang Hui and two other teachers, Wang Xitian, the chief chef of the Great Hall of the People, and Hou Ruixuan, the chief chef of Diaoyutai, at a banquet in the Guangdong Hall of the Great Hall of the People to bid farewell to them. I personally cooked for the three of them dishes such as Donkey-hide gelatin with Sea Cucumber, the "three black and three white" dishes, Salt-baked Chicken with Sand Ginger, Seawater Tofu, and a dish with creative decoration called "Vigorous Spirit of the Aged". During the dinner, we drank two bottles of Moutai liquor exclusively available at the Great Hall of the People. We opened up our hearts and shared anecdotes about cooking at home and abroad, which were so intriguing that I didn't want to leave...

I remember that on the Mid-Autumn Festival in 1998, I went to your home at No. 15 Xiagongfu in Dongcheng District and cooked a meal for you. You were gracious enough to comment on the dishes. You also invited Hou Ruixuan, the chief chef of the Diaoyutai Guesthouse, Ye Huanlin and Luo Guorong from the Beijing Hotel, and Zhu Dianhua, Premier Zhou Enlai's personal hairdresser, to a meal together. The palace medicinal dishes that I cooked, such as Eight-Dainty Cakes, Donkey-hide Gelatin Moon Cakes, Deerskin Gelatin with Sea Cucumber, Tortoise-shell Gelatin with Fish Maw, Peach Gum with Hasma, Datong Deerskin Gelatin with Moutai Liquor and Court Pu'er, were highly praised by you.

You encouraged me and said, "Song Zigang, you are a cultured man. Your teacher, Professor Wang Rong, is a good friend of mine. Few chefs ever studied in the Heilongjiang Business School, and even fewer graduated from a master's degree. As the heir to the palace medicinal food of Yude Restaurant, you must carry forward the legacy if you have the opportunity to do so..."

You also said, "I am retiring this year and plan to return to my hometown of Shunde, Guangdong to open a school so that I can make use of my remaining energy and make a difference in my old age."

In 2019, when I funded the publication of the picture album Passing on the Fire—Chinese Culinary Masters by the Beijing Municipal Commission of Commerce and the Beijing Cuisine Association, I also suggested to President Yun Cheng that they edit and publish an exclusive picture album for Mr. Kang Hui in order to pass on his exquisite culinary skills!

Today, I heard that Mr. Kang Hui, a culinary master of his generation and a leading figure in Cantonese cuisine, passed away, and I sorrowfully mourned his death. May your soul rest in peace! As the 16th-generation heir to Datong Yude Restaurant and Jinfeng Restaurant, I will always remember your teaching to put the cultivation of my moral standing before learning, and contribute to the development of Chinese dietary therapy!

国宴菜

宋：学菜的时候，有几位老师给予了我很大的启发和帮助。第一位是我在人民大会堂学习期间认识的王锡田，我跟着他学习国宴菜。印象最深的是学做毛氏红烧肉。那个时候大家都爱吃这道菜，我学会后，就回去给领导做。更多的时候是听他们讲选料，因为国宴菜的关键在于“精”。就拿五花肉来说，需要选纯精五花肉，太厚的有点肥、太薄的有点瘦，所以要把五花肉的上面部分去掉、下面部分也去掉，只选取中间那一块纯五花三层。然后还有烧、蒸的步骤，做毛氏红烧肉需要将近五个多小时。现在外面餐馆一般的红烧肉都有油，而正宗毛氏红烧肉基本上都是脱油、脱脂的，这都是我跟他学到的特色。王锡田对餐食的精致有很高的要求，比如，猪肉要求是从湖南、江西、湖北一带送过来的散养猪的肉。

苏：为什么一定得是那边送过来的猪肉？

宋：不同地域生产出来的产品，口感不一样，味道也不一样。首长小时候在那边长大，喜欢那种猪的特色口感，其他地方的猪稍微差点。后来我琢磨，这跟孔子说的“食不厌精，脍不厌细”是一个道理。制药也讲究道地药材，考量的是产地、质地、标准、规格。国宴菜从全国各地选取最上乘的材料这点跟制药也是一样的，这对我以后做药膳产生了很深的影响。

苏：您主要跟他学习选料方面？

宋：王锡田老先生平时不怎么做菜，都是底下人做，他主要负责讲解、监督。但我也看过他做菜，还跟他学过一道水炒鸡蛋。拿四个鸡蛋加点盐，锅里放水烧开，把鸡蛋倒进去，搁手勺轻轻推，鸡蛋就自己飘上来了，飘上来后捞起搁碗里头，倒点汤汁，加点香油和香菜就完事。这菜领导特别喜欢吃，因为既清淡、好看，又美味。这种技法外边没有，属于国宴独创菜。王锡田老先生说过越简单的方法，做出来的菜品质量越高。还有做鱼，他不用烧，而用蒸。蒸有两种，有一种叫隔水蒸。原料洗净过一遍水，放水封好后上锅蒸，蒸的过程，始终在那儿煨着。一般蒸五个小时左右，出来的菜就已经达到脱骨的酥烂程度，所有的营养成分都溢出来，吃起来味道也非常好。我们平时做老鸭汤，实际上也不是炖的，而是蒸的。因为蒸更能保持食材的状态，出来的菜品质量更好。包括我们在人民大会堂做的皮冻、水晶冻，也是蒸出来的，而不是熬的。

苏：这个是怎么做的呢？

宋：先把肉皮洗净、去油，焯洗干净后放到托盘里，加入水，放上葱、姜、调料油和料酒，拿保鲜膜封好搁笼屉里蒸，一般蒸三到五个小时，皮化了

State Banquet Dishes

Song: When I was learning to cook, I had several teachers who inspired and helped me a lot. The first one was Wang Xitian, whom I met during my time at the Great Hall of the People. I learned how to cook state banquet dishes from him. It was learning how to make Mao's Braised Pork that I remember most. At that time everyone loved this dish, so I learnt it and went back to make it for the leadership. More often than not, I would listen to them talking about the selection of ingredients, because the key to state banquet cuisine is "precision". Take streaky pork for example. We need to choose pure streaky pork. It cannot be too fatty or too thin, so we need to remove the top part and the bottom part, and use only the middle. Then there are the steps of braising and steaming. It takes nearly five hours or more to make Mao's Braised Pork. Nowadays, the average braised pork in restaurants outside is oily, while the authentic Mao's Braised Pork is basically de-oiled and fat-free, which are the characteristics I learned from him. Wang Xitian is known for his sophisticated standards for meals. Take pork as an example. He required free-range pork delivered from Hunan, Jiangxi and Hubei.

Su: Why does it have to be pork sent from there?

Song: Products produced in different regions have varying tastes and flavors. The senior officer grew up there as a child and liked the taste of pigs over there, which were slightly better than those in other places. Later I figured out that this is the same principle that Confucius mentioned, "To be fastidious about one's food". The preparation of medicines is also concerned with the selection of authentic herbs, taking into account their origin, texture, standards and specifications. State banquet dishes are made from the best ingredients from all over the country, which is the same as pharmaceuticals, so it had profound influence on my cooking later on.

Su: Did you learn mainly from him about selecting ingredients?

Song: Mr. Wang Xitian usually didn't cook much. It' s all done by the people under him, and he was mainly responsible for supervision. I've also seen him cook, and I learned how to cook scrambled eggs with water from him. He picked up four eggs and added some salt, then put water in the pot and boiled it. He poured the eggs into it, gently nudged it with a spoon. The eggs would float up on their own. He then put them in a bowl, poured the soup in the bowl, added sesame oil and cilantro. This dish was especially popular with the leadership because it was light, nice-looking, and tasty. This technique cannot be found anywhere else in the world, and it is a unique state banquet dish. Mr. Wang Xitian said the simpler the method, the higher the quality of the dish. And to cook fish, he never braised it, but steamed it. There are two types of steaming, one is called water-proof steaming. The ingredients are washed once in water, and then put into a pot to steam after being properly blocked from water. During the steaming process, they were always simmered there.Generally, they are steamed for about five hours until they're mushy and squishy. By this time the dish is done, the ingredients are cooked perfectly and all the nutrients ooze out and taste fantastic. The duck soup that we usually make is not actually stewed, but steamed. Steaming keeps the ingredients in better condition and produces dishes of better quality. The pork rind jelly we made at the Great Hall of the People was also steamed, not boiled.

Su: How is this done?

Song: We first wash the pork rind and remove the fat. After blanching it, I put it into a tray, add water, scallion and ginger, seasoning oil and cooking wine. Then I seal it with plastic wrap and

即可。这样蒸出来的皮冻更清澈、不浑浊。

苏：还有什么菜您觉得特别值得讲一讲？

宋：人民大会堂的汤特别到位。一个是选料精细，二个是时间足够。人民大会堂的汤分成高汤、清汤、中汤、毛汤。有的汤需要吊两三天，而不是像咱们平常那样熬一会儿就完事。

苏：毛汤是指？

宋：毛汤指一般的吊汤，用于炒普通菜。人民大会堂的炖汤发展有三个阶段，开始是黄汤，然后变成浓汤，后来又变成清汤，我在不同时期跟他们学习了不同的汤。最早在1984年，我刚跟他们学习做菜的时候都是黄汤，就是用老鸡炖的汤。到1991年、1992年的时候，就变成了用鸡、肘子、牛肉、鲍鱼煲的浓汤，不是那么黄，油也更少。等到1996年以后，就变成了清汤，一般都是用蘑菇、海鲜来吊。1998年，我从部队转业的时候，王老师在人民大会堂请我吃饭，喝的就是清汤。

苏：中间跨越了将近十年，您觉得这种变化是因为什么呢？

宋：第一个原因是人们的生活品质越来越高。第二个原因是人们对健康和营养的需求发生了变化。二十世纪八九十年代生活条件差，人们喜欢喝鸡汤、鸡油补身体。后来加入一些海产品做成浓汤，营养价值更高，同时减少了油腻。等到九十年代末的时候，清汤就比较普遍了，尤其粤菜的清汤更多。原来是黄汤、浓汤比较流行，目前则是清汤成了主流。我觉得“汤”的大变化跟药膳很像。原先的药膳都有药味，药量占比大，现在药剂越来越小，且凸显单一配方，注意突出食材的主味。像我们做的补益药膳、养生长寿药膳，不是什么药都往里放，而是更具针对性，大部分都是以单一配方为主。

苏：您多次提到人民大会堂的烹调方法，他们的烹调方法到底特别在哪儿呢？

宋：人民大会堂讲究兼收并蓄。举个例子，过去国宴有道菜叫佛跳墙，涵盖了全国各地的食材，海参、鲍鱼、鱼翅、鱼肚、元蘑、口蘑、竹笋……烹饪手法集炖汤、吊汤、烧、蒸为一体。人民大会堂做菜还讲究精致，特别注重摆盘，码得很精细。凉菜都是带图案的，而且每一个菜都非常入味，大部分都是卤或酱后再加调味汁。这就是技术，调味时间、卤制时间、腌制时间都得精准掌握，非常值得学习，因为药膳中也有凉菜。八珍鹿肉就既可以热吃，也可以凉吃，热菜的烹调方法就是吊汤、烧、扒、蒸、烤，凉菜就是用卤和酱的烹调方法。

steam it in a steamer. The steaming usually takes three to five hours until the rind melts. This way the jelly is much clearer and less murky.

Su: Are there any other dishes you think are particularly worth talking about?

Song: The stock used at the Great Hall of the People were particularly spot on. They were made from carefully selected ingredients, and their timing was perfect. They include refined stock, broth, bouillon and raw broth. Some soups need to be cooked for two or three days, rather than simmering for a while like we usually do.

Su: What does raw broth mean?

Song: Raw broth refers to the general broth for stir-frying ordinary dishes. There are three stages of development for the broth at the Great Hall of the People. It started out as yellowish soup, then refined broth, and later broth, which are the different kinds of stock I learned to make at different times. As early as 1984, when I first learned to cook, I used yellowish soup, which was a stew made with aged hens. In 1991 or 1992, it became a concentrated soup made with chicken, ham hock, beef and abalone, not quite as yellow and far less oily. In 1996, it changed to broth, which was usually cooked with mushrooms and seafood. When I retired from the military in 1998, Mr. Wang invited me to dinner in the Great Hall of the People. The dishes we had were accompanied by a course of broth.

Su: It spanned almost a decade in between, what do you think caused this change?

Song: The first reason is the improvement of people' lives. The second reason is the change in people's needs for health and nutrition. Back in 1980s and 1990s when the living conditions were tough, people liked to drink oily chicken soup to tonic their bodies. Later they added seafood to make soup richer and more nutritious, while reducing greasiness. Towards the end of the 1990s, bouillon became more common, especially in Cantonese cuisine. It took the place of the once popular yellowish soup and refined broth. I think the development of broth is quite similar to that of dietary therapy. In the past, all medicinal dishes had a strong smell because of the large proportion of herbs. Nowadays, as the portion of medicinal substances gets smaller and smaller, and single-ingredient formulas are promoted, attention is paid to highlighting the main flavor of ingredients. We never put all kinds of medicine into our tonic dishes and longevity dishes. Rather, they are more specific and most of them are based on single-ingredient recipes.

Su: You mentioned the cooking method of the chefs at the Great Hall of the People several times, what is so special about their cooking method?

Song: The chefs at the Great Hall of the People emphasized eclecticism. As an example, in the past, the state banquets had a dish called Buddha Jumps Over the Wall, encompassing ingredients from all over the country such as sea cucumber, abalone, shark fins, fish maw, mushrooms and bamboo shoots. The cooking method combines stew, stock making, roasting and steaming a whole. The chefs of the Great Hall of the People are meticulous in their cooking, especially focused on elaborate plating. The cold dishes are all patterned and each one is incredibly flavorful. Most are marinated, or sauced and then flavored. This is their technique. Their time of seasoning, marination and curing have to be controlled precisely and are well worth learning. There are also cold dishes in dietary therapy. For example, the Eight Dainties and Venison can be served either hot or cold. Hot dishes are cooked with broth. They are made by roasting, grilling, steaming or baking, while cold dishes are cooked with marinades and sauces.

人民大会堂让我感受最深的还有面点的烹调方法。当时人民大会堂、钓鱼台国宾馆和北京饭店的点心被称作“美点双辉”。他们在给领导上菜的时候，不是单独一个菜，而是一套组合菜品，每道菜都配有全国各地的小点心和小吃。现在大通饭庄的鹿全席就是采用国宴的这种方法，将各种形式综合起来，有凉菜、热菜、正菜、茶和点心。如果我没有在这些地方的工作经历，我做的鹿全席和药膳就会变得很普通。

粤菜

宋：粤菜清淡，康辉老先生常用爆炒、清炒的方式做菜，我觉得药膳也很适合用爆炒和煲汤的方法来做，就把跟他学到的很多粤菜技法移植、转化到药膳当中。

苏：您举个具体例子？

宋：我们现在做素胶、素菜就多用爆炒。胶熬好后，在炒菜过程中像放调料似的迅速加上胶汁，这样尽可能地保持了食材本身的营养。举个简单的例子，我们做山药，先把山药切成片，舀点熬好的胶汁，搁点盐，入锅迅速爆炒后盛出，上菜的时候再撒上一点枸杞子即可。

还有粤菜里的面点手法——冻，也就是各种龟苓膏、什锦果膏……我们学习了粤式的这种烹调方法，把龟鹿二仙膏放入粤式早点、早茶里，反响特别好。我们还有阿胶茶、鹿胶茶、宫廷普洱，喝茶的时候附赠一块蜂胶，相当于小点心，调节口味，提高营养价值。

广东还有一种技法叫焗。用内蒙古的紫皮小葱（类似于圆葱）为主料，再用广东的生姜，或者山东本地生姜切成片，一起在锅里炒出香味后放上鹿肉，就是姜葱焗鹿肉。鹿肉不用腌制，直接用新鲜鹿肉搁上葱和姜，再搁点酱和盐，一炒就完事，特别好吃、特别香，突出原汁原味。

川菜

苏：您再讲几个川菜中具有代表性的菜，尤其是对您后面做药膳有影响的菜。

宋：川菜大师陈松如有一个非常特别的菜叫开水白菜。我后面做的鹿胶白菜，就借鉴了他这道菜的制作方法。

苏：您具体讲一讲怎么做的。

宋：其实有三道菜，鹿胶白菜、阿胶萝卜和牛胶豆腐，根据季节的不同更

What I found most impressive about the dishes at the Great Hall of the People was the way the pastry was made. The dim sum of the Great Hall of the People, the Diaoyutai Guesthouse and the Beijing Hotel were called "the twin glories of beautiful desserts" at that time. The dishes they served to the leadership were arranged in sets, and each dish was accompanied by refreshments and snacks from all around the country. Now, the venison banquet at the Datong Restaurant is similar to a state banquet, with a combination of dishes, including cold dishes, hot dishes, main course, tea and dim sum. Without my experience working in these places, the venison banquet and medicinal dishes I made would have been mediocre.

Cantonese Cuisine

Song: Cantonese cuisine is all about being light and fresh. Mr. Kang Hui used to cook dishes by stir-frying. I think stir-frying and soup-making are also suitable for cooking medicinal dishes, so I learned a lot of Cantonese cuisine techniques from him and used them in medicinal dishes.

Su: Can you give us some examples?

Song: We now cook vegetarian gum and vegetarian dishes by stir-frying them mostly. After making the gelatin, we add the gelatin as quickly as we put the seasoning in the stir-fry process, so that we can preserve the nutrition of the ingredients themselves. Let me give you a simple example. When we cook yam, we will first cut the yam into slices, ladle boiled gelatin sauce, add salt, stir-fry them quickly in the pan, sprinkle some wolfberries on them before serving the dish.

We also use the technique of making Cantonese jelly, such as tortoise jelly and assorted fruit paste. We put Guilu Erxian Ointment into the Cantonese breakfast and morning tea, which is particularly well-received. We also have donkey-hide gelatin tea, deer skin gelatin tea and court Pu'er tea. We serve a piece of propolis when we serve tea, which is equivalent to a snack to temper the taste and enhance the nutritional value.

Cantonese cuisine also has a technique called "baking". We use small purple shallots (similar to Spanish onions) from Inner Mongolia as the main ingredient, then cut Guangdong ginger, or local Shandong ginger into slices, and stir-fry them together in a wok to bring out the aroma. We then add the venison, hence the Baked Venison with Ginger and Shallots. There is no need to marinate the venison. It is directly flavored with shallots and ginger. And then with sauce and salt we stir-fry the venison. The dish is particularly delicious, with the original flavor accentuated.

Sichuan Cuisine

Su: Can you name a few more representative dishes of Sichuan cuisine, especially those that have influenced your medicinal cuisine later on?

Song: Sichuan cuisine master Chen Songru is famous for a very special dish called Boiled Water and Cabbage. I borrowed his technique for the Deerskin Gelatin and Cabbage that I made later.

Su: Tell us exactly how it's cooked.

Song: The dish comes in three forms, deerskin gelatin and cabbage, donkey-hide and turnip, and bovine-hide gelatin and *tofu,* which varies according to the season. But the cooking method and

换食材，但烹饪方法和调味都是借鉴了川菜。开水白菜是一道四川名菜，也是当时的一道国宴菜，关键在于吊清汤。我把熬胶的汤跟鹿胶、阿胶、牛胶结合起来，放点白菜、萝卜、豆腐。颜色有点微黄、微红，特别好看，而且口感和营养都比较好。

苏：比如说鹿胶白菜所用的高汤是您熬胶的汤？还是鸡肉的汤？

宋：用鹿骨头、鹿筋熬的高汤配上白菜。鹿筋煮到八成熟的时候就捞出来，所以最后成品的口感比较清澈。熬汤过程中加入鹿筋主要是借用它的一部分营养。

苏：在借鉴川菜调味方面，您能讲得再细致一些吗？

宋：还有用川菜干烧的调味方法，把咸口变成咸辣口。我跟陈松如学了几种口味，麻辣味、咸辣味、咸香味、鱼香味、葱姜蒜味还有宫保鸡丁那种咸甜酸辣兼备的口味……通过变换药膳的不同口味来满足不同人群的需求。我现在的专利——鹿胶海参（男）和阿胶海参（女）就是如此。我会先询问顾客是否喜欢吃辣，如果不喜欢吃辣，我就弄成咸口，如果喜欢吃辣，就弄成辣口。这样调整后，无论南方、北方的客人都能满意。

以前做的药膳80%都是咸口和清汤，注重体现本色、本味。现在的药膳口味比较丰富。加入辣口也是因为客人的需求，尤其对于常客，需要变换一下口味。比如利用麻婆豆腐的味道、味型，来做海参、肉、蔬菜。

做药膳的彭铭泉也是四川人，他对我的影响也比较大，到现在我还保存着他的书。

苏：比如说有什么影响呢？

宋：他用枸杞叶、红薯叶炒菜。这些在我们老家没人要、遍地扔的东西，他却说都是好东西。我们家的红薯叶特别紫，炒完盘子底都流紫色的汤汁，花青素含量特别高。他用煎出来的药汁去炒菜，没有药味，就像花椒水似的。他还有一道菜叫杜仲猪肝，将树上的茶叶摘下来后，一熬一泡，拿茶炒猪肝。他还拿银杏叶子泡茶喝，那是我第一次接触，但一看就学会了，我们小院里有很多银杏树，回来我就拿树上的白果炒芹菜。

鲁菜

宋：我还跟负责北京市政府宽沟招待所的鲁菜大师张文海学了不少菜，油爆双脆、糟熘三白、虾子葱扒大乌参、蟹黄扒鱼唇、扒鱼翅……我后来做萝

seasoning are inspired by Sichuan cuisine. Boiled Water and Cabbage is a famous dish in Sichuan and a state banquet dish at that time. Its key is in the bouillon. I combined the soup from making gelatin with deerskin gelatin, donkey-hide gelatin and bovine-hide gelatin, and add cabbage, turnips and *tofu*. This dish is a bit yellowish and slightly red. It is especially nice-looking, with superior texture and nutritious value.

Su: For example, in the Deerskin Gelatin and Cabbage, does the broth come from the soup you make the gelatin in? Or is it from the soup you cook the chicken with?

Song: I used deer bones and tendons to make the broth with cabbage. I take out the deer tendons when they are medium well, so the texture of the final product is still crisp. The main reason for adding deer tendon in the soup is to leverage its nutrition.

Su: Can you go into detail about the seasoning of Sichuan cuisine?

Song: Use the dry braising in Sichuan cuisine to add a spicy touch to salty dishes. I learned to cook dishes with multiple flavors from Chen Songru. Spicy dishes, salty dishes, savory dishes, sweet and sour dishes, alliaceous dishes, and dishes with a variety of flavors such as Kung Pao Chicken. By changing the flavor of the medicinal dishes, we can cater to the requirements of different people. It's the same with the dishes that I have patented, including the Deerskin Gelatin and Sea Cucumber for men and Donkey-hide Gelatin and Sea Cucumber for women. When entertaining customers, I would first ask them if they like spicy food. If they don't like spicy dishes, I'll make them salty. If they do, I'll make them spicy. After adjustment, customers from either the south or the north are satisfied.

In the past, 80% of the medicinal dishes we made were salty and based on bouillon, emphasizing the original colors and flavors of the ingredients. Nowadays, we make medicinal dishes with more flavors, not just one. We added spicy flavors because of customer demand, especially for regulars, who need a change of taste. For example, we incorporate the flavor and taste of Mapo Tofu into the cooking of sea cucumber, meat, and vegetables.

Peng Mingquan, who cooked medicinal dishes, was from Sichuan and had a great influence on me, and I still have his book.

Su: What is the influence, for example?

Song: He cooked stir-fries with wolfberry leaves and sweet potato leaves. Back in my hometown, nobody would eat these things. But in his eyes, they were wonderful ingredients. The sweet potato leaves we grew in our hometown were exceptionally purple. The purple broth flowed at the bottom of the plate when sweet potatoes were served, indicating high content of anthocyanins. Peng used the decoction to make stir-fries without the taste of medicine, just like pepper water. He was known for another dish called Du Zhong's Pig Liver, for which he plucked tea leaves from the trees and made them into tea. Then he used the tea water, to fry the pig's liver. He also drank tea made of ginkgo leaves. That was the first time I knew how to do that and I learned quickly. We have many ginkgo trees in our yard. When I returned home I would take the ginkgoes from the trees and stir-fry them with celery.

Shandong Cuisine

Song: I also learned to cook quite a few dishes from Zhang Wenhai, a master of Shandong cuisine, who worked at the Kuangou Guesthouse of the Beijing Municipal Government. The dishes included Fried Gizzards and Goat Tripe, Sautéed Three White Slices with Rice Wine Sauce, Braised

卜、豆腐就是用的扒鱼翅的做法。豆腐切好摆盘里，把汁、牛胶还有各种调料放在里头，再搁上宽汤——宽汤就是用鸡蓉走过一遍的清汤——没过原料，菜在锅里小火煨着，大约煨40分钟，汤都煨进食材里，少量勾芡，加上胶汁，一大翻勺出来，这种烹调方法就叫扒，用这个方法做豆腐和萝卜都特别好吃。我经过反复试验，最后选择用扒的方法做豆腐，因为萝卜、豆腐跟鱼翅类似。虽然一个是动物原料，一个是植物原料，但根茎类的植物原料耐烧、耐入味，我用这种方法进行调整，举一反三，烧得非常好吃。

苏：这个豆腐实际上已经不是您家原来“三黑三白”的做法了。

宋：不是。我结合了人民大会堂、北京饭店、宽沟招待所、钓鱼台国宾馆的烹调方法，结合了不同的味型，经过了多次调整和试验。因为大部分时间我跟大师们都只是互相交流，他们并不能在现场指导我做菜，也不像现在有手机能拍照片，我只能告诉他们做完后菜是什么样的。

苏：您说的这几个地方之间的区别是什么？

宋：区别还是很大的。北京饭店的菜品没有人民大会堂的广泛，以谭家菜、淮扬菜居多。人民大会堂菜品广泛，什么地区的都有，涵盖中餐、西餐。宽沟招待所主要是请内部领导吃饭，以鲁菜为主，家常菜居多，讲究北京本地的田园特色菜，像水库鱼、本地烤全羊。钓鱼台国宾馆以粤菜、淮扬菜为主，少量川菜和一部分西餐。

苏：还有什么菜，您觉得值得一讲？

宋：我做鹿全席比较多，鹿的不同部位用不同的方法烹制，烧、炒、扒、蒸、卤……综合借鉴了粤菜、鲁菜、人民大会堂还有西餐的一些烹调方法。比如用西餐的方法煎鹿排、烤鹿排，客人反映都不错。餐饮的关键是老百姓爱吃，不愿意吃都是白扯。光有个好名字也没用，关键还得味道好。好看又好吃，这样才行得通。

西餐

宋：领导特别喜欢我做的带馅儿八珍糕，后来我又将它改良成了红、白月饼，红色的是阿胶月饼，白色的是鹿胶月饼，北京烹饪协会和中国药膳协会将它评为北京名菜，还曾获国家质量金奖，征战德国，卖80欧元一块。我的月饼皮不同于普通月饼，采用了中西结合的手法。

苏：请您具体讲一讲如何结合？

Jumbo Sea Cucumber with Shrimp Roe, Braised Fish Lips with Crab Roe, and Braised Shark's Fin. Later on, I cooked turnips and *tofu* using the technique of Braised Shark's Fin. I cut up the *tofu* and put it on a tray, add the sauce, bovine-hide gelatin and various seasonings, and then pour the broth over it. The broth is made from chicken bouillon without any other ingredients. The ingredients are simmered in a pot over low heat for about 40 minutes or so until they are soaked with the flavor of the soup. And then I thicken the soup with mixture of cornstarch and water, add gelatin, and then take the ingredients out. The turnips and *tofu* are particularly delicious when cooked this way. This cooking method is called braising. I experimented repeatedly before choosing braising to cook *tofu*. This is because turnips and *tofu* are similar to shark fins. Although shark fins are a type of animal ingredients, turnips are roots which are resistant to roasting and flavoring. Therefore, I leveraged their characteristics and refined the cooking technique to make the dish quite tasty.

Su: The *tofu* in this dish is actually not the same as your family's original "three blacks and three whites" dish.

Song: No, it's not. I incorporated the cooking methods of the chefs of the Great Hall of the People, Beijing Hotel, Kuangou Guesthouse and Diaoyutai Guesthouse, modified and experimented with the different flavor types for many times. In the past the chefs and I could only talk to each other after I made the dishes. They could not come and tell me how to do it, and I didn't have a cell phone that can take pictures. I could only tell them what the dish was like when I was done.

Su: What are the differences between these places that you mentioned?

Song: The differences are significant. The cuisine of Beijing restaurant is not as extensive as that of the Great Hall of the People, with Tan's dishes and Huaiyang dishes being the most popular. The Great Hall of the People has a wide range of dishes from all over the world, including Chinese and Western food. Kuangou Guesthouse mostly serves in-house leadership. It mostly offers Shandong cuisine, featuring more home-cooked dishes and idyllic specialties produced locally in Beijing, such as fish from reservoirs and roasted sheep from the local area. Diaoyutai Guesthouse mainly serves Cantonese and Huaiyang cuisine, with a small amount of Sichuan cuisine and some Western food.

Su: Are there any other dishes that you think are worth talking about?

Song: I have cooked many venison banquets, using various methods to cook different parts of a deer, such as roasting, stir-frying, braising, steaming and marinating... I have borrowed some of the cooking methods from Cantonese cuisine, Shandong cuisine, the Great Hall of the People and Western cuisine. For example, fried venison steak and grilled venison steak in the Western way are well received by customers. The key to successful catering is that customers love your food. If they don't like your food, it's all for nothing. For any dish, having a pleasant name alone is useless. The key is to taste good. A nice dish that looks and tastes good will do the trick.

Western Food

Song: The leadership especially liked my stuffed Eight-Dainty Cake. Later, I refined it into red mooncakes and white mooncakes. The red ones are stuffed with donkey-hide gelatin, and the white ones with deerskin gelatin. They were honored by the Beijing Cuisine Association and the China Association of Health Protection Food as one of Beijing's famous dishes. Having won China's Gold Medal for Quality, they're sold for 80 euros a piece in Germany. The crust of my mooncakes is different from that of regular mooncakes, which is a combination of Chinese and Western techniques.

Su: Could you tell us more about the combination?

宋：我跟其他厨师不一样的地方在于我会做西餐。我曾在国际饭店、国际俱乐部、建国门专家公寓学过半年西餐，主要学习法餐，包括主菜和烘焙，虽然不是很精通，但掌握了全部的技法。我的月饼皮就是采用了西餐面包的原料和制作方法。

苏：红、白两种月饼除了胶以外，里面的馅料是一样的吗？

宋：都是九种果仁馅儿，基本主料相同，比如说核桃、松子、榛子、杏仁、花生米、黑芝麻、白芝麻。区别在于白的是用冬瓜蓉，红的是用莲子蓉，营养上也有所区分。

苏：您能稍微讲讲怎么创造阿胶雪梨丸子这个菜的吗？

宋：之前有个委员长来大通饭庄吃饭，拿了一些莱阳梨搁在我这儿。过了一段时间后，梨搁不住、要变质了，也不能因为这个梨就去找领导。我就把梨子洗干净，拿擦子擦成细丝。然后熬好阿胶，化好后放一点芝麻、一点青红丝。再拿梨丝包在芝麻和阿胶外面，蘸上鸡蛋，又用馒头给它包上。全部包完后放入冰箱速冻。过段时间，委员长再来餐厅，我跟他说："领导，我把梨子试验成了菜，您试试。"他说："试验什么菜，你给我水煮煮就行。"我说："咱能老搁水煮吗？我做了点别的东西，您看看。"我把冻起来的雪梨丸子拿出来搁锅里炸，领导吃过后觉得这丸子跟元宵似的，还淌着汤汁，就问我是什么，我说这是阿胶，他直呼好吃，我就让领导给这道菜题个字，他写下了"阿胶雪梨丸子最精彩"，直到现在这个牌匾还在店里。

杨：您当时怎么想到用阿胶来搭配梨子的呢？

宋：梨清火清肺，阿胶补气补血，从药理、食理上比较搭配，然后它俩又都产自一个地区——山东。但我的烹饪手法是用的西餐手法。

苏：您是参考西餐的什么菜来做的？

宋：西餐有一道西子排炸，比如麦当劳炸鸡腿、炸鸡排，这都叫排炸。西餐是用面包裹着炸，我给改成了用馒头裹着，因为咱们这儿没有面包，只有馒头。这个菜谁都乐意吃，过段时间，我准备将这道菜投入工业化生产，做完后立刻速冻，再配送到各地，吃的时候当场一炸就行。现在我们山东老家有人开馆子还用我这道菜呢。这道菜就是将西餐的技法和药膳相结合的典型。

宫廷菜

宋：我还有两位宫廷菜老师：金喜升和潘喜发。他们原本跟着溥仪，后又

Song: What makes me different from other chefs is that I can cook Western food. I learned to cook Western cuisine for six months at Beijing International Hotel, Beijing International Club and Jianguomen Outer Diplomatic Residence Compound. I mainly studied French cuisine, including entrées and bakeries. However, I was not that proficient, and only learned all the steps. My mooncake crust is made with the same ingredients and methods used to make Western bread.

Su: Are the fillings inside the red mooncakes and white mooncakes the same, except for the gelatin?

Song: They are all nine kinds of nuts, with the same basic main ingredients, such as walnuts, pine nuts, hazelnuts, almonds, peanuts, black sesame and white sesame. The difference is that white mooncakes are stuffed with winter melon paste and red mooncakes are stuffed with lotus seed paste. Their nutritional benefits are also different.

Su: Can you tell us a little bit about how you created the dish of Donkey-hide Gelatin Pear Balls?

Song: Once a commissioner came to Datong Restaurant for dinner, and brought some Laiyang pears. After a period of time, the pears started to go bad, I didn't dare to complain to him about the pears.. I then washed the pears first and sliced them into fine shreds. Then I melted donkey-hide gelatin and added sesame seeds and candied flavedo and other citrus rinds. Then I wrapped sesame seeds and gelatin with pear shreds, dipped them in egg mixture, and put them into steamed buns. After all was done, I put them in the freezer. After some time, the commissioner came to the restaurant again. I said to him, "I made the pears into a dish. Do you want to have a try?" He said: "You shouldn't have bothered. I would eat them even you only boil them in water." I said: "It's not my style to cook something in the same old way. I made it into something else. Have a try." I took the frozen pear balls out and fried them in the pot. After trying them, the commissioner thought they were like sweet dumplings. He saw broth dripping out of them, and asked me what they were. I said it was donkey-hide gelatin. He highly praised them, so I asked the commissioner to write an inscription for this dish. He wrote "The Most Wonderful Donkey-hide Gelatin Pear Balls", and now this plaque is still in the restaurant.

Yang: How did you come up with the idea of using donkey-hide gelatin with pears at that time?

Song: Pears can relieve heat and clear the lungs, while donkey-hide gelatin can replenish qi and blood, which makes them a perfect match in terms of pharmacology and dietary science. In addition, both of them are produced in Shandong. But I cooked the dish in a Western style.

Su: What Western dish inspired you?

Song: In Western cuisine, there is a technique called deep-frying. For example, McDonald's deep-fried chicken legs and chicken cutlet. In Western cuisine, they're deep-fried with bread crumbs. I replaced them with crumbs of steamed buns, because we don't have bread here. This is a dish that anyone would be interested in enjoying. In the future, I am going to produce this dish industrially. After they're made, they'll be quick-frozen and distributed. Customers only need to fry them before eating. Even now we have restaurants in our hometown in Shandong that serve this dish. This dish is a typical combination of Western techniques and medicinal dishes.

Palace Cuisine

Song: I had two teachers of court cuisine: Jin Xisheng and Pan Xifa. At first, they followed

去了台湾。后面回到家乡，分别在吉林和北京待了一段时间。我在部队的时候跟他们学习了一些东西，大概是1995年或1996年，那会儿他们都已经80多岁。金喜升和潘喜发都是少将级别，一位是吉林朝阳人，一位是吉林辽源人，都来自鹿乡，所以他们都擅长做鹿肉。

苏：您是在什么场合认识他们的？

宋：1995年前后，金喜升和潘喜发来北京跟我们部队进行交流，就住在京西宾馆。我听说他们是宫廷里的御厨，就老跟他们唠嗑，他们跟我讲了大量关于鹿的制作方法。我跟他们里里外外待了两星期，学到了很多做药膳的方法。

苏：您具体讲讲是怎么学的？

宋：我跟他们学了鹿的屠宰方法，还有几个基本的制法：炖、烤、烧。他们最引以为荣的菜就是鹿鞭王。他们杀鹿的手法也跟别人不一样，通常我们杀鹿要么拿刀砍，要么就捅。但他们不是，他们先用板子把鹿头夹住，再拿剪刀把喉咙处的毛全部剪掉。剪完后先用盐水洗，再用酒洗，洗得干干净净。最后拿刀一捅，血"哗"一下流出来，直接灌进酒瓶子里头。鹿血酒，酒和鹿血都不能落地，就是杀鹿的时候，血不能搁一边儿，得直接拿酒接着。割鹿茸的时候也一样，鹿茸里的血也得滴到酒里。另外鹿鞭、鹿尾泡人参酒，也不是用水洗，得用酒洗，洗完了直接泡酒里头。

杀鹿的时候，要先把后腿抻起来，把血控出来，血控干净后才炖。因为他们不会熬胶，所以全是带皮炖鹿、烤鹿。制作出来的鹿不勾芡、不放草药，靠大酱去腥，用的调料比较多，他们说溥仪喜欢吃烤鹿里脊。他们有时候还会用西餐的做法煎鹿排。鹿肉硬，切的时候要用斜刀切。鹿肉一般要吃新鲜的，存放不能超过两三天，因为也存不住。

苏：他们怎么会愿意教您这些东西呢？

宋：我的叔叔宋来鲁和他们一起共事过，算师兄弟。虽然我没见过我叔叔，但因为这一层关系，打开了话匣子。再加上我们家里以前给故宫提供鹿胶，他们也是故宫的御厨，有同样的渊源。

苏：这个单子上的鹿全席，没有写具体的菜式。

宋：鹿做的菜有上百个，都是口味、方法、形状上的变化。

苏：您的鹿全席除了跟他们学的这部分，还有哪些是从您家学的？

宋：烀，就是在锅里炖成鹿冻。烀在鹿全席里占了很大位置，甚至超出了炖。他们之间的区别在于：炖的时间短，烀的时间长，火力大小也不一样。

Puyi They then went to Taiwan. After returning home, they spent some time in Jilin and Beijing respectively. I learned something from them while I was in the army, probably in 1995 or 1996, when they were in their 80s. Both Jin Xisheng and Pan Xifa are major generals. One is from Chaoyang, Jilin, and the other is from Liaoyuan, Jilin. Chaoyang and Liaoyuan were habitats of deer, so they were both good at cooking venison.

Su: On what occasion did you meet them?

Song: Around 1995, Jin Xisheng and Pan Xifa came to Beijing for an exchange with our troops and stayed at the Jingxi Hotel. I heard that they were royal chefs from the palace, so I kept chatting with them. They told me a lot about how to cook venison. I spent two weeks with them and learned a lot about the way they make medicinal dishes.

Su: Tell us exactly how you learned from them?

Song: I learned from them how to slaughter a deer, and a few basic ways to cook it: stewing, roasting, and braising. The dish they were most proud of was the deer penis. They slaughtered deer differently than others. Usually we do it by either cutting or stabbing. First they clamped the head of the deer on a board and then cut off all the hair at the throat with scissors. After cutting, he first washed it with saline and then with wine. Finally, they stabbed it with a knife, and the blood poured out directly into a wine bottle. This is called the deer blood wine. The wine and the deer blood must not fall to the ground, that is, when a deer is slaughtered, its blood must be put into a wine bottle directly. The same goes for its antler. The blood in the antler has to be dripped into the wine bottle. In addition, before soaking deer penis and tail in ginseng wine, they washed them with wine instead of water, and then directly put them in the wine.

When they slaughtered a deer, they tied up the hind legs first to drain the blood and stewed it after. They don't know how to make deerskin gelatin, so they stewed or roasted the deer with its skin. They cooked the deer without cornstarch powder and herbs. They used soybean paste and a lot of seasoning to remove the pungent smell. They said that Puyi liked grilled deer tenderloin, and sometimes they would cook fried deer steak in a western style. Venison is hard, so they cut it in an oblique way. Venison is generally eaten fresh. It does not last more than two or three days.

Su: How would they be willing to teach you these things?

Song: My uncle Song Lailu worked with them together, which makes them disciples of the same mentor. Although I have never met my uncle, his connection with them helped introduce me to them. In addition, our family used to make deerskin gelatin for the imperial family, and they were the imperial chefs, which made them more accessible.

Su: The list of venison banquet has no specific dishes written on it.

Song: There are hundreds of dishes made from venison, with variations in taste, method and form.

Su: Apart from the things you learned from them, is there anything you learned from your family to cook venison banquet?

Song: I learned how to make venison jelly stew with a small amount of water. This technique is called "*hu*" in Chinese. It's used more often than stewing in venison banquet. Hu takes longer than stewing and their heat varies.

Yang: I start to realize that in the very beginning, it seemed you knew little about cooking. But you were surrounded by talented men who offered you guidance, so you grew particularly fast.

杨：我现在有一个体会，其实最开始的时候，您对烹饪并不了解。但您周围很多的高人都给了您指点，所以您成长地特别快。

宋：任何我不明白的事情，都可以直接去问他们，他们也不能对我隐瞒。因为我的身份，给我提供了机会。通常我这种职位的人，对做饭并没有兴趣。

杨：但是您对这个有兴趣。

宋：是的。上周我还跟几位大师开了一个米饭研讨会，研讨米饭怎么蒸才好吃。第一，米饭要根据产地特点，比如说长粒、短粒，新米、陈米，调整放水量。第二，蒸米饭的时候可以加佐料油增香。常见的是加猪油、鸡油等动物油，比如我跟康辉老先生学的海南鸡油饭，除此之外，我还曾经尝试加过鸭油、鹅油还有鹿油。

苏：您具体再说说东北大米怎么做好吃？

宋：用东北大米的新米做米饭时，需要加入没过米面一指半的水，陈米则需要多加点水，因为它已经失去了油性。

杨：您只吃东北大米吗？

宋：不一定。天津小站稻米、玉泉山稻米、上海崇文大米也都非常好吃。南方的米生长时间短，所以口感、质量、营养比北方的略差，但也有好处，像蟹稻米、鱼稻米，在稻田里养了鱼虾蟹，在自然环境下生长，再加上这些植物、动物的配合，生态环境好，米的质量就好。这种米一般来说更适合熬粥、做米糕，或者磨碎后做米粉、米线。

在部队研发菜品

杨：您是进部队后再上的大学？

宋：我非常感谢部队、感谢中国共产党，没有他们，我们家翻不了身。部队领导看我在学厨方面很用心，就一点一点地培养我，让我去国际饭店、国际俱乐部学习法餐，还送我去读大学，学习文化知识。我在部队工作两三年后，1983年，部队给我提了干，并送我去广州炮兵学院读专科。学了不到三个月，我立功入党，又送我去黑龙江商学院读本科。虽然我文化课成绩不好，但我达到了部队

Song: I could ask them about what I didn't understand at the time, and they were more than happy to share their experiences with me. Because of my background, there was an opportunity. Usually people in my position are not interested in this.

Yang: And you're interested in that.

Song: Yes. Last week I even held a rice seminar with some masters. We discussed how to steam rice to make it taste good. First, the amount of water put into the rice should be adjusted according to the characteristics and place of origin of the rice. Secondly, when steaming rice, you can add condiment oil to enhance the flavor. It is common to add lard, chicken oil and other animal oils. For example, I learned to cook Hainanese Chicken Rice from Mr. Kang Hui, and I myself have tried to add duck oil, goose oil, and deer oil.

Su: Tell me more specifically, how to make delicious steamed rice from northeast China?

Song: New rice needs the amount of of water equivalent to one and a half fingers over the surface of the rice, and more water for aged rice because it has lost its oiliness.

Yang: Do you eat rice from northeast China all the time?

Song: Not necessarily. Tianjin Xiaozhan Rice, Yuquanshan Rice, and Shanghai Chongwen Rice are also very tasty. The rice in the south has a short growth time, so the taste, quality and nutrition are slightly less than ours. However, there are also advantages, such as crab rice and fish rice, which are raised in the rice fields with fish, shrimps and crabs, the natural environment of growth, coupled with the complement of these plants and animals. The ecological environment makes the quality of the rice. Generally speaking, this kind of rice is suitable for boiling porridge, making rice cake, or grinding it to make rice flour or rice noodles.

Developing Dishes in the Army

Yang: Did you go into the army and then go to college?

Song: I am very grateful to the army and the Communist Party of China. Without them, our family could not make a turnaround. The leadership of the army saw that I was very dedicated in learning cooking, so they trained me little by little, including letting me learn French cuisine in Beijing International Hotel and Beijing International Club, and also sending me to university to learn cultural knowledge. After I worked in the army for two or three years, in 1983, the army gave me a promotion and sent me to the Guangzhou Artillery Academy to pursue a technical degree. After less than three months of study, I was sent to the Heilongjiang Business School for my undergraduate studies because of my meritorious entry into the Party. I didn't even need to take the test. Although my cultural performance is not good, but in the army I was up to standard. I was a member of the party with military excellence, and also achieved merit. I studied food engineering and then cold chain processing in the Department of Tourism and Culinary Arts at the Business School. There are summer and winter vacations in school. Generally, anyone who is promoted will go home on

的指标，军事优秀又是党员，还立过功，所以不需要考试，直接保送。我在商学院旅游烹饪系先学习了食品工程，后又学习了冷链加工。学校有寒暑假，一般提了干的人放假都会回家，但我一次也没回去过，直到大学毕业四年后才回家。我放假的时候就回去继续为首长服务，首长撵我回家我都不去，因为我不知道该怎么感谢领导，只有继续为首长服务。有一次回来我跟领导说想学营养配餐，领导同意了，并让我学成回来后保障首长。就这样我又去了大连陆军总院，学完后分配到了棒棰岛，在棒棰岛工作一段时间后，又跟着首长回到了北京。

苏：在学校的学习对您从事餐饮行业有什么影响吗？

宋：影响深刻。待人接物更系统、更规范。我学的是旅游烹饪。旅游，我原来并不知道咱们国家有哪些旅游地点、人文景观，国际上的更不懂。但是通过学习，我的理论知识得到了很大的提高。烹饪，我原来只知道做菜，通过学习才知道，烹饪是一种文化、是一门科学、是一种艺术、是一个非常广泛的学科。理论和实践相结合使得我视野更开阔、应用更广泛。

苏：您在大连待了几年？

宋：我在棒槌岛待了两年多。但不是一直在那待着，因为我的工作是给首长提供保障，首长去哪儿我们就得跟着去哪儿。

杨：按您所说，首长对每一样吃的东西都有非常严格的把关，您怎么敢把自家的药和菜结合起来给首长做药膳呢？

宋：我最早开始做药膳是在大连陆军营养部，当时我在那儿学习营养配餐。有一次回老家，父母给我熬了胶放在玻璃瓶里，让我拿回部队吃，可以补身体。我每种都拿了一些，回到部队后跟主任说，我们家的鹿胶、阿胶也能做菜。他认为这些都是好东西，我就给当时负责我的领导尝了尝。领导尝完后觉得挺好，就说等首长来了，给首长也尝尝。

各位首长来了后，我就给他们做药膳。旁边还有医生，都知道阿胶、鹿胶是好东西。后来胶吃没了，领导就让我们自己在部队里熬胶，我就让他们去大兴安岭找鹿皮、鹿筋还有驴皮，我在部队现熬。后来我跟我父亲说，我做的胶比你做的还好。拿给他一看，我做的胶的确更亮、更好，因为部队的设施条件比老家好。熬好胶后就分别送到领导家里。这个胶对身体的好处立竿见影，尤其是腿脚、说话的声音，都有明显的改善。就像我，你看我现在说话声音多洪亮、眼睛多亮。我就老吃我们家的鹿胶膏、阿胶膏。昨天没吃饭，我就吃了一片鹿胶。

vacation, but I didn't go home once until four years after I graduated from college. I went back on vacation to continue to serve the senior officer. I was so determined that I would disobey his order to go home, because I did not know how to thank the leader, only to continue to serve him. Once I told the leadership that I wanted to learn nutrition and meal preparation, the leadership agreed, and let me finish my studies and come back. I went to the Dalian Army Academy of the Chinese People's Liberation Army. After I finished my studies, I was assigned to Bangchui Island, where I worked for a while and then returned to Beijing for the senior officer.

Su: Did these things you learned in school have any influence on your career in the catering industry?

Song: They had a profound impact. I learned to be more systematic and disciplined. I studied tourism cooking. I didn't know much about our country's tourist sites and cultural landscapes, and I didn't know much about international ones. But through the study, my theoretical knowledge has been greatly improved. I originally only knew how to cook, but through my studies, I realized that cooking is a culture, a science, an art, and a very broad discipline. By putting theory into practice, I am able to broaden my horizons and apply them more widely.

Su: How many years did you spend in Dalian?

Song: I spent more than two years on Bangchui Island. But I wasn't always stuck there, because my job was to provide security for the senior officer, and we had to follow him wherever he went.

Yang: According to you, the senior officer was very strict about everything he ate. What inspired you to combine your family's medicine and dishes to make medicinal meals for him?

Song: I first started doing medicinal cuisine at the Army Nutrition Department in Dalian, where I was studying nutritional meal preparation. Once I went back home, my parents made me gelatin and put it in a glass jar, so that I could take it back to school. I then took a little of each and told the director that my family's deerskin gelatin and donkey-hide gelatin could be used for cooking. He thought they were wonderful, and I gave them to the leader who was my supervisor at the time to try. After my supervisor tasted them, he thought they were tasty as well, and said that when the senior officer came, he would like to have a try.

When the senior officers came, I made medicinal meals for them. They were accompanied by doctors, who understood that the dishes I made were good when they heard me talk about making donkey-hide gelatin and deerskin gelatin. Later, when we ran out of gelatin, the leadership let us make our own gelatin here. I asked them to go to the Daxinganling region to find deerskin, deer tendon and donkey hide, and I made the gelatin in the army. I told my father, "I made better gelatin than you did." He took a look, and the gelatin I made was brighter and better. The army was well equipped, but not back home. After the gelatin was finished, it was sent to the leader's home separately. This really works well and has immediate effect. There were obvious improvements on their legs and feet in particular, and their voices. Take myself for example. Look how loudly I speak and how bright my eyes are now. I'm a big fan of our family's deerskin gelatin and donkey-hide gelatin. I didn't eat yesterday and took a piece of deerskin gelatin.

杨：过去好多官员见皇帝怕上厕所，所以不吃不喝，就是含参茸、鹿茸这些东西。

宋：对，我们家还有清宫的代茶饮。以前我的父亲和母亲会用胶熬好了茶，倒在壶里背着，当作食物和水。因为他们给人看病，老在路上。

杨：您是怎么知道胶能入菜的？

宋：有一年回家，我父亲正在熬胶，锅、盆底下粘着一些剩下的肉渣。我在部队干净惯了，就给刷干净倒了。我父亲就说我干净不到正地方，药食同源，熬胶剩的渣子底都是可以吃的，从那以后我就慢慢地开始做这方面的试验。

杨：哪些胶首长觉得比较不错？

宋：鹿胶、牛胶、阿胶、龟胶都不错。蜂胶、桃胶用得比较少，领导不爱吃，他愿意吃辣的。桃胶没什么口感，跟饮料似的。桃胶可以熬粥，但是炒菜不行，因为有桃的甜味，水果味整成咸口不好吃，只能做甜口。

杨：有什么菜是首长比较喜欢的呢？

宋：鹿胶可以单独直接吃，我熬好后，搁小塑料盒里，每次切一块，首长吃饭前或者平时茶歇就这样拿着吃。也可以做成鹿胶海参、阿胶海参。炖牛肉、烧鱼、炖鱼、做豆腐萝卜的时候加点胶，都能起到很好的补益作用。胶可以熬粥、烧菜都没问题，但不能放太多，一般不超过两克。

苏：您做药膳开发的时候会考虑口味问题吗？

宋：那当然，我做的所有药膳都没有药味，我也反对菜里面有药味。有些人做菜喜欢把人参、枸杞子都往里面搁，我从不这样做，我做的胶类菜都是单一配方。因为胶是起修合作用，本身已经很突出，不需要再加其他辅料。我很反对有人无休止地搁人参，这不是谁都能吃的食材。这些都是父母告诉我的，他们不允许乱添加东西。

苏：在大连的时候您已经开始掌厨了？

宋：那会儿我是干部，也不能老在这儿做菜。有时候领导来了，我就做一两个菜。平时我做一次胶可以放很长时间，早晨起来喝茶拿刀一切就好。

苏：那您家这么丰富的菜品，是什么时候研发出来的呢？

宋：有80%的菜是在部队研发出来的，后来恢复大通饭庄后又研发了20%。在大通饭庄恢复前，很多菜都已经成型，现开发哪来得及。

杨：举几个例子，哪些是您在部队开发的？

Yang: In the past, many officials were afraid to use the toilet when they met with the emperors, so they would not eat or drink before the meeting. Instead, they took ginseng and antlers.

Song: Yes, we also have Court Tea substitute from the Qing Palace. My father and my mother boiled the tea with gelatin and poured it into a pot to carry it as meals and drinks. This was because my parents gave medical attention and were always on the road.

Yang: How did you know that gelatin could be used in dishes?

Song: One year when I was home, my father was boiling gelatin. Some leftover meat dregs were stuck under the bottom of the pot and basin. I'm used to being clean in the army, so I brushed it clean and dumped them. My father said it was a waste of materials. Because of the homology of medication and diet, the leftovers were edible, so I slowly started experimenting.

Yang: Which gelatin did the senior officers find preferable?

Song: Deerskin gelatin, bovine-hide gelatin and turtle-shell gelatin. But they didn't like propolis and peach gum. They liked spicy food. Peach gum has little taste, similar to a drink. Peach gum can be used in making congee, but not in stir-fries, because it's sweet and cannot be used in dishes.

Yang: What are the dishes that the senior officers enjoy more?

Song: Deerskin gelatin can be eaten directly alone. I put it in a small plastic box and cut a piece each time. They ate it before meals or during tea breaks. They can be cooked with sea cucumbers as well. If we stew beef, roast fish, stew fish, or make tofu and turnips with gelatin, the dishes can be quite tonic. We can make congee and cook dishes with gelatin. But we can't add more than two grams each time.

Su: Do you consider taste when you develop medicinal dishes?

Song: Of course, none of the medicinal dishes I make have a medicinal taste, and I'm against having a medicinal taste in them. Some people like to put ginseng and wolfberry in their dishes, which I never do. The gelatin I use in dishes had only a single ingredient. Because gelatin is acting as a repair agent, it is already very prominent and does not need to be supplemented. I'm very much against someone endlessly putting ginseng in the dishes. It's not for everyone. That's what my parents told me. They warned me not to add ingredients at my will.

Su: You were already in charge of the kitchen when you were in Dalian?

Song: At that time I was a cadre, I could not always be cooking. Sometimes when the leaders came, I cooked one or two dishes for them. The gelatin that I make once can be preserved for a long time. Every morning when I get up to drink tea, I cut a piece off it.

Su: So when did you develop such a wide variety of dishes?

Song: 80% of the dishes were developed when I was in the army, and 20% were developed after the restoration of the Datong Restaurant. Many dishes were already in place before the restoration of the Datong Restaurant. There is no time to develop them after that.

Yang: Can you name some of the ones developed by you in the army?

鹿胶海参

宋：1996年，我在商学院念书的时候，写了一篇论文：《试论活海参的制作》。那时候鲜海参很少见，大部分人做菜用的都是干海参，需要现发。因为我在棒棰岛学习工作，接触过活海参，就去问牟传仁怎么做活海参。牟传仁是中国做海鲜菜的一把手，也是中国十大名厨之一，当时在大连市政处机关宾馆，也就是渤海饭店当总厨。他说做不了，活海参又硬又涩。我查了很多书籍寻找关于活海参制作的内容，但都没有找到，我想这是一个空白。我就问海边的人有没有吃活海参的？他们说渔民在海里抓住海参，开膛洗洗就直接生吃。我说那我得去看看，于是就找时间去了海边。

黑石滩、黑石礁、大连……一共去了四个地方，询问当地村里的治保主任。等到早上七八点船回来了，那是我第一次看到活海参，绿色的，有点发黄，全是刺，手一抓都是黏液。我想这可怎么吃啊！渔民就拿剪子，这头一剪，那头一剪，再用水把沙子冲出去，直接就放嘴里嚼。我也跟着吃了一个，特别咸，但是艮、脆，我觉得挺好吃，连吃了两根。中午的时候，他们做凉拌海参，我过去看，他们拿刀把海参剁碎，洗干净后，放在大块冰里冷藏，等到吃的时候，再剁点儿生菜、辣椒，搁点酱油、醋，把冰海参直接放在这里头。我一吃，凉凉的口感，再加上醋、酱油和辣椒的调味，真好吃。

等我回去，首长来后，我也给他做了一碗凉拌活海参，他也觉得挺好吃，这就成了我们棒棰岛的特色。1986年，从春天到冬天，所有来的客人，吃的第一个菜都是凉拌活海参。但有一次，一个领导请客，吃完饭闹肚子。可能是吃得太凉了，我想着下次做个热的海参尝一尝。结果做成热菜后，硬邦邦，根本吃不了。

杨：焯一下也不行？

宋：根据我学过的知识，应该是海参的蛋白质含量太高，火候没掌握好，温度过高，蛋白质就会紧缩变硬。后来我尝试了不同的水温，75℃下去，拿上来的海参不发硬。焯完后我又把它放在凉水里回软，但再烧的时候又变硬了。就这么反复地试验了一个多月，有一天，我刚把海参焯完水就有人来找我，底下的战士就把焯过水的海参放在冰箱里冻着。等我下午去做的时候，一摸海参，扎手但吃起来特别软和、特别嫩。从那以后，海参焯完水，我就会把它搁冰箱里回软，就像发面似的，大约四个小时，再拿出来把水控干。用川菜的做法，锅里炒个汁，搁点辣酱、豆豉、笋丁、肉末，我叫它肉末活海参，做了几

Deerskin Gelatin and Sea Cucumber

Song: In 1996, when I was a student in the business school, I wrote a thesis titled *Experimenting with the Cooking of Fresh Sea Cucumbers*. At that time, fresh sea cucumbers were rare, and most people used dried sea cucumbers for cooking, which required soaking first. Since I was studying and working at Bangchui Island and came into contact with fresh sea cucumbers, I asked Mou Chuanren about how to cook them.Mou Chuanren at that time was the best chef in making seafood cuisine in China and also one of China's top ten chefs. He was also the chief chef at the hotel of the Governmental Affairs Office of Dalian, the Bohai Hotel. He said he couldn't do it because fresh sea cucumbers are hard and astringent. Then I looked it up in many books about cooking fresh sea cucumbers, but I couldn't find any, so I guessed it was a void. I then asked the people at the beach if anyone eat fresh sea cucumbers. They said that fishermen caught sea cucumbers from the sea and ate them raw. I replied that I had to go and see, so I paid the beach a visit.

Heishitan, Heishijiao, Dalian... I went to four places and asked the security officer of the local village. When the boat came back at 7 or 8 in the morning, I saw fresh sea cucumbers for the first time. They looked green, slightly yellowish, with thorns and mucus. I didn't have a clue how to eat it! The fisherman took the scissors to cut both ends of it, poured sand in with water, and directly put it in his mouth to chew. I ate one also in his way. It tasted very salty, but crispy. I thought it was delicious, so I ate two in a row. At noon, they tossed sea cucumbers in sauce. I went there and saw that they used a knife to chop the sea cucumbers. After washing them, they put them in a large piece of ice and refrigerated them. Before eating, they chopped up some lettuce and chili, added some soy sauce and vinegar, and directly put the iced sea cucumber into them. As soon as I put it in my mouth, I was totally delighted by the fresh taste, a mixture of the vinegar, soy sauce and chili.

When I went back, the senior officers came. So I made him a bowl of tossed fresh sea cucumbers in sauce. He also thought it was delicious. This is the characteristic of our Bangchui Island. In 1986, from spring to winter, the first dish for all the guests who came was mixed fresh sea cucumbers with sauce. But one time, a leader entertained us but had a stomachache after the dinner. Maybe it's because the dish was too cold for him. Then, I planned to try cooking it hot the next time. But the heated dish was too hard to eat at all.

Yang: Won't it work even if it's blanched?

Song: According to what I have learned, the reason should be the high protein content of sea cucumbers. If cooked in too high a temperature, the protein would turn hard. Later, I tried different cooking temperatures and found that the sea cucumber wouldn't turn hard in 75℃. After blanching, I put it in cold water to soften it again, but it hardened again when I boiled it again. After repeated trials for more than a month, one day when I had just blanched the sea cucumbers, someone came. The soldiers under my charge had to put the blanched sea cucumbers in the refrigerator to freeze them. When I tried to cook it in the afternoon, the sea cucumbers felt prickly, but very soft and tender. After the sea cucumber was blanched, I put it in the refrigerator to soften it, just like the dough. About four hours later, I took it out to dry it. Taking the Sichuan cuisine's cooking method, I stir-fried the sauce in the pot, added some chili sauce, fermented black bean, diced bamboo shoots and minced meat. I called it fresh sea cucumber with minced meat. All my several trials turned out successes. For later visits by the leaders, I served hot fresh sea cucumber

次都比较成功。领导再来的时候，我就不上凉拌活海参，改上热的肉末活海参，领导觉得很好吃。我就写了一篇论文，当时获得了商学院的最佳论文，发表在《中国食品》和《烹调知识》上。

我是中国第一个做活海参的大厨。做完了活海参，就开始做活虾、活鲍鱼、活龙虾，全是活的海鲜，然后在报纸、杂志上发表文章，现在网上都能查得到。但有个问题，时间一长都叫别人学了去，甚至达到什么程度呢？我在部队负责管理单位旗下的五星级酒店，有一次我去酒店考察，他们告诉我这是他们公司发明的新菜——活海参制作。我一看，不能说什么。但回去后我就思考，我们家有胶，我可以把胶加到菜里面再申请专利。后来我就不怎么做活海参了，我研制了鹿胶海参、阿胶海参、牛胶海参、龟胶海参等，现在我有很多菜的专利。大连晓芹海参想给我500万买下阿胶海参的专利，我都没有卖。所以中国烹饪协会、北京烹饪协会春节开团拜会的时候，都会叫我过去做咱们自己开创性的菜品。

杨：是根据不同的参配不同的胶吗？

宋：根据不同的季节配不同的胶吃。比如，冬至一过，就吃羊胶烧海参；秋天是牛胶海参；夏天是龟胶海参；春天是鹿胶海参……而且男女吃的也不同。后来就被评为北京名菜。其实胶并不是熬出来的，而是蒸出来的，是慢工夫。胶蒸出来后再调制，我们家大部分都是拿酒和红糖、冰糖调，有时候还拿醋调。我父母给人配药的时候就分这三种，把它分到不同的食品里，相当于药引子，比如搁一勺到姜汤里，一和就可以喝。

苏：放入食品中，口味是不是会有变化？

宋：口味没啥太大变化，因为胶是原味的。而且放得很少，1吨酒才搁3斤胶。它是起一个长期保健的作用，我记得我们家有银勺、铜勺，就是用来固定每次放胶的量。

杨：那您做的阿胶海参其实就是拿胶勾芡？

宋：我们很早就把胶浸到海参里头煨着，跟葱烧海参一个道理，我一般搁胡椒粉、姜还有黄酒调味。鹿胶海参有用活海参做的，也有用干海参。大的是水发的，有型。活的海参没有型，一般用小碗，一人来一碗。大家都愿意吃活的，不愿意吃水发的。我还将鹿胶海参和荞麦面搭配在一起做。荞麦面煮完加两根芦笋，然后放烧好的鹿胶海参，大家也挺乐意吃。

苏：您是怎么想到这种搭配的呢？

with minced meat to replace the cold dish. The leaders were well pleased. Then I wrote a paper, which was selected the best of the business school at that time, and published in *China Food* and *Cooking Knowledge*.

I became the first chef in China who specializes in cooking fresh sea cucumbers. After fresh sea cucumbers, I started to try other fresh seafood such as shrimps, abalones and lobsters. Relevant articles were published in newspapers and magazines, which can still be retrieved now online. But there is a problem. The cooking methods are learned by others over time. How far do they go? I was in charge of the five-star hotel affiliated with the unit when I served in the troops. When I visited the hotel, they told me it's a new invention of their company–making of fresh sea cucumbers. I saw it and found no words to comment. But when I went back, I thought I had gelatin. So I added gelatin to the dish and applied for a patent. Afterward, I didn't do many fresh sea cucumbers. I developed deer gelatin sea cucumbers, donkey-hide sea cucumbers, cattle gelatin sea cucumbers, turtle gelatin sea cucumbers, etc. Now I have many dish patents. The Dalian-based Xiaoqin Sea Cucumber offered me RMB 5 million for the donkey-hide sea cucumber patent, but I refused. Many times the China Cuisine Association and Beijing Cuisine Association held gatherings to celebrate the coming of Spring Festival, and I was invited to showcase these original dishes.

Yang: Are different gelatins added to different sea cucumbers?

Song: Different gelatins are added according to different seasons. For example, after the Winter Solstice, sea cucumbers with goat hide gelatin are recommended; sea cucumbers with cattle hide gelatin are best in autumn; those with turtle gelatin are preferred in summer; spring is the season for sea cucumbers with deer gelatin... Men and women shall eat differently. Mine was later rated the Beijing's Famous Dish. In fact, the gelatin is steamed, but not boiled out. It takes time. After steaming, it's mixed with wine, brown sugar, rock sugar, and sometimes vinegar. When my parents dispensed medicines, they put these three kinds into different foods, like the guiding drug. For example, put a spoonful into the ginger soup and drink it after mixing.

Su: Will the taste change when it is put into food?

Song: No big changes, because it has no special flavor. And a very small quantity is added. 1.5kg gelatin for 1t of wine. It contributes to health care in the long run. I remember that silver spoons and copper spoons were used in my family, but the quantity added was fixed.

Yang: So you just cook the sea cucumber and use donkey hide gelatin to make the gravy?

Song: We dipped the gelatin in the sea cucumber and simmered it very early. It cooks the same way as the sea cucumber with green onions. I usually season with pepper, ginger and yellow wine. Sea cucumber with deer gelatin can be made with either fresh sea cucumbers or dried ones. The big are dried ones, which are easier to shape. Live sea cucumbers have no shape. So these are served with small bowls, one bowl per person. Everyone prefers to eat fresh ones and refuses the soaked ones. I also mixed sea cucumbers with deer gelatin into buckwheat flour. After the soba noodles are boiled, add two pieces of asparagus and the stewed deer gelatin sea cucumber. It's also spoken highly of among the eaters.

Su: How did you come up with this combination?

宋：粗粮细作，精和粗要结合起来。《黄帝内经》有五畜为益，五谷为养，五果为助，五菜为充，按照这个配餐理念来做的。

苏：您曾经学过的营养配餐对您做药膳有什么样的作用？

宋：作用很大，使我懂得了理论跟实践相结合，食物的相生相克原理。原先我做菜的思维都是单一的，学习营养配餐后变成了双向的。我养成了一个习惯：从来不做单菜。我的特点就是每样东西里面配料全是两种，海鲜和蔬菜的搭配、和主食的搭配、和水果的搭配。比如，海参配上谷物和蔬菜。像我这样把菜搭上主食的人很少。

海水豆腐

宋：在棒棰岛的时候，有一次首长说这里的豆腐没有青岛舰队做得好吃，我就上心了。部队之间可以互相学习，我叫青岛舰队的人到棒棰岛来教我们做豆腐。来了后，我看那人拿着一个小瓶，等豆酱熬好后，就把瓶子里的水倒盆里头，水是绿色的，我问他是什么？他说是卤水。我们这儿的卤水是黑色的，我说怎么跟我们这儿的不一样？我担心他什么玩意儿都往食物里搁。他说你看吧！

我们做的豆腐一般都是白色的，他用绿色卤水做出来的豆腐有点发暗、发绿，形状也跟我们不一样，比较松散，不像我们的豆腐压得实，吃起来口感也不同。我就让战士去市场买绿色的卤水，但没有找到。几天后，正好有机会去青岛，就让他们带我去市场转转，一看，这边的卤水都是绿色的。我就问卖豆腐的人如何制作这种卤水？我以为搁了什么化学原料，结果人家说这是纯天然的海水卤！我就去晒盐池子看，礁石那儿的水被太阳晒热、晒干，最后剩下一些绿了叭叽的沉淀物，像海藻一样。我拿回来一看，和绿色卤水一样，只是舰队拿的那个比这要更浓。我就买了一些拿回来做海水豆腐，但领导还是觉得我做的豆腐有问题，吃着跟他们做的不一样。

我想怎么还不一样呢？过了一段时间，舰队正好停在崂山脚下，我就去崂山溜达，渴了买崂山矿泉水喝，这是我们中国三大名水之一，味道果然不一样。我就问他们是不是营房也安的这种水，他们说对，天天都喝矿泉水。我一琢磨，豆腐整不好可能是因为水。就拿了一些水回大连做豆腐，领导再来吃的时候就说有那味了。因此我们有了一个新菜海水豆腐，就是用海水卤和崂山水做的，这种豆腐的海藻清香味比较突出。

Song: Coarse grains should be made finely. It means the fine and coarse grains should be combined. The "Inner Canon of Yellow Emperor" proposes five animals for benefit, five grains for nourishment, five fruits for help, and five vegetables for replenishment. It is made against this catering concept.

Su: What effect does the nutritional diet you have learned impose on your medical diet?

Song: It imposes a great effect. It teaches me how to understand the combination of theory and practice, and the mutual growth and restraint of foods. I followed a simplex way of thinking originally, and changed to a two-way method after learning the nutritional diet course. I have developed a habit: never cook with a single ingredient. It's my signature to add two ingredients in each dish, seafood plus vegetable, plus staple food, or plus fruit. For example, sea cucumbers go with grains and vegetables. Few people would mix the dish with staple food like me.

Seawater Tofu

Song: When I was in Bangchui Island, once the senior officers complained that tofu there didn't taste as good as in the Qingdao fleet. I remembered it. Chefs in troops may learn from each other. Then I invited chefs of the Qingdao fleet to teach us how to make tofu in the Bangchui Island. When he arrived, I found him holding a bottle in hand. When the bean paste was finished, he poured water in the bottle into the basin. The water looked green. I asked, what was it? He replied it's brine. Our brine was black. So I asked why it looked different in color? I was cautious about food ingredients. He said, look!

The tofu we make is generally white. The tofu he makes with green brine is a bit dark and green, in different shape from ours. It is loose, not as compact as ours, and tastes different. So I sent my soldiers to buy green brine in the market, but they didn't find any. A few days later, when I had the opportunity to go to Qingdao, I asked them to take me to the market. I saw the brine there was all green. I asked the tofu seller how did he make the green brine? I thought certain chemical materials were put in, but he replied it was purely seawater brine! I checked at the pond for salt sunning and saw that the water around the reef was heated and dried by the sun, leaving some green sediment like seaweed. I took it back and found it the same with the green brine, except that it looked thinner than the one brought by the fleet. I bought some to make seawater tofu, but the leader still felt there was something wrong with the tofu I made, which tasted different from theirs.

I wondered why it still tasted different. After a while, the fleet happened to stop at the foot of Laoshan Mountain. I went to the mountain for a stroll. I was thirsty and bought a bottle of Laoshan mineral water. As one of the three famous waters in China, it truly tasted good. So I asked them if the barracks were supplied the same water, they replied yes and soldiers drank the mineral water every day. I guessed the problem of my tofu may be resulted from the water. So I took some water back to Dalian to make tofu. For afterward visits, the leaders said it tasted basically the flavor required. Thus, we have a new dish, seawater tofu, which is made with seawater brine and Laoshan water. This sort of tofu features a thick smell of seaweed.

杨：您要在北京长期做这豆腐，制作成本可够高的。

宋：这是一款高端豆腐，就算在山东青岛做成本也一样高。

苏：现在北京有卖这个菜吗？

宋：内部有时候卖。我还在参加比赛的时候做过，但人家不给我评分。他们觉得自己不会做这个东西，没办法鉴别到底是不是海水豆腐。而且他们都是厨师，不会做药膳，让我别难为他们。但这个豆腐味道很好，我就给它申请了专利。

宋子刚制作的宫廷药膳鹿胶海参、阿胶海参被《中国烹饪》杂志选登

Song Zigang's palace dietary specialties, Deerskin Gelatin and Sea Cucumber and Donkey-hide Gelatin and Sea Cucumber, were published on *Chinese Cuisine*

Yang: You're mass-producing this tofu in Beijing. The cost would be heightened.

Song: This is high-end tofu. It cost high even if made in Qingdao.

Su: Does it sell in Beijing now?

Song: It's available internally sometimes. I once brought it to a competition, but the judges refused to give it a score. They admitted they couldn't do it, so they couldn't judge it. They asked me not to embarrass them. They were just general chefs, with no clues on how to cook medicinal dishes. But they agreed this tofu tasted very good. So I applied for a patent for it.

"海水豆腐"发明专利证书

The patent for invention of "Seawater Tofu"

宋子刚制作的宫廷药膳“阿胶海参杂粮面”展示

“Donkey-hide Gelatin and Sea Cucumber Plus Grains Noodle”, a palace dietary specialty by Song Zigang

宋子刚制作的宫廷药膳“鱼胶饽饽”展示

“Steamed Bun with Fish Gelatin”, a palace dietary specialty by Song Zigang

宋子刚和他的膏

Song Zigang and his ointment

宋子刚制作的宫廷药膳“金锅全家福”展示

Song Zigang's “All Poon Choi”, a palace dietary specialty

宋子刚制作的宫廷药膳“牛胶萝卜”展示

Song Zigang's “Bovine-hide Gelatin and Turnip”, a palace dietary specialty

大通鹿茅酒

Datong Lumao Wine

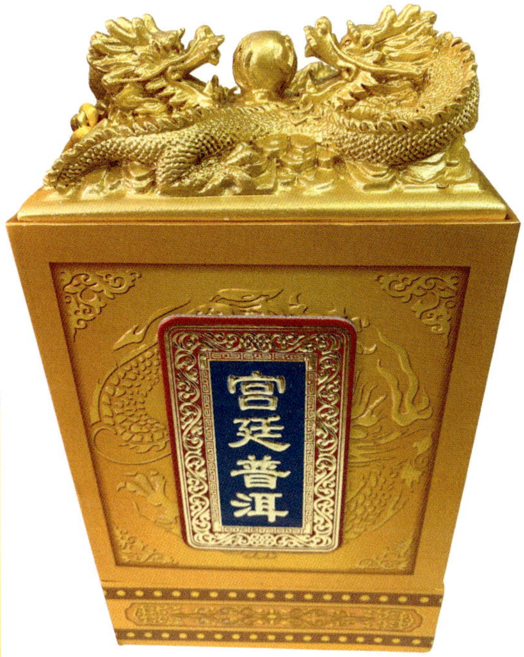

宫廷普洱茶

Court Pu'er Tea

宋子刚在奥运博览会上展示药膳产品仙鹿膏、凤凰膏、鹿茅酒、阿胶酒、宫廷普洱茶

Song Zigang displayed medicinal food products such as Xianlu Ointment, Fenghuang Ointment, Lumao Wine, Donkey-hide Gelatin Wine and Court Pu'er Tea at the Olympic Expo

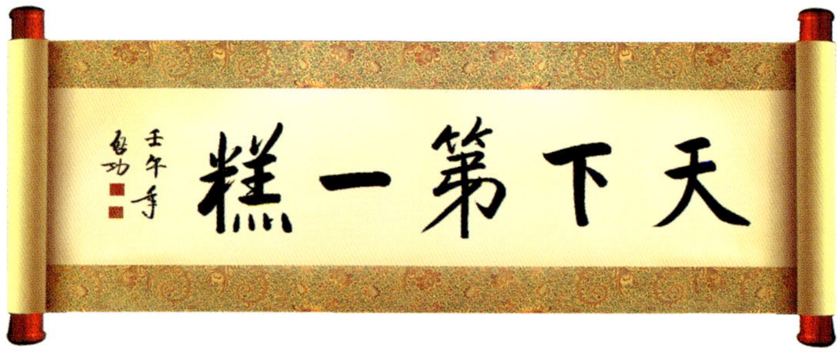

宋子刚在故宫“御膳房”主理时，爱新觉罗·启功品尝仙鹿膏、凤凰膏后为宋子刚题词

When Song Zigang was running the “Yushan Restaurant” in the Forbidden City, Aisin-Gioro Qigong sampled the Xianlu Ointment and Fenghuang Ointment and then wrote an inscription for Song Zigang

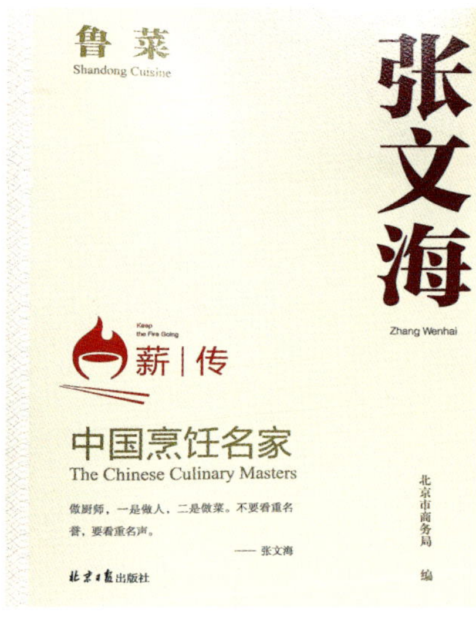

北京市商务局原副局长刘梅英、北京烹饪协会会长云程、张文海之子张宝庭参加宋子刚为纪念恩师张文海出资出版的《薪传——中国烹饪名家张文海》新书发布会

Liu Meiying, former Deputy Director of Beijing Municipal Bureau of Commerce, Yun Cheng, President of Beijing Cuisine Association, and Zhang Baoting, son of Zhang Wenhai, attended Zhang Wenhai's publication ceremony of *Passing on the Fire—Chinese Culinary Masters* Zhang Wenhai funded by Song Zigang in memory of his mentor

宋子刚在故宫“御膳房”主理时，爱新觉罗·恒德为宋子刚题写宋氏老牌匾“御德堂”

When Song Zigang was running the “Yushan Restaurant” in the Forbidden City, Aisin-Gioro Hengde inscribed on the Song’s plaque “Yude Restaurant”

宋子刚在故宫“御膳房”主理时，爱新觉罗·恒德为宋子刚题写“御德堂堂训”

When Song Zigang was running the “Yushan Restaurant” in the Forbidden City, Aisin-Gioro Hengde inscribed the Yude Restaurant motto for Song

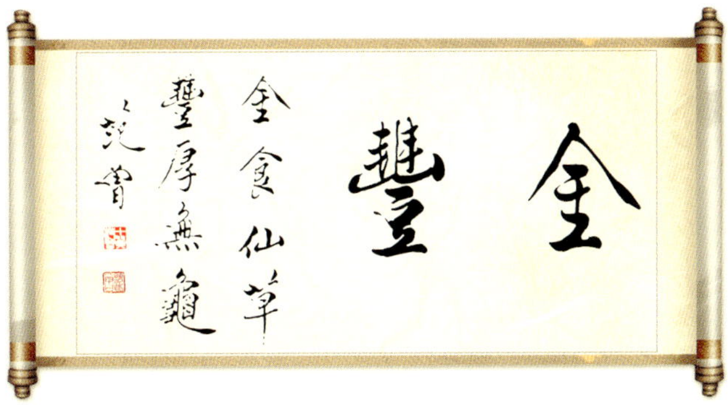

宋子刚在故宫“御膳房”主理时，国学大师文怀沙和国学大师、书法家范曾品尝仙鹿膏、凤凰膏后为宋子刚题词

Inscription for Song Zigang by Wen Huaisha, master of Chinese culture, and Fan Zeng, master of Chinese culture and calligrapher after tasting the Xianlu Ointment and Fenghuang Ointment when Song Zigang was in charge of the “Yushan Restaurant” of the Forbidden City

宋子刚承接国家科研课题，打造中国药膳第一品牌，并成为餐饮界杂志的封面人物

Song Zigang undertakes the national scientific research project to build the first brand of Chinese medicated diet, and has been featured on the cover of magazine

宋子刚荣登多期报刊封面人物

Song Zigang has been featured on the cover of multiple newspapers and magazines

第三章

Chapter 3

开启团餐事业

Start the Group Meal Business

【访谈者按】 药膳是我们访谈的起始点，也是本书的重点，但如果不谈团餐，我们对宋先生的认识就失于片面了。对于宋先生的事业来说，团餐和药膳是相辅相成的两个重要组成部分。药膳是团餐的亮点，团餐则为进一步发展药膳打下了基础。这部分访谈收录了宋先生早年的创业经历，让我们十分钦佩的是，即使曾为部队的干部，宋先生还是选择从基层做起，事事亲力亲为，不假手于人。他的精细化管理，对菜品、服务的高要求让他的团餐迅速脱颖而出。少有人敢于承接服务的2008年奥运会对他来说是个巨大的挑战，但同时也是机遇。圆满完成任务之后，他的事业迎来了第一个高峰。

部队转业后

苏：1998年从部队转业后您做过什么呢？

宋：从1998年到2000年，大约有一年多的空档期，我在外面打工，干炒菜和管理，直到1999年年底才去原信息产业部上班。我从部队学到的东西都在社会上进行了实践。

苏：都是在哪些公司干过？

宋：我曾在大型计算机集团公司的食堂做过厨师长。

第二个，1998年的下半年，北京全益达在丰联广场联合大厦有一个美食广场，当时它有20多个食堂，给外交部、政府机关、银行、华润、嘉里中心等供餐。我朋友介绍我去做技术总监，每个月三万块钱，主要负责指导菜品、做菜。

苏：您还要亲自炒吗？

宋：必须炒，我得给他们进行培训、打样。我在全益达工作到第二年4月份，就去了原信息产业部做行政二处处长，管理赛迪酒店。

苏：实际上您真正担任厨师这个岗位做炒菜的工作，就是那一年多的时间吗？

宋：那一年可以说把我在部队学到的东西全用上了。我所有的时间都在钻研炒菜，白天上班，下班后我就骑自行车到西单图书大厦抄全国各地的烹饪书，一直抄到书店打烊才走。就这样看了有一年吧，那里的人都认识我。那时候我爱打球，周六日除了上午打球以外，其他时间全都在那儿学习，还学习了

[Interviewer's note] Medicinal diet is the starting point of our interview and the focus of this book. But if we skip the group meals, our understanding of Mr. Song will be one-sided. For Mr. Song's career, group meals and medicinal meals are two important components that complement each other. While the medicated diet marks the highlight of the group meal, the group meal lays the foundation for the further development of the medicated diet. This part of the interview introduces Mr. Song's early entrepreneurial experience. What we admire is that even though serving a cadre in the army, Mr. Song chose to start from scratches and do everything by himself, without bothering others for no excuse. His refined management and high standards on dishes and services made his group meals quickly stand out. The 2008 Beijing Olympic Games, which few people dare to undertake, turns out a huge challenge and also an opportunity for him. After successfully completing the task, he ascended to another peak of his career.

After Retirement from the Army

Su: What have you done since you transferred to civilian work from the army in 1998?

Song: From 1998 to 2000, there was a gap of more than a year. I worked outside, acting as chef or manager, and went to work in the Former Ministry of Industry and Information Technology in 1999. What I learned from the army has been put into practice in the society.

Su: Which companies did you work for?

Song: I served as head chef of the canteen in a large computer company.

Second, in the second half of 1998, the Beijing-based brand Quanyida had a food plaza in the Unity Building at the Fenglian Plaza. It had more than 20 canteens then, which served the Ministry of Foreign Affairs, government organs, banks, China Resources, Kerry Centre... My friend introduced me to be a technical director, RMB 30,000 a month, mainly responsible for dish instructions and cooking.

Su: Did you cook in person?

Song: Surely. I also had to give them training and sampling. I worked with Quanyida until April of the next year, and then I went to work as the director of the Administrative Division II of the Former Ministry of Industry and Information Technology to take charge of the Saidi Hotel.

Su: Actually, you worked as a chef merely during that period of time?

Song: It can be said that I used all the things I had learned in the army that year. I spent all my time studying cooking. I went to work in daytime, and rode a bike to the Beijing Book Building to copy the cooking books after getting off work until the closing time. I went there for a year, and everyone there knew me. At that time, I loved to play balls. Except for playing in the morning on Saturdays and Sundays, I studied there all the time. I also learned modern management, which helped me a lot. One is that I don't cook big-pot dishes because I have to guarantee the quality of my

现代化管理，这些对我帮助很大。一是我不做大锅菜，菜出来的品质有保证。二是我的精细化管理，成本控制得比较好，给老板挣了钱，老板高兴。最后我走的时候，全益达的老板不想我走，给我20%的股份挽留我继续跟他干。我说不行，我得回去上班。那时候我就想多挣点钱，实在没办法了才回去上班。后来我在原来的信息产业部上了几年班后也辞职了。

苏：您在非典期间表现特别卓越，当时是主要负责食堂的管理工作吗？

宋：当时的信息产业部有三个酒店，北京一个，外地两个，我负责管理北京昌平的赛迪会议中心。当时信息产业部的食堂跟通信兵总部在一起，非典的时候，领导曾想把食堂停了。但我想好好干，不想刚负责就被停办。我自告奋勇说学过防护，再加上我家的祖传药方，用姜配上鹿胶、牛胶给大伙喝，主要是补气血，提高免疫力。就这样，整整九个月，我们单位没有出现过一例病例，后来就被评为国务院红旗食堂。

非典时期我还发明了两项专利。那时候国家食品药品监督管理总局来我们这儿总结经验，我就把3块毛巾保洁法和餐具2次消毒法讲给他们听，他们听完后说这可以申请专利。国家实用新型专利很快就批下来了，从那时候开始，我们的食堂环境保洁就一直沿用这些方法直到现在。后来中央电视台、国家食品药品监督管理总局都想找我们承包食堂，我们就给接过来了，但领导说信息产业部不能接这些工作，那我想我就辞职干吧，于是，我就成了中央国家机关里第一个辞职的处级干部。

从食堂做起，从服务做起

苏：您辞职后的第一份工作是什么呢？

宋：承包中国海关的食堂进行社会化改革。当时我从原信息产业部带了160个人出来，没到三个月全跑了回去。人家跟我说："宋总，我媳妇儿不让，怕没了铁饭碗，领导也说如果在外干一年半载不行就赶紧回来。"我说："你们回去吧，我不回去。"我就想挣点钱去做药。

杨：还是因为您有在外打工的经验，知道可以挣钱。

dishes. The second is my refined management well controls the cost. I made money for the boss, and he was pleased. When I decided to leave, the boss of Quanyida didn't want to let me go and offered 20% shares of the company to show his intention. I said no, I have to go back to work. At that time, I just wanted to make more money. I wouldn't get back until I had no ways out. Later, I worked with the Former Ministry of Industry and Information Technology for a couple of years and resigned.

Su: You performed exceptionally well during the SARS period. At that time, were you mainly responsible for the management of the canteen?

Song: The Former Ministry of Industry and Information Technology has three hotels, one in Beijing and two in other places. I was responsible for managing the Saidi Conference Center in Changping, Beijing. At that time, the canteen of the Ministry of Industry and Information Technology was located at where the canteen of the headquarters for signalmen was. When SARS hit, the leadership wanted to quit the canteen. But I wanted to do something, and didn't want it to be suspended when I just took charge of it. I volunteered to claim that I had learned the prevention and protection. Also, I followed my family's ancestral prescription to braise deer and cattle hide gelatin with ginger, and offered them to drink to replenish qi and blood and improve their immunity. In this way, there was not a case confirmed in our unit for nine months. So ours was rated the State Council Red Flag Canteen later.

During the SARS period, I also invented two patents. When the State Food and Drug Administration came to us to sum up the experience, I told them the 3-towel cleaning method and the 2-time disinfection method. Hearing them, they advised that I apply for patents. My application for the national new utility model was soon approved. From them on, our canteen had been using my methods for cleaning until now. Later, CCTV and the State Food and Drug Administration asked us to operate canteens, and I agreed. But as a civil servant with the Ministry of Industry and Information Technology, I was not allowed to do business outside. So I resigned, as the first regiment-level cadre that quit job from a governmental organ.

Start from the Canteen, Start from the Service

Su: What was your first job after resigning?

Song: I took over the canteen of China Customs for socialization reform. At first, I brought 160 people with me from the Former Ministry of Industry and Information Technology, but all of them returned to the ministry in less than three months. They told me, "Mr. Song, I'm sorry but my wife said no. She's afraid my job outside the governmental organ may not last long. My former leader also promised my job's still available for me." I said: "You go back, but I won't." I just want to make some money and go back to make medicine.

Yang: It's because you have the experience of working outside and know that working outside could make money.

宋：对，我看到这是一个产业，但那时候社会上没人有这个意识。我还有实践经验，当时我给信息产业部一年挣了三百多万，那个年代的三百多万是什么概念！盒饭里就放俩菜，搁一个米饭，弄一瓶可乐，弄个水果，连酸奶都没有，就15块钱一份，多么高的利润啊！

1998年，我就开始涉足团餐行业，跟酒店、餐馆相比，做团餐：第一，风险小；第二，投入少；第三，我有文化知识。那时候我经常上网，了解到世界500强中就有3家企业是做团餐的——美国的爱玛客、英国的康帕斯和法国的索迪斯，这是当时世界上三个比较大的团餐公司，他们都有上百年的历史。但中国还没有历史如此悠久的团餐企业，连做团餐的都很少。再加上我经济条件有限，部队转业发的钱很少，我又没有家底，但我有机会承包了宣传部、中央电视台和国家食品药品监督管理总局的食堂，所以就选择了做团餐。

苏：团餐跟酒店、餐馆的经营成本有什么不一样呢？

宋：我认为团餐是餐饮中最难干的。因为团餐的标准低，客户群体又固定。如果菜品没有变化、管理不到位、精细化算不好就会赔钱。因此要想做好团餐，对技术管理的要求更高、更严。刚开始做的时候全是我一个人盯，我既是服务员，又是厨师，又是采购，啥都亲力亲为。能够做到今天，都是因为我的团餐理念和配餐理念，到今天也是称得上全国最先进的中餐、西餐和养生药膳。

杨：您从那时候就开始做药膳了？

宋：1998年我就开始做药膳，母亲教我的红糖馒头配小米粥在我们餐厅卖得最快。小时候，别人上我们家来看病，女同志缺气血，母亲就让回去吃这个，她还告诉别人往红糖里加阿胶、枣。枣蒸熟、捣碎后和红糖、白面搓一起，像包包子似的包起来，再熬小米粥喝，或者有时候直接就拿这些熬小米粥。我记得那时候母亲就用红皮鸡蛋，不用白皮鸡蛋，她说坐月子就得用红皮鸡蛋。到今天，我都认为这些是很经典的方子。

杨：古代中医理念是讲究药食搁在一起，但很少有人懂得，只有少数有条件的人才会去做。您是怎么想到这个的？

宋：我本来想回家熬药做保健品，鹿胎膏、九昼夜阿胶……但是等我辞完职，国家对保健品进行了管控，出台了各种药字号、食字号的文件，没有资质不能做，我只能做食品类的东西。但我不能闲着，就被逼着一步一步走出来了。

杨：我觉得您跟那些大厨学的东西，在团餐上用不到。

宋：太用得上了，我总结越高档的菜做法越简单。比如白菜、萝卜、豆腐

Song: Yes, I thought it was an industry, but no one else thought the same way with me. I also had practical experience. Back then, I contributed annual revenue of RMB 3 million to the ministry. That's an astronomical figure at the time! A lunch box, containing two dishes, a rice, a bottle of coke and a fruit, not even a yogurt, cost RMB 15. What a high profit!

As early as in 1998, I started to get involved in the group meal industry. Compared with hotels and restaurants, it features such advantages: I) small risks; II) less investment; and III) I'm educated. At that time, I used to surf the Internet a lot and learned that three of the world's top 500 companies were doing group meals–Aramark in the United States, Compass in the United Kingdom and Sodexo in France. They were major practitioners in the group meal industry at the time, which were all established some 100 years ago. But I found no Chinese group-meal company had been run for so long, and the number of group-meal companies was limited. Though my budget was small, with a handful of allowance for transfer to civilian work from the army and no financial support from family, I seized the opportunity to take over the canteens of the Publicity Department, CCTV, and the State Food and Drug Administration to offer group meals.

Su: What is the difference in the operating costs between group meals, and hotels and restaurants?

Song: I think group meals are the hardest of catering businesses. Because group meals feature low standards and fixed customers. If there is no change in the dishes, or there is poor management and budgeting, you will lose money. So, group meals require higher and stricter requirements on technical management. I took charge of all things at first. I was a waiter, a chef, a purchaser... My business lasts today because I adopt the most advanced group meal and meal design concepts that involve Chinese, western and medicinal dishes.

Yang: When did you start to do medicinal diet business?

Song: I started the medicated diet in 1998. The brown sugar steamed bun with millet porridge my mom taught me sells the best in my canteen. In my childhood time, when female patients lack of qi and blood came to our clinic, my mom would suggest them eat the steamed buns with porridge, added with donkey-hide gelatin and date. Steamed dates, mashed brown sugar and white flour are packed or directly poured into the porridge for boiling. I remember my mom preferred eggs with red shells, claiming that this sort was taken by women in confinement. Even today, I think these are classic recipes.

Yang: The ancient Chinese medicine philosophy proposes to mix medicine with food. But only a few people understood the theory and fewer practiced it. How did you come up with this idea?

Song: I originally scheduled to go home and boil health care products, such as deer placenta ointment, nine-day donkey-hide gelatin... However, when I resigned, the state issued various "medicine"- and "food"-titled documents to control the health care products. Without qualifications for health care product production, I can only do food. I had to do something, so I delved deeper and deeper into the food industry.

Yang: I don't think you can use the things you learned from those senior chefs for your group meal business.

Song: Too useful, I concluded that higher-grade food has a simpler way of making it. For example, for cabbage, radish, tofu and other such ordinary ingredients, the chef cook them differently from what the ordinary people do. The chef's cooking quality and thinking are different

这些稀松平常的食材，大厨做出来的跟普通人做出来的截然不同。大厨做菜的质量和思路跟别人不一样，他将平常的东西弄出花来，这就是艺术，并且不需要特别高级的烹饪技术。举一个简单的例子，王锡田做过一个箱子豆腐，就是把豆腐炸一下后掏空，做几种料放进去，再盖上，上锅蒸。领导吃起来就觉得这很不一样。我跟他们交流，学习他们的思路，举一反三地把这些应用在团餐上。

我是靠两样东西把团餐做起来的。第一个，特别讲究服务。我始终西装革履，其他做食堂的人没有一个西装革履。第二个，坚决反对做大锅菜团餐，恰恰相反，食堂要做精品菜。原先都是做一大盆，我告诉他们一次只做10份、20份，炒和炸的尤其不能做太多。

炒、蒸、烧、炖、烤、炸这六种烹调方法是做热菜最常用的烹调方法，因为我讲究营养，大部分用烧、蒸、炖、炒，到今天我基本不做过油的菜，除了烧菜、做鱼类、做肉类会过油，现在都用新鲜鱼，鱼也不用过油了。我也是餐饮业第一个提倡用混合油的人，因为这个有营养。

杨：您要是一次只做10份，会不会供应不上？

宋：精细化做菜需要技术支撑。我把菜按烹调方法、出餐时间进行分类。蒸的菜、烧的菜、炖的菜可以是大锅，越炖越好吃，但我不允许炒大锅菜，我们这儿没有一次炒超过20份的菜。开菜谱的时候，主荤菜一个用炖或者烧，一个用蒸，这两个都不用炒，可以批量生产。然后把所有调味分为汁料、粉料、调料、小料四种和加热前调味、加热中调味、加热后调味、辅助性调味四种，所有材料都提前备好。我是第一个提倡在前台做“营养加油站”的人，就是摆一大堆调料在前台，花生米、海米、姜丝、醋、辣椒、豆豉，包括榨菜都有。菜炒出来后不搁辣椒，也不搁那么多盐，只有基本底味，顾客根据自己的口味往里加盐、生抽、老抽，顾客也很高兴。现在的火锅自助料台，估计都是跟我学的。

很多准备工作一早我就给分开来，食堂的工作人员，前厅的准备前厅，后厨的准备后厨。这些都是我跟人民大会堂、钓鱼台国宾馆学的。我说过一句话“卓越温馨的服务，是金丰生存的唯一理由”。这就来自于我太爷爷宋相如，他开创了全国服务台由后头挪到前头的先例。除了服务，还有一个“首接负责”。

杨：这个怎么讲？

宋：意思是只要我接手了，这个事就得在我这儿结束，一次性把事情做好。比如，我接到这个菜，就要一次性把菜做好，不能回锅。我要求精，因此写了团餐菜品特点18条。第一，设计中求全面。设计的菜需要兼顾东南西北、

from others. He likes to make ordinary things special, and this is art, and does not need particularly advanced cooking techniques. To give a simple example, Wang Xitian made a box-type tofu, that is, fried tofu, hollowed it out, put some ingredients in it, covered it again, and steamed it in a pot. The leader feel different when he tasted it. I communicated with them, learned their ideas, and applied these dishes to group meals by analogy.

I got my group meals going by two things. First, pay special attention to service. I always wear a suit and tie, and none of the other canteen workers wear a suit and tie. Second, I firmly oppose preparing mediocre group meals, instead, a canteen shall make refined dishes. They used to cook a large pot of dishes,but I told them to cook for only 10 or 20 people at a time, especially for stir-fried and fried dishes.

Stir-frying, steaming, braising, stewing, roasting and frying are the most commonly used cooking methods for hot dishes. I cook most of the time by braising, steaming stewing and frying, because I care much about nutrition, I seldom cook any oily dishes. Except for making fried dish, fish dish and meat dish to which I fried it with oil first, now I use fresh fish and never fried it with oil. I am also the first person in the catering industry to advocate the use of mixed oil, because it is nutritious.

Yang: If you only make 10 copies of dish at a time, can you supply your customers?

Song: Fine cooking needs technical support. I classify the dishes according to cooking method and meal time. Steamed dishes, braised dishes and stewed dishes can be made in a big pot, and the more they are stewed, the better they are. However, I do not allow to cook big-pot dishes. We never cooked 20 copies of a dish at one time here. When preparing the menu, main meat dishes can be cooked with stewing or braising or steaming rather than stir-frying, so dishes can be mass-produced. Then all seasonings are divided into four kinds: juice, powder, seasoning and small seasoning, and four kinds: seasoning before heating, seasoning during heating, seasoning after heating and auxiliary seasoning, which are all prepared in advance. I was the first person to advocate to make a nutrition gas station before cooking. I put a lot of spices in front of me, including peanuts, dried shrimps, shredded ginger, vinegar, peppers, fermented soya beans, including pickled mustard tuber. The dish is stir-fried without chili pepper and not so much salt, only the basic base flavor, and customers are happy to add salt, light soy sauce and dark soy sauce to it according to their taste. Now the hot pot buffet material table, I guess are learned from me.

I assigned a lot of preparation work to the cafeteria staff early in the morning, and those in the front room prepared the front room, and those in the back kitchen prepared the back kitchen. I learned all these from the Great Hall of the People and the Diaoyutai State Guesthouse. I have said that "excellent and warm service is the only reason for Jinfeng's survival". This comes from my grandfather, Song Xiangyu, who started the national service desk by moving it from the back to the front. In addition to service, we have a "first call" system.

Yang: How do you explain this?

Song: It means that as soon as I receive this task, it has to end up with me and get it done at one time. For example, when I receive a task to cook a dish, I have to cook it well at one time, re-cooking is not allowed. I am seeking for delicacy, so I wrote 18 characteristics of group meals. First, seek comprehensiveness in design. The designed dishes need to take into account the tastes of the southeast, northwest, domestic and international people. Second, seek standards in cutting and serving dishes. Cutting and serving dishes are made based on standards. Third, seek bright colors.

国内、国际人群的口味。第二，切、配中求标准。切菜、配菜讲究标准化。第三，色彩中求鲜艳。第四，出品中求清爽，我不允许出现油乎乎、黏糊糊、黑乎乎的菜。第五，口味中求柔和，不能太麻太辣。第六，检查中求严格。上菜之前装盘要讲究……一共18条，还有一个“出餐十不上”，在我管理五星级酒店时就写过“上菜十不上”。

苏：都是什么呢？

宋：心情不好不能上。我对这个理解跟别人不一样，服务员今天不高兴，还去给客人端菜，这是让客人看脸色吗？所以，心情不好就换到别的岗位。另外制作不达标不能上。我对菜是定有标准的，做黑了、煳了、没熟都不行，不能上。还有切配不标准不能上、装盘不讲究不能上，等等。

杨：这得下大功夫培训。

宋：我天天培训，开例会、开总结会、开培训会。全员都要参加，总结当天早晨、中午客人对菜的反映，好的表扬，不好的改进。

苏：一次开会有多少人？

宋：刚开始人少，才一百多人，现在都上万人了，必须坚持开会培训。

苏：您还做过“御膳房”是吗？

宋：我在故宫里面开了五年半的“御膳房”，这个和团餐是同时进行的，它俩还能互补。很多菜品都是我在故宫里恢复开发的。[1]“二十四节气宴”就是我退伍开公司后，在故宫“御膳房”研发的。部队里没有“宴”，因为不能给首长上很多菜，都是上单品菜。

苏：全牛宴、全羊宴都是您自己创立的吗？

宋：对，这是属于我自创的东西。故宫里有几个宴，比如千叟宴，但不多。[2]我觉得不行，就根据二十四节气配制不同的宴席。按照节气做菜补益身

1 宋子刚注：宫廷美食“细八件”——仙鹿膏、凤凰膏、定升糕、定胜糕、八珍糕、八仙糕、状元糕、千叟糕；还有太乙紫金锭、宫廷普洱茶、宫廷代茶饮、鹿茅酒、阿茅酒、樱桃煎、顶皮酥、益寿糕、琼玉糕、碧玉糕、固元膏等，就是在故宫“御膳房”研发的。

2 清代宫廷宴席重于礼仪繁复和场面盛大，吃食反而并不重要（参见杨原：《如果故宫会说话》，社会科学文献出版社2020年版，第211页）。这里所提到的“千叟宴”，所设膳品主要分两个等次，以乾隆五十年（1785年）为例，最高等供皇帝、王公、一二品大臣、外国使臣食用，有火锅及羊、猪肉片、鹿尾烧鹿肉、煺羊肉各1品，另有荤菜4碗，蒸食、炉食各1盘，小菜2盘及肉丝汤饭。次等供三至九品官员、蒙古台吉、顶戴、领催、兵民等饮宴，照高等少了羊肉，鹿肉改为烧狍肉，其余一致（参见杨建峰编《千古食趣：说说吃的那些事》，汕头大学出版社2016年版，第221页）。

Fourth, we should seek freshness in our products. I will not allow oily, sticky and dark dishes. Fifth, seek softness in taste, not too hemp or too spicy. Sixth, to be strict in inspections. Care shall be given before serving the dish..., altogether 18 rules, plus ten no-serving rules, and I also wrote ten no-serving rules when I managed a five-star hotel.

Su: What are they?

Song: No dish serving when in a bad mood. My understanding of this is different from others. The waiter is not happy today and still serves food to the guests. Is this for the guests to look at his face? Therefore, if you are in a bad mood, you will change to another position. In addition, no serving when the cooking is under standard. I have a standard for dishes. Burnt or undercooked food is not allowed and cannot be served to customers. In addition, a dish with under-standard cutting and preparing is not allowed to be served, and dishes with below-standard traying are also not allowed to be served, etc.

Yang: This needs great effort into training.

Song: I train them every day, including in regular meetings, summary meetings and training sessions. All the staff should attend the regular meeting, sum up the guests' reaction to the food in the morning and noon, and praise the good ones and ask for improvement for the bad ones.

Su: How many people are there at a meeting?

Song: At the beginning, there were fewer persons, more than 100, and now there are tens of thousands, so we must insist on meeting and training.

Su: Did you run a "Yushan Restaurant"?

Song: I ran a "Yushan Restaurant" in the Forbidden City for five and a half years, which was operated simultaneously with group meal, which can complement each other. I developed many new dishes in the Forbidden City. [1]"Twenty-four Solar Terms Banquet" was formed by me in Yushan Restaurant after I retired from the army. There was no "banquet" in the army, because it's not allowed to serve many dishes at once to senior officers. Only single dishes were served.

Su: Did you create the whole beef banquet and the whole sheep banquet by yourself?

Song: Yes, these are my creations. There are several banquets in the Forbidden City, such as the Thousand Old Men Banquet, but not many.[2] I didn't like this, so I prepared different banquets according to the twenty-four solar terms. Make dishes according to the season to nourish the body,

---

1 Note by Song Zigang: Court food "Eight Pieces" includes Xianlu Ointment, Fenghuang Ointment, Promotion Cake, Victory Cake, Eight-Dainty Cakes, Eight Immortals Cake, Scholar Cake, Thousand Old Cake; and Taiyi Zijin Tablet, Court Pu'er, Court Tea, Lumao Wine, Amao Wine, Cherry Fri, Top Skin Crisp, Yishou Cake, Qiongyu Cake, Biyu Cake and Gelatin Ointment were developed in the Imperial Kitchen of The Imperial Palace.

2 In the Qing Dynasty, the palace banquet paid attention to elaborate ceremony and the grand scene, but the food was not important (See Yang Yuan: *If the Forbidden City Could Talk*, Social Sciences Academic Press, 2020, page 211). In the "Thousand Old Men Banquet" as mentioned here, the food was divided into two levels. Taking the 50th year of the Qianlong reign (1785) as an example, the highest level food was for the emperor, princes and dukes, the first and second ministers, and foreign envoys, including hot pot and sheep, pork, roasted deer tail, ham mutton, four bowls of meat dishes, one plate of steamed food and one plate of stove food, two plates of snacks and shredded rice soup. The second level food was to provide for officials from three to nine grades, Mongolian Taiji, official cap, civil officials, soldiers and civilians. In addition to mutton and deer, other food was the same as mentioned above (See Yang Jianfeng, *Eating in the Past: Talking about the Eating*, Shantou University Press, 2016, page 221).

体，比如，立冬要吃羊肉，就做黑羊宴。

我在故宫跟别人交流的时候，看到一些摆着的小袋子，就问这是做啥的？他们告诉我，乾隆出行的时候，会往袋子里装各种咸菜、肉、果仁——各种干果搁一起炒好入味。后来文怀沙来吃饭，我就把花生、榛子、松子搁一起做了一个干果拼盘，他觉得好吃，问我这是什么？我寻思也不能就叫干果，就给取名叫乾隆果仁。

苏：您当时是怎么知道故宫要开“御膳房”？

宋：我是侦察兵出身，挺喜欢通信，没事儿就喜欢上网看看，无意间浏览到了他们在网上公布的招标信息。文化部在网上公示，故宫经营部准备恢复跟故宫过去饮食相关的项目，然后我就报了名。那时候还不能网上报名，得到现场去。三个月后通知我去面试，去的时候有七八家跟故宫饮食相关的企业，大部分都是故宫内部推荐的。面试的时候有十多个专家在现场，我什么资料都没有，只能给他们转述我们家的历史。他们提的第一个问题就是，你家跟故宫有什么关系？我说我们家是太医院做胶的，九昼夜阿胶就是我们家做的。这个专业性很强，我估计其他人说的都是一些炒菜方面的事情，跟我这稍微有一些层次上的差距。领导一听，觉得我比较靠谱，就这么中标了。

承接奥运团餐

宋：奥运会后我的企业有了巨大的变化。奥运会结束以后，我就买了房、车，有了车队和大丰物流、大通饭庄。

苏：您还有一个物流公司？

宋：大丰物流、海赋国际酒店管理有限公司……我一共成立了九家公司，金丰现在是名副其实的全业态、全品类的集团公司，提供闭合式一站服务，到今天，中国都只有我这一家。如果没有新冠疫情，工厂也早开起来了。

苏：您做团餐这几年觉得市场有什么样的变化？

宋：竞争越来越激烈。现在有很多公司都是外国企业控股、中国人经营，很多时候我都感觉孤军奋战、无能为力，因为外国企业舍得砸钱。但我对于我们企业充满着必胜的信心，一定能在外国企业之中厮杀出自己的天地。

for example, if you want to eat mutton at the beginning of winter, make a black mutton feast.

When I was communicating with others in the Forbidden City, I saw some small bags on display and asked what they were for? They told me that when Qianlong was traveling, he would put all kinds of pickles, meat and nuts–all kinds of dried fruits and stir-fry them together. Later, when Wen Huaisha came to dinner, I put peanuts, hazelnuts and pine nuts together to make a dried fruit. He felt delicious and asked me what it was. I thought I couldn't just call it dried fruit, so I named it Qianlong Nut.

Su: How did you know that the Forbidden City was going to run a "Yushan Restaurant"?

Song: I was a scout before, quite like communications. If I have nothing to do, I like to look on the Internet, and I accidentally browsed the bidding information they published on the Internet. According to the online announcement of the Ministry of Culture, the Forbidden City Business Department was ready to resume the projects related to the past diet of the Forbidden City, and then I signed up. At that time, I couldn't register online, so I had to go to the site. Three months later, I was informed to go for an interview. When I went, there were seven or eight enterprises related to the diet of the Forbidden City, most of which were recommended by the Forbidden City. During the interview, there were more than ten experts at the site, and I had no document but to tell them the history of our family. The first question they asked was, what is the relationship between your home and the Forbidden City? I said that our family made gelatin at the academy. The nine-day donkey-hide gelatin was made by us. This is very professional. I guess all the other people are talking about cooking, which is slightly different from me. Hearing this, the leader thought I was reliable, so I won the bid.

Undertake Olympic Group Meals

Song: Great changes have taken place in my enterprise since the Olympic Games. After the Olympic Games, I bought a house, a car, a motorcade, Dafeng Logistics and Datong Restaurant.

Su: You still have a logistics company?

Song: Dafeng Logistics, Haifu International Hotel Management Co. ... I have established a total of nine companies, Jinfeng is now a veritable all-industry, all-category group of companies, providing a closed one-stop service, to this day, I am the only one in China. If there was no COVID-19, the factory would have been opened long ago.

Su: What kind of changes do you think the market has seen in the past few years of doing group meals?

Song: The competition is getting fiercer. Nowadays, many companies are controlled by foreign companies and run by Chinese people. Very often, I feel that I am alone and powerless, because foreign companies are willing to throw money. But I am confident that our company will win, and we will be able to make our own way among foreign companies.

苏：那您准备怎么开创自己的天地？

宋：区别竞争力。我们企业正从餐饮业逐渐向食品加工业转型，我还开办了培训学校，每个月举办菜品品鉴会、服务品鉴会。

杨：北京奥运会的时候，您是负责哪一部分？

宋：我们负责奥运村、国奥村的官员、媒体和一部分教练员、运动员，还有安保部门和志愿者的餐饮。那时候我们一天服务十来万人。奥运会之前我们给市政府服务，做过国家科技部立项的“十一五”大城市营养配餐科研工作的课题，这些给了我服务奥运会的信心。

苏：奥运期间，有发生过什么印象深刻的事吗？

宋：那时候我的中餐加西餐加药膳的配餐理念已经成形，并在奥运会中得到了检验，尤其是药膳特别受欢迎。举个例子，我跟彭铭泉学了枸杞子蒸蔬菜。河北、山东出产枸杞子，新鲜的枸杞叶摘回来以后和萝卜、白菜一起蒸，蒸好后再撒上枸杞子，立刻就比绵阳蒸菜提升了档次。我认为药膳千万不能离开国家药食同源目录的范围，目录上有的东西就可以做，没有的不要乱整，属于违法。

我把国家药食同源目录和我们家的胶药门、我在中医药大学学的药膳学相融合，再结合中国特色来做奥运团餐。我认为奥运团餐一定要有中国特色，提供北京烤鸭就是我提出来的。

杨：那时候也做外国菜吗？

宋：不是只有一家企业做奥运团餐，有好多家企业一起中标，服务不同的人群，像美国的爱玛客中标后，就不做中国菜。

苏：您能中标是不是跟您之前的部队经历有些关系？

宋：没有部队的经历，我做不了这些东西。我给北京市市政府、中央党校、中央电视台等服务的经验也为做奥运团餐提供了帮助。这段经历锻炼了我的心智，心更加坚定、思路更加开阔。

苏：这段经历是如何锻炼了您的心智呢？

宋：在奥运会之前的筹备期，我去了美国、英国、德国、日本、法国等国家考察。考察美国佳美航空的机餐，发现他们都是找航空食品公司做的，国外都是在工厂里加工。考察回来后设计菜谱就具有针对性，要不我弄不了土耳其烤肉套餐。后来我还弄过啤酒套餐、热红酒套餐、欧洲香肠套餐……考察的时候，面包、香肠都是四五袋地往回提，切开一样一样尝，尝完后，对以后自己采购的食品品质就心里有数了，有了质量标准。没吃过、没看过，就不知道咋回事。

Su: And how are you going to create your own world?

Song: Differentiating competitiveness. Our company is gradually transforming from catering to food processing industry, and I have also opened a training school, holding monthly dish tasting sessions and service tasting sessions.

Yang: Which part of the Beijing Olympics were you in charge of?

Song: We were responsible for the officials, media and part of the coaches and athletes in the Olympic Village and National Olympic Village, as well as the security department and volunteers. In those days, we served about 100,000 people a day. Before the Olympic Games, we served the municipal government to do the research project of the Ministry of Science and Technology of China for the "Eleventh Five-Year Plan" on nutritional food distribution in large cities, which gave me confidence to serve the Olympic Games.

Su: Did anything memorable happen during the Olympics?

Song: By that time, my Chinese plus Western plus medicinal food meal preparation concept had been developed and tested at the Olympic Games, and the medicinal cuisine was particularly popular. For example, I learned to steam vegetables with Lycium barbarum from Peng Mingquan. Hebei and Shandong specialize in producing Lycium barbarum. After picking fresh Lycium barbarum leaves, we steamed them together with radishes and cabbages. After steaming, we sprinkled Lycium barbarum, which immediately improved the grade compared with Mianyang steamed vegetables. In my opinion, medicinal diet must not deviate from the national list of homology of medicine and food. You can make any item included in the list, and it is illegal if not included in the list.

I integrated the national list of homology of medicine and food with The Songs' School of Medicinal Gelatin and the medicine and food science I studied in the University of Traditional Chinese Medicine, and then combined it with Chinese characteristics to make Olympic Group Meals. I think the Olympic Group Meals must have Chinese characteristics, and provide Peking duck is what I proposed.

Yang: Were you still cooking foreign food at that time?

Song: There is not only one company doing Olympic group meals, there are several companies winning the bid together, serving different people, like the U.S. Aramark won the bid, which did not cook Chinese food.

Su: Does your winning bid have something to do with your previous military experience?

Song: I can't do these things without the experience of the army. My service experience to serve Beijing Municipal Government, Central Party School, CCTV, and so on, also helped to prepare Olympic group meals. The experience of Olympic Games have strengthened my mind, strengthened my heart and broadened my thinking.

Su: How did this experience train your mind?

Song: In the preparatory period before the Olympic Games, I went to the United States, Britain, Germany, Japan and France for investigation. I went to the American Camry Airlines to inspect the machine meals, and found that they were all made by aviation food companies and processed in factories abroad. Back from the study tour my design of recipe then had a target, otherwise, it will be like Turkish kebab set, which I cannot do. Later, I also made beer package, hot wine package, and European sausage package... During the inspection, I bought bread and sausage in four or five bags, cut them and tasted them one by one. After tasting, I would have a general understanding of the quality of my purchased products, so I had a food quality standard in mind. Not having eaten or seen it, I don't know what's going on.

苏：考察是很多家一起去吗？

宋：考察全是我自己出资去的，我有自己的针对性，直奔运动员餐饮，想去看看欧洲人吃啥、美国人吃啥，弄清楚他们的需求和特点，都搞清楚了，回来我才能做。

杨：这跟您原来在部队学的还不一样？

宋：他们的标准要求不一样。首先，原材料制作标准不同。给首长服务的时候，餐饮的标准也很高，但方向不一样，首长吃的原材料都是自己种的。而奥运团餐是采买的，全国各地的原材料都有，需要筛选一些出来做兴奋剂检测，像牛羊肉里就不能有任何添加剂，所有肉类都有科学检验指标。我一般都用三个供应商、备三个供应商。

其次，服务标准不同。我非常讲究服务礼仪，我们员工的服装跟别的公司不一样，都穿得跟空姐似的，白衬衣、戴丝巾，丝巾还是清华大学的李老师设计的，体现了中华女性的含蓄美。

最后，菜品的特点、口味不同。我在菜谱中标出河北省、河南省、山东省、四川省、安徽省等，以省为单位进行配餐，更贴近大家的口味。因为要提供将近一个月的奥运团餐，我们还按照节气配餐，同时我也是第一个把中国非遗美食放进去的。那个时候还叫老字号食品，像狗不理包子、香河肉饼、老边饺子，都是我放进奥运团餐里的。因为我经营老字号，所以我要推广老字号。

杨：您家那时候就是老字号了吗？

宋：那时候我们家大通饭庄还没恢复。直到2008年才恢复，但我一直在积极地推广中华老字号的产品。

Su: Did many enterprises go together for the study tour?

Song: I paid for the study tour solely by myself. I have my own pertinence. I went straight to the athletes' dining. I wanted to see what Europeans and Americans eat. I figured out their needs and characteristics. I will do it when I come back.

Yang: this is different from what you have learned before in the army?

Song: Their standards are different. First, the raw material production standards are different. When serving the senior officers, the standard of food and beverage is also very high, but the direction is different. The senior officers eats raw materials of his own, and the Olympic meals are purchased. Raw materials are available all over the country, so it is necessary to screen out some for doping test. For example, there cannot be any additives in beef and mutton, and all meats have scientific inspection indicators. Generally, I used three vendors and reserved three vendors for standby.

Second, the service standards are different. I pay great attention to service etiquette. Our employees' clothes are different from those of other companies. They are all dressed like stewardesses. White shirts and scarves are designed by Teacher Li of Tsinghua University, which reflects the subtle beauty of Chinese women.

Lastly, the characteristics and taste of the dishes are different. I marked Hebei Province, Henan Province, Shandong Province, Sichuan Province, Anhui Province, etc. in the menu, and the catering was carried out on a provincial basis, which was closer to everyone's taste. We are going to provide Olympic group meals for almost a month, and we also match meals according to the festive seasons, and I am also the first one to put in Chinese intangible heritage cuisine. At that time, it was also called time-honored food, Goubuli steamed stuffed bun, Xianghe meat pie, and Laobian jiaozi, which I put into the Olympic group meal. Because my brand is a time-honored brand, so I promote it.

Yang: Is your brand a time-honored brand at that time?

Song: My Datong Restaurant had not been restored from a time-honored brand. It was not restored from a time-honored brand until 2008, but I have been actively promoting Chinese time-honored products.

宋子刚在工作总结会上主持发言

Song Zigang presided over the work summary meeting

金丰餐饮集团第十五届烹饪技能大赛，2019年

2019 Jinfeng Catering Group 15th Cooking Skills Competition

宋子刚带领团队参加奥运会服务，召开誓师大会

Song Zigang led the team to take part in the swearing-in meeting for Olympic service

国际奥委会副主席、北京2022年冬奥会和冬残奥会组织委员会副主席于再清考察金丰集团大通饭庄药膳，并赠送奥运冠军集体签名

Yu Zaiqing,Vice President of the International Olympic Committee and Vice Chairman of the Beijing 2022 Winter Olympic and Paralympic Games Organizing Committee, inspected the medicinal meals of Datong restaurant and Jinfeng Group, and presented the collective signature of Olympic champions

国际奥委会副主席、北京2022年冬奥会和冬残奥会组织委员会副主席于再清，率领一众奥运健儿到奥运训练餐厅就餐并鼓励金丰餐饮全体员工发扬中国体育精神和奥林匹克精神

Yu Zaiqing,Vice President of the International Olympic Committee and Vice Chairman of the Beijing 2022 Winter Olympic and Paralympic Games Organizing Committee, led a group of Olympic athletes to the Olympic training restaurant for dinner, and encouraged all staff of Jinfeng to carry forward the Chinese sports spirit and Olympic spirit

国际奥委会副主席、北京2022年冬奥会和冬残奥会组织委员会副主席于再清向荣获奥运工作荣誉奖的宋子刚表示祝贺并合影留念

Yu Zaiqing, Vice President of the International Olympic Committee and Vice Chairman of the Beijing 2022 Winter Olympic and Paralympic Games Organizing Committee, congratulates Song Zigang, who won the honorary award for his devotion to the Olympics, and poses for a group photo

金丰餐饮服务北京2022年冬奥会期间，中国滑冰协会主席李琰莅临金丰餐饮考察指导，宋子刚向李琰主席赠送《中国团餐科技标准》系列丛书

During Jinfeng Catering's service for Beijing 2022 Winter Olympic Games, Li Yan, President of China Skating Association, visited Jinfeng Catering, and Song Zigang presented a series of *Scientific and Technological Standards for Chinese Group Meals* to Li Yan

宋子刚带领团队参加奥运会服务，召开誓师大会

Song Zigang led the team to take part in the swearing-in meeting for Olympic service

宋子刚保留的外国友人表扬信

Letters of commendation from foreign friends retained by Song Zigang

金丰集团为中国奥运健儿准备的“决战东京，为中国加油”大蛋糕

Jinfeng Group prepared a big cake of “decisive battle in Tokyo, cheer for China” for Chinese Olympic athletes

北京奥运总指挥部赠予北京金丰餐饮有限公司锦旗

The Silk Banner from the Beijing Olympic Headquarters to Beijing Jinfeng Catering Co., Ltd.

国际奥委会文化与奥林匹克教育委员会原主席何振梁为宋子刚题词

Former IOC Culture and Olympic Education Commission Chairman He Zhenliang inscribes Song Zigang

服务奥运获得的各项荣誉证书

Certificates of honor for serving the Olympic Games

“薪传—中国烹饪名家”系列丛书首发式

The first issue of the series of “*Keep The Fire Going - The Chinese Culinary Masters*”

宋子刚在“科技部‘十一五’大城市现代营养配餐技术研究与产业化”课题研讨会中与课题组专家合影

Song Zigang in the Group photo of the research project of “the Ministry of Science and Technology of China for the ‘Eleventh Five-Year Plan’ on modern nutritional Catering Technology in large cities”

中国财贸轻纺烟草工会二级巡视员张晓冬向金丰集团董事长宋子刚颁发“工人先锋号”荣誉奖牌

Song Zigang was awarded the “Worker pioneer” Citation by Zhang Xiaodong, the Secondary inspector of National Committee of the Trade Union of Financial and Commercial Workers, Light Industry and Textile Workers, Tobacco Industry Workers

第四章

Chapter 4

大通药膳

Datong Medicinal Dishes

【访谈者按】“中华老字号”的认证工作最早启动于1991年，当时百货、中药、餐饮、服装、调味品、酒、茶叶、烘焙食品、肉制品、民间工艺品和其他商业、服务行业共有1600余家品牌被授予了牌匾和证书。2006年4月，商务部启动实施“振兴老字号工程”，将“中华老字号”定义为：历史悠久，拥有世代传承的产品技艺或服务，具有鲜明的中华民族传统文化背景和深厚的文化底蕴，取得社会广泛认同，形成良好信誉的品牌；并要求拥有商标所有权或使用权，品牌创立于1956年（含）以前，有传承的独特产品、技艺或服务等七个认定条件，评审委员会由多个行业的专家共同组成。北京老字号协会则是在2005年8月成立。2013年9月16日，“北京老字号”认定工作正式启动，在此之前，国家商务部曾分两批认定了北京市117个“中华老字号”。大通饭庄则是在2014年进入第一批“北京老字号”名录。

宋先生恢复自家老字号的过程是坎坷的，但他始终没有放弃继承药膳文化的一颗赤诚之心。在团餐事业走上轨道之后，他将自己的时间和精力更多地放在了钻研药膳上，不但在自己的公司内部普及药膳知识，帮助培养了120名持证的药膳师，还赞助、协办了全国“药膳杯”大赛。求知欲在这些合作项目中又给他带来了新的收获，他既是老师，又是学生。传统的医和药，再加上营养学、炮制学的知识使他在创制药膳时，既尊古法、讲科学，又有新意。他对药膳的认识也发生了根本转变，过去的药膳讲究食材高级、精致，但这导致造价不菲，难以走入寻常百姓家，现如今，他更倾向于面向大众，用最常见、普通的食材打造最补益的效果。他所掌握的多种烹调技法、医药知识也使药膳更贴合现代人的口味和个体需求。最难得的是，他对食材的重视不亚于怀有“医者父母心”的祖上，走遍大江南北去考察最好的原料，始终坚持品质至上，这也正是老字号不灭的精神和追求。

[Interviewer's Note] The certification of "China Time-honored Brand" was first launched in 1991, when more than 1,600 brands in department stores, traditional Chinese medicine, restaurants, clothing, condiments, wine, tea, baked goods, meat products, folk handicrafts and other commercial and service industries were awarded with plaques and certificates. In April 2006, the Ministry of Commerce launched the "Revitalizing Time-honored Brands Project", which defined "China Time-honored Brands" as: a brand with a long history, products, skills and services passed down from generation to generation, distinct Chinese traditional cultural background and profound cultural heritage, which has won wide recognition from the society and formed a good reputation; It is also required to own the trademark ownership or use right. The brand was founded before 1956 (inclusive), and it has seven identification conditions such as unique products, skills or services inherited. The evaluation committee is composed of experts from many industries. Beijing Time-honored Brands Association was established in August 2005. On September 16, 2013, the identification of "Beijing Time-honored Brands" officially started. Before that, the Ministry of Commerce had identified 117 "China Time-honored Brands" in Beijing in two batches. Datong Restaurant was included the first batch of "Beijing Time-honored Brands" in 2014.

The process of Mr. Song's restoration of his own time-honored brand was bumpy, but he never gave up his sincere heart of inheriting the medicinal diet culture. After the group meal business went on track, he devoted more time and energy to studying medicinal diet, which not only popularized medicinal diet knowledge in his own company, but also helped train 120 certified medicinal dieters, and sponsored and co-organized the national "Medicinal Diet Cup" contest. The thirst for knowledge has brought him new gains in these cooperative projects. He was both a teacher and a student. Traditional medical science and drugs, coupled with the knowledge of nutrition and processing science, made him respect ancient methods, follow scientific approaches and have new ideas when creating medicinal diet. His understanding of medicinal diet has also undergone a fundamental change. In the past, medicinal diet paid attention to the high-quality and exquisite ingredients, but this led to high cost and difficulty in entering the homes of ordinary people. Now, he is more inclined to face the public and use the most common and ordinary ingredients to create the most beneficial effect. His mastery of various cooking techniques and medical knowledge also makes the medicinal diet more suitable for modern people's tastes and individual needs. The most rare thing is that he attaches no less importance to food materials than his ancestors who have the heart of "doctors are parents". He has traveled all over the country to inspect the best raw materials and always insisted on the supremacy of quality, which is the immortal spirit and pursuit of old brands.

唯一的药膳老字号

苏：在复建老字号的过程当中，有什么让您印象深刻的事情吗？

宋：在故宫“御膳房”开业以后，我几次去找商务部但始终都不给我批老字号。因为老字号需要溯源，而我拿不出太多的材料。我们家过去没有留下什么资料，为了找这些记录我费了很大劲，先是回山东找县志里的记载，没有找到，又去找山东省档案，也只找到了不太确切的记载，因为我们只是一个饭铺，不是什么大事，没有人记载。后又去了德州找人，但很多人都已经去世了。最后找到《国宝同仁堂》[1]这本书，才算有了真正的证据，最起码证明了我们家的的确确是做这个的。整个过程中，我一直不断地提交材料，直到最后成功了。

苏：还需要什么材料？

宋：要求我们有字号，字号找着了：大通饭铺、大通饭庄；还要有地址，我们家在运河边上的地址也提交了；关键还得有产品，我们家有九昼夜阿胶、大通阿胶……再加上我太爷爷的信息，有了这些溯源，人家才能批。

苏：具体有哪些专家来参与老字号审批的过程呢？

宋：都是北京市的专家，但不会告诉我们具体是谁，我们只是提交材料，材料合格了，就给你批。

苏：每年有一个具体的评选时间吗？

宋：每年一次，一般是春天开始，到冬天的时候评完。

苏：您是一直在关注这个吗？

宋：对，我想恢复我们家的传统，就得坚定信心。

苏：拿到老字号认证的时候，您父母还健在吗？

宋：父母早就去世了。【停顿】

宋：我是第一个在北京提出开馆子做药膳养生菜的人。

苏：大通饭庄具体在什么地方？

宋：最早是在故宫里卖我们家的东西，后来在车公庄开了一家，中关村开了一家，气象局开了一家，当时一共有三家，号称“天下第一黑店”，因为里面出售的全是“黑色食品”。

---

1 边东子著，人民出版社2010年版。

The Only One Time-honored Medicinal Diet Brand

Su: What impressed you in the process of rebuilding the old brand?

Song: After opening the Yushan Restaurant in the Forbidden City, I went to the Ministry of Commerce several times, but never approved a time-honored brand to me. Because old-honored brands need to be traced back, and I can't provide too many documented materials. Our family didn't leave any written records in the past. In order to find these records, I spent a lot of effort. First, I went back to Shandong to find the records in the county annals, but I didn't find them. Then I went to the archives of Shandong Province and only found the inaccurate records, because we were just a restaurant, not a big deal, and no one gave them a record. Later, I went to Dezhou to find anyone concerned, but many of them have passed away. Finally, we found the book *National Treasure Tong Ren Tang*[1], and then we got real evidence, which at least proved that our family really did this business. During the whole process, I kept submitting documented materials until I finally succeeded.

Su: What other documented materials do they need?

Song: They asked us to provide a shop name, and I found it: Datong Dinning House and Datong Restaurant; then asked us to provide the address, and I gave the address near the Great Canal; importantly, asked us to provide the products, our family produced Nine-day Donkey-hide Gelatin, Datong Donkey-hide Gelatin......, plus the information about my grand-grandfather, they will not approve a time-honored brand unless you provided all this source information.

Su: Which experts will participate in the examination and approval process of time-honored brands?

Song: They are experts from Beijing, but they won't tell us who they are. We are required to submit the documented materials. If the documented materials are qualified, they will approve a time-honored brand for you.

Su: Is there a specific time every year for this?

Song: Once a year, it usually starts in spring and ends in winter.

Su: Are you always keeping an eye on this?

Song: Yes, if I want to restore our family tradition, I must strengthen my confidence.

Su: Were your parents still alive when you got the time-honored certification?

Song: My parents passed away long time ago. [Pause]

Song: I was the first person in Beijing who proposed to open a restaurant to make medicinal diet.

Su: Where is Datong Restaurant located?

Song: We first sold our family's food products in the Forbidden City, and later opened one restaurant in Chegongzhuang, one in Zhongguancun and one in Meteorological Bureau. At that time, there were three, which were called "No.1 black restaurant in the world", because it seals "black food" products.

1 By Bian Dongzi, People's Publishing House, 2010.

苏：为什么选在这些地方开饭庄？

宋：离公司注册地点、厨师学校、办公地点近。

苏：获批老字号认证后，花了多长时间开这三家店呢？

宋：两年，需要找合适的地方。

苏：您还能回想起当时开第一家店的心情吗？

宋：我们家老字号批下来后，我非常高兴，觉得自己能对得起父母、对得起家人的期望了。但没想到当初我租了别人的房子，用的是别人的营业执照，国家不允许用别人的营业执照挂自己的招牌，而且营业执照也不能改名，于是干了三年就关门了，因为这个我赔了不少钱，装修费用和其他费用加起来三百来万。经历过这件事情后，我走上了另外一个模式，不在外面弄，现在我都是在各个单位的食堂里弄，中餐、西餐加上药膳，这样推广起来也快。

苏：都有什么药膳？

宋：都是补益类药膳和长寿类药膳，我只做这两样，别的不做。

苏：具体有些什么菜呢？

宋：有蛋类的、畜类的、禽类的、海鲜水产类的，也有果蔬类、蘑菇类、豆制品类，还有酒、茶，全方位涵盖。

苏：给不同的单位配餐，是他们自己挑选菜品？还是您给他们搭配？

宋：我给他们配的。我把药膳和团餐进行结合，整理了大量适合做团餐的药膳品种。红糖馒头、红糖小米粥，配红皮鸡蛋，可以成套卖也可以单卖。还有就是用各种胶和豆腐、萝卜、水果进行搭配，比如素胶炖豆腐、阿胶雪梨丸子、蜂胶雪梨丸子、桃胶雪梨丸子。按照季节，用不同的东西来调制。很早我就在做这个研究，根据二十四节气去养生、去做配餐。因为我们家是胶药门，胶的种类比较多，别人家一般只有一两种，我们有十多种。

苏：您现在做的团餐药膳面向普通大众，而之前恢复的大通饭庄则是面向高消费人群，对吗？

宋：我早前做团餐、药膳的道路非常坎坷，但是现在已经理顺了。一开始我认为药膳是给高端人群吃的，但现在我的理念发生了转变，药膳是给老百姓吃的。我在故宫开“御膳房”全是高端人群去消费、大通饭庄也全是高端人群，

Su: Why did you choose these places to open your restaurant?

Song: These places are to the company's registered address, chef's school and office.

Su: How long did it take to open these three restaurants after being certified as a time-honored brand?

Song: Two years, we need to find the right place.

Su: Can you recall the mood when you opened your first restaurant?

Song: After our time-honored brand was approved, I was very happy, and I felt that I could live up to my parents' and my family's expectations. But unexpectedly, because I rented someone else's house and used someone else's business license, the government was not allowed to use someone else's business license to operate its own brand products, and the business license could not be renamed, so I closed the restaurant after three years. I lost a lot of money because of this, and the renovation cost and other expenses add up to more than RMB 3 million. After this experience, I have embarked on another mode, not operating outside. Now I operate in the canteens of various units, with Chinese food and western food combined with medicinal food, which can be popularized quickly.

Su: What kind of medicinal food is there?

Song: They are tonic dishes and longevity dishes, I only produce these two, but nothing else.

Su: What are the specific dishes?

Song: There are eggs, livestock, poultry, seafood and aquatic products, as well as fruits and vegetables, mushrooms and bean products, as well as wine and tea, covering all aspects.

Su: When catering to different units, they choose their own meals? Or, you choose the meals for them?

Song: I choose the meals for them. I have combined medicinal meals with group meals, and sorted out a large number of medicinal meals suitable for group meals. Brown sugar steamed bun, brown sugar millet porridge, and eggs with red shells can be sold in sets or separately. There are also various gelatins to match with tofu, radish and fruits, such as Vegetarian Gelatin with Stewed Tofu, Donkey-hide Gelatin-stuffed Pear Balls, Propolis Pear Balls and Peach Gum Pear Balls, which are prepared with different things according to seasons. I've been doing this research for a long time, and I've been making meals based on the 24 solar terms. Because our family is a School of Medicinal Gelatin, and there are many kinds of gelatins, others generally only have one or two kinds, and we have more than ten kinds.

Su: The group meals you are making now are for the general public, while Datong Restaurant that was restored from a time-honored brand is for the high-spending people, right?

Song: I had a very rough road to making group meals and medicinal meals earlier, but now I have straightened it out. At first, I thought that medicinal diet was for high-end people, but now my idea has changed, and medicinal diet is for ordinary people. The Yushan Restaurant I opened in the Forbidden City is full of high-end people to consume, and Datong Restaurant is also full of high-end people. However, it is very different when medicinal food and health-preserving dishes are

但是食堂里推出药膳、养生菜就很不一样，来的全是老百姓，他们很高兴。[1]

苏：针对不同的单位，配制的药膳有什么区别吗？

宋：养生要因人而异，我是按性别、年龄、季节来区分，部队、运动员、学校都有区别。部队是以牛胶、羊胶、鹿胶、阿胶为主；学校是以补益补脑的胶为主，如牛胶、羊胶、驴胶，桃胶、蜂胶、树胶，不能用鹿胶，因为孩子不适合吃鹿；运动员是以强身健体为主，必须得吃鹿胶、牛胶，女运动员还可以吃龟胶滋阴。龟胶还分两种，一种是鳖甲胶，一种是龟板胶。鳖的上面是滋阴的鳖甲胶，下面是壮阳的龟板胶。就像鹿似的，黄毛鹿胶有助怀孕，青毛鹿胶对怀孕帮助不大，不同的原料有不同的作用，不能乱吃。我是全国第一个提出男用鹿胶海参、女用阿胶海参的人。

苏：为什么要这么分呢？

宋：这就回到了中医的“望闻问切”。人的素质不一样，需求也不一样。女同志要滋阴，需要把气血补上来。有的女性手脚冰凉就是因为血气不通，滋阴才能潜阳，得把潜在的阳气激发出来。而男同志则要壮阳，而不是潜阳。

苏：您现在已经做了哪些方面的配餐？

宋：我们已经做了春夏秋冬的儿童配餐，现在研发的方向有：补钙的、长身体的、保护视力的……花青素含量比较高的食品就适合提供给中小学生和科研工作者。

苏：现在您主要给哪些单位配餐？

宋：我们现在给一百多家单位提供团餐，北京的很多高校也有我们的团餐。清华百年校庆的时候，我做的胶可受欢迎了。但提供给学校的餐点中，做成菜的不多，大部分做成甜品供应，像鹿胶膏、阿胶膏这种，或者做成月饼和点心，用小盒装上直接拿着吃，这样的东西更受大众欢迎，牛胶萝卜和豆腐之类的也挺受欢迎，这都是大众食品。如果弄个鹿胶海参，那就没人吃了。这次

---

1 宋先生这里所讲与《周礼》天官一章的记载很合，过去的“食医”主要服务王公贵族，“掌和王之六食、六饮、六膳、百羞、百酱、八珍之齐……凡君子之食恒放焉。”按节气配餐的理念也是一脉相承的：“凡食齐视春时，羹齐视夏时，酱齐视秋时，饮齐视冬时。凡和，春多酸，夏多苦，秋多辛，冬多咸，调以滑甘。凡会膳食之宜，牛宜稌，羊宜黍，豕宜稷，犬宜粱，雁宜麦，鱼宜菰。”

introduced in canteens. Consumers going there are ordinary people and they are very happy.[1]

Su: Is there any difference in the medicinal meals prepared for different units?

Song: Health care varies from person to person. I distinguish it by gender, age and season. There are differences among soldiers, athletes and students. Bovine-hide gelatin, sheepskin gelatin, deerskin gelatin and donkey-hide gelatin are mainly for soldiers; gelatin for nourishing the brain is mainly for students, such as bovine-hide gelatin, sheepskin gelatin, donkey-hide gelatin, peach gum, propolis and gum, but deerskin gelatin cannot be used, because school students are not suitable for eating donkey; athletes mainly keep fit, and must eat deerskin gelatin and bovine-hide gelatin. Female athletes can also eat turtle-shell gelatin to nourish yin. Turtle gelatin is also divided into two types, one is turtle-shell gelatin and another is tortoise-plastron gelatin. Turtle top is turtle-shell gelatin for nourishing yin, and turtle bottom is tortoise-plastrorn gelatin for strengthening yang. Just like deer, yellow-haired deer is helpful to pregnancy, while green-haired deer is not helpful to pregnancy. Different raw materials have different functions and cannot be eaten indiscriminately. I was the first person in China to propose deerskin gelatin with sea cucumber for men and donkey-hide gelatin with sea cucumber for women.

Su: Why did you have to divide it that way?

Song: According to traditional Chinese Medicine "Looking, hearing, asking and observing". People have different qualities and needs. Women need to nourish Yin, because women need to get their Qi and blood up. Some women's hands and feet are cold because the blood gas is blocked, so nourishing yin can subdue yang and stimulate the latent yang. Men, on the other hand, should be aphrodisiacs, not latent yang.

Su: What aspects of catering have you done now?

Song: We have made children's meals for spring, summer, autumn and winter, and now the research and development directions are: calcium supplementation, body-building and eyesight protection food … and foods with higher anthocyanin content are suitable for primary and secondary school students and scientific research workers.

Su: What are the main units you are now supplying catering service for?

Song: We now provide group meals to more than 100 units, and many universities in Beijing also receive our group meals. When Tsinghua University celebrated its centenary, the gelatin products made by us were very popular. However, among the meals provided to schools, few are made into dishes, and most of them are made into desserts, such as deerskin gelatin ointment and donkey-hide gelatin ointment, or made into moon cakes and snacks, which are directly eaten in small boxes. Such products are more popular with the public, and bovine-hide gelatin and turnip and tofu are also very popular, all of which are popular foods. If you make deerskin gelatin and sea cucumber, no one will eat it. In this epidemic, I also donated three tons of deerskin gelatin and three

1 What Mr. Song said here is very consistent with the records in the Tianguan chapter of *Rites of Zhou*. In the past, "food doctors" mainly served princes, dukes and nobles, and managed "six kinds of meals, six kinds of drinks, six kinds of meat, all kinds of delicacies, all kinds of sauces and eight kinds of delicacies. Every meal of the gentleman is prepared according to this principle" According to the concept of food according to the solar term, it is also consistent: "Food in the spring, soup in the summer, sauce in the autumn, drink in the winter. More sour in spring, more bitter in summer, more spicy in autumn and more salty in winter, with a smooth sweet. For blending meat and vegetarian diet, beef should be matched with rice, mutton with millet, pork with millet, dog with sorghum, goose with wheat, and fish with Manchurian wild rice."

疫情我还给雷神山、火神山捐了三吨鹿胶、三吨阿胶，下一步我想把我们的胶送到西藏，让士兵们也吃上牛胶、鹿胶、阿胶。

苏：这些养生菜是不是跟养老院合作会更容易推广？

宋：不单是养老院，还可以从医院、养老、社区构建整个业态。

苏：金丰餐饮现在的服务规模具体有多大呢？

宋：全国有不到300家店，大通饭庄也包括在内。

苏：您的公司现在有什么国际业务吗？

宋：我们给一些合作单位的驻外办事处派厨师。比如国航、电建、水建、公安部、新华社等。

尊古与创新

苏：您推出了很多种药膳菜品，这个过程中有没有什么让您觉得比较困难的地方？

宋：那倒没有，因为我只做膏，当然膏也分很多种类，我只做补益、长寿类，没有做那么多。我就天天研究这类膏方，驴的膏方是我从祖上继承下来的，而鹿的膏方是我自己发扬光大的。我父亲说我们家就做了一个驴菜——八珍驴肉，我要是也按这个思路去做鹿就白瞎了鹿。鹿的不同位置，作用是不一样的，为此我做了一个鹿结构与食用功效图，本想申请专利，但没批。

苏：您家以前是怎么做鹿全席的？

宋：我们家在扎赉诺尔做鹿全席的时候，需要客人来我们这儿住一段时间，买下一整头鹿，分几天吃鹿肉、喝鹿血酒，而不是一天把一头鹿全吃完。有的客人一待半个月，能慢慢地把身体养好。

苏：来的都是一些什么人呢？

宋：有生病的、有断胳膊或腿的、有没法生小孩的……

杨：你们家怎么保存鹿呢？

宋：不保存，我们那儿都烧木头，鹿就在锅里一直炖着。

杨：不是按照传统宴席做的？

tons of donkey-hide gelatin to Huoshenshan and Leishenshan hospitals. Next I want to send our gelatin products to troops in Tibet so that soldiers there can also eat bovine-hide gelatin, deerskin gelatin and donkey-hide gelatin.

Su: Are these health-care dishes easier to promote if cooperating with nursing homes?

Song: It's not just nursing homes, but you can build the whole business from hospitals, nursing homes and communities.

Su: How big is the service scale of Jinfeng Catering now?

Song: There are less than 300 outlets in China, including Datong Restaurant.

Su: Does your company have any international business now?

Song: Sending chefs to the overseas offices of some cooperative units. For example: Air China, Power Construction, Water Construction, Ministry of Public Security, Xinhua News Agency, etc.

Respect for the Past and Innovation

Su: You have introduced many kinds of medicinal dishes, is there anything in this process that you find more difficult?

Song: No, because I only make gelatin ointment. Of course, there are many kinds of gelatin ointments. I only make tonic and longevity gelatin products, and I don't make other types of gelatin. I studied the prescriptions of these gelatin ointments every day. I inherited the donkey gelatin prescription from my ancestors, and I carried forward the deer gelatin prescription myself. My father said that our family donkey series has only one dish made–the Eight Dainties of Donkey Meat; if I follow this thinking to create donkey meat products, it will be in chaos. Different positions of deer have different functions. Therefore, I made a deer structure and edible efficacy map. I wanted to apply for a patent, but I didn't get approval.

Su: How did your family make deer banquet before?

Song: When our family made a deer banquet in Zalainuoer, guests were required to come and stay with us for a period of time, buy a whole deer, and eat the meat and drink deer blood wine for several days, instead of eating the whole deer in one day. Some guests stayed for half a month and slowly mended their bodies.

Su: Who were the people coming?

Song: Some were sick, some had broken arms or legs, and some was unable to have children...

Yang: How did you store the deer in your family?

Song: we didn't store deer, we all burned wood there, and deer was always stewing in the pot.

Yang: Not according to the traditional banquet?

宋：现在条件好了，可以做得很精致，用不同的部位来做不同的菜。鹿血可以泡酒、蒸鸡蛋、灌肠。蒸鸡蛋本来只有一种颜色，我创新了一个鹿血膏，把鸡蛋黄搁在鹿血里，蒸出红色部分，鸡蛋清单独拿出来，蒸出白色部分，然后把白色部分放在红色外面，效果特别好。

鹿脸上的部件都可以单独做，烧眼睛、烧嘴……鹿耳朵割下来，酱好后放锅里烧，特脆特好吃，鹿脑也能拿来单独炖。

鹿前腿，炸的比较多；鹿里脊，排烤的比较多。还有一个菜叫大汗九保锅，就是鹿全锅，这个菜也非常受欢迎。我曾经在内蒙古待过，内蒙古有一个叫九保的地区，当时有九个蒙古包，他们炖鹿肉就是拿砂锅炖。鹿筋、鹿皮、鹿尾、鹿鞭这四样是单独熬膏，有时候会往里加鹿脊髓，我们家还有鹿全膏，就是整头鹿连骨头带肉全放进去一起炖，烀得烂烂的，熬成膏放凉后，拿刀切。这都是过去草原、林区里的吃法。

鹿的肠我们家就做成鹿茸膏，搁瓦罐里焙干了可以治肠炎。鹿心、鹿肺焙干后也可以磨成粉，每一个部位都有不同的作用。

杨：您现在做的鹿全席其实是根据自己家里的经验做的？

宋：父母跟我讲是一部分，还有就是我在故宫也看了很多关于补益药膳的记载，都是以鹿为先，没有说把猪、牛、羊、海鲜放前面的。

苏：现在您的饭庄里面也有这个鹿全席吗？

宋：有，而且卖得非常好。全国只有我有鹿全席的菜谱，写着所有部位的做法，有很多人专门加盟我们的鹿全席，加盟后我会把全套资料和原材料给他，教他制作鹿全席。

苏：您家现在用的鹿也是从大兴安岭那边买的吗？

宋：有两个地方，一个是大兴安岭，一个是双阳、四平、西丰、东丰那块。新疆产的是马鹿。

苏：一般都是些什么人来吃鹿全席？

宋：什么人都有，南方人更喜欢吃。但主要还是面向高消费人群，像兰博基尼车友会、劳斯莱斯车友会、哈雷摩托车友会的会员等，他们就喜欢吃鹿全席。鹿肉太贵了，宰杀完的成本，一斤大约在80块钱，这还没算上加工费用，所以我们的定价是三千块钱一位。

苏：他们是怎么找到您的？

Song: Now that the conditions are good, you can cook it very delicate and use different parts to cook. Deer blood can be made into wine to drink, used for making steamed eggs and sausage. Steamed eggs have only one color. I have also innovated a deer blood cream. I put the yolk in deer blood, and make the red part. I take out the egg white separately, and make it into the white part. Then I put the white part around the red part. The effect is particularly good.

The parts of the deer face can be cooked separately, such as fried deer eyes, fried deer mouth… We can cut the deer's ears off, sauce them and put them into a pot for braising, which would make the dish crispy and delicious. The deer brain can be stewed separately.

The front legs of deer are fried more; and deer's tenderloin is roasted in most cases. There is also a dish called Da Han Jiu Bao Guo, which is the whole pot of deer meat. This dish was also very popular. I used to stay in Inner Mongolia, where there was a place called Jiubao. At that time, there were nine yurts. They stewed deer meat in a casserole. Deer tendon, deerskin, deer tail and deer whip are boiled separately for making ointment, and sometimes deer spinal cord is added. We still have deer whole ointment in our family series, that is, the whole deer with bones and meat is put in for stewing together, which is rotten. After boiling into ointment and cooling down, cut it with a knife. These are the ways of eating in grasslands and forest areas in the past.

Deer intestines are made into velvet paste in our family series, and baked in crock can cure enteritis. The heart and lung of deer are also ground into powder after baking, and each part has different functions.

Yang: Your present deer banquet is actually based on your own family experience?

Song: What my parents told me was part of it. Besides, I also read a lot of records about tonifying in the Forbidden City, which put deer first, but didn't put pigs, cattle, sheep and seafood in the first place.

Su: Do you have this deer banquet in your restaurant now?

Song: Yes, and it sells very well. I'm the only one in the country who has a recipe for deer banquet, which says how to make all parts. Many people join our deer banquet specially. After joining, I gave him a full set of documented materials and raw materials to teach them how to make deer banquet.

Su: Did you buy deer from the Daxinganling region?

Song: There are two places to buy deer, one is the Daxinganling region, and the other is the place where Shuangyang, Siping, Xifeng and Dongfeng are located. Xinjiang produces red deer.

Su: Who usually comes to eat deer banquet?

Song: All kinds of people, but southerners prefer it most. But most of them are high-spending people, such as the members of Lamborghini car club, Rolls Royce car club, Harley Motorcycle club, etc., and they like deer banquet. Deer meat is too expensive, and the cost is about 80 yuan per 500g after slaughtering, and we haven't even counted the processing cost, so our price is 3,000 yuan for each customer.

Su: How did they find you?

宋：口碑。一个传一个，吃了都觉得有效，而别人没有这东西，只有我这儿有。

苏：你现在在哪儿做鹿全席？

宋：各大院里都可以做。

苏：您是怎么给车友会做鹿全席的呢？

宋：我们派厨师去他们自己组织的场地里做鹿全席，给他们整个活动提供餐点。他们买来一头鹿、自己备上酒，鹿杀完后就泡酒，然后其他不同的部位做成不同的菜。一般一头鹿能做三四回。

杨：您是怎么想到做月饼的呢？

宋：以前宫廷里的季节性食品很多。我来北京观察发现驴打滚、艾窝窝、京八件等并不能代表皇室点心。我就老琢磨什么样的点心能够体现皇宫特点呢？因为皇室讲究的是未病先治、补益，在没有毛病之前就先补身体。

我在故宫的时候，他们告诉我南方人考了状元后要吃状元糕。当时我们在黄山有酒店，我就问他们有没有状元糕，过了十来天，他们没找着状元糕，找到了跟月饼有些相似的定升糕、定胜糕。原来在浙江的嘉定地区，考学或者升官的时候就要吃这种糕点。用米粉制成，有圆形和方形，白的是定胜糕，红的是定升糕。我买回来一看，都不带馅儿，就想给它们加上馅儿，但在加馅儿的过程中，发现米粉不好弄，就换成了咱们的面，做成了现在的月饼。如果我不在里面放鹿胶、阿胶和果仁，就是定胜糕、定升糕。

苏：您这月饼和您家祖传的鹿胶膏有关系吗？

宋：有关系，但它俩不是一回事。鹿胶膏前面标了一个宫廷非遗美食，是海淀区替我上报，经过国家认定的。非遗只需要报一个，就可以把其他的胶都涵盖。

苏：您所做的仙鹿膏、凤凰膏、黑牛固原膏，口感都有点类似于牛皮糖？

宋：有两种做法。我在家里熬胶，就放一个主料加黄酒，不放其他东西，熬好后装瓶子里，半液态半凝固，吃的时候拿小勺舀。另一种塑料包装的固体是方便食品，因为流状的不好拿。

杨：您把这些膏都做成了糕点？

宋：对。当时故宫的郑欣淼院长给过我一本书，里面有很多方子。父亲以前跟我讲明朝时候的“细八件”，八珍糕、八仙糕是以男、女、老、少分类，然后按照二十四节气来做，跟那书上写的不一样。我就问父亲书里的八珍糕、

Song: Word of mouth, passed from one to another, is effective after eating, but others don't have it, only I have it here.

Su: Where do you make deer banquet now?

Song: It can be made in every major place.

Su: How do you make deer banquet for car clubs?

Song: We sent chefs to make deer banquet in their own venues, and provided them with meals for the whole activity. They bought a deer, prepared their own wine, soaked the wine after the deer was killed, and then made different dishes from different parts of deer meat. Usually a deer can be cooked for three or four times.

Yang: How did you come up with the idea of making moon cakes?

Song: There used to be a lot of seasonal food in the palace. When I came to Beijing, I observed that snowballing usury, Aiwowo and Beijing Eight Pieces, etc., did not represent royal snacks. I always figure out what kind of snacks can reflect the characteristics of the palace? Because the royal family pays attention to treating diseases before they are ill, and making up for them, I will make up for this body before I have any problems.

When I was in the Forbidden City, they told me that people in the south have to eat scholar cake after taking the scholar's exam. At that time we had a hotel in Huangshan, I asked them if there was a scholar cake, after ten days, they did not find the scholar cake, found with the moon cake some similar to promotion cake and victory cake. It is made of rice flour, round and square shape, the white one is promotion cake, and the red one is victory cake. When I bought it, I saw that there was no stuffing in it, so I wanted to add stuffing to them. However, in the process of stuffing, I found that the rice flour was not easy to handle, so I replaced them with our flour and made it to present moon cake. If I don't put deerskin gelatin, donkey-hide gelatin and nuts in it, it will be promotion cake and victory cake.

Su: Is this moon cake related to your ancestral deerskin gelatin ointment?

Song: Yes, but they are not the same thing. Deerskin gelatin ointment is marked with palace intangible heritage food, which application was submitted reported by Haidian District for me and recognized by the government. only one intangible heritage food application is required to cover all gelatin products.

Su: Xianlu Ointment, Fenghuang Ointment and Black Cow Guyuan Ointment made by you all taste like sticky candy?

Song: There are two ways of making it. When I boil gelatin at home, I put a main ingredient and yellow wine, and don't put anything else. After cooking, I put it in a bottle, which is semi-liquid and semi-solidified. When I eat it, I take a small spoon. Another solid packaged in plastic is a convenient food, because it is not easy to take in the form of flow.

Yang: You made all these ointment into cakes?

Song: Yes. At that time, Dean Zheng of the Forbidden City gave me a book with many prescriptions in it. My father used to tell me about the "Eight Pieces" in Ming Dynasty, Eight-Dainty Cakes and Eight Immortals Cakes were classified by their use for male, female, old and young, and then they were made by the twenty-four solar terms, which was different from what was recorded in the book. I asked my father about Eight-Dainty Cakes and Eight Immortals Cakes only eight in the book. How come there are more than ten in our family? And there is no stuffing as recorded

八仙糕就八个，咱们家的怎么有十多个？而且书里的也没有馅儿，咱们家的怎么有馅儿呢？他说，书上是御膳房的方子，不是太医院的，自然不一样，所以我做的八珍糕跟别人不一样。

杨：乾隆八珍糕是茶点类，而且专门有旨意写得很明确，“熬茶以后，随上。”

宋：我在西直门中医科学院跟陈士林老师专门学习过一段时间，这种点心的专利在他们手里，我吃着觉得像绿豆糕，回来后就进行了改良，改得更适合于老百姓吃。一年四季我用了四种水果、鲜花来做八珍糕的馅料，平谷开春的桃、海南的芒果、海南的香蕉、云南的鲜花，做出来的馅儿特别受欢迎。这次我去四川考察，准备把状元饼的生产搁在四川，因为状元饼就源自于四川，我讲究原产地。

苏：您具体讲讲。

宋：状元饼是用黑芝麻和黑豆烤熟后，捣碎加上红糖，然后搅拌包馅儿制成的。

苏：您为什么想做状元饼？

宋：这是我们家祖传下来的宫廷太医院食品，原来是状元糕，现在我给改良成了饼，包上了馅儿。一开始只有黑芝麻炒香捣碎加糖，这次我加入了黑豆，因为水属黑，肾属水，这样补肾的效果更强。我们家有一句话“尊古不泥古，创新不失宗”。父亲经常说，做的东西再好，也不能把老祖宗的东西丢掉，但可以在原始方子的基础上增加新的东西，总结成四个词：“完善”“巩固”“充实”“提高”。

培养120名药膳师

宋：大通饭庄是药膳协会的理事单位、副会长单位，跟同仁堂合作培养了120名药膳师，这在全国都是绝无仅有的。

苏：你们是怎么合作培养的？

宋：就在中医药大学、同仁堂研究院还有北京职业研究院上课。培训是我牵头，一共出资50多万。除了出资，我还负责教他们怎么做药膳。

in the book. How can there be stuffing in our family series? He said that the book recorded the prescriptions of the imperial kitchens, not those in imperial hospital, which is naturally different, so the Eight-dainty cake I made is different from others.

Yang: Qianlong Eight-dainty Cake is a kind of refreshment, and there is a clear decree which reads "enjoy it after tea".

Song: I studied with Chen Shilin in Xizhimen Academy of Traditional Chinese Medicine for a period of time. The patent of this snack is in their hands. I feel like mung bean cake when I eat it. After I came back, I improved it and made it more suitable for ordinary people. All year round, I use four kinds of fruits and flowers to make Eight-Dainty Cakes. Stuffing made of peach in Pinggu in spring, mango in Hainan, banana in Hainan and flowers in Yunnan are especially popular. This time I went to Sichuan for a study tour, ready to put the production of the scholar pies in Sichuan, because the scholar pies are originated in Sichuan, I pay attention to the origin.

Su: Tell me more about it.

Song: Scholar pie is baked with black sesame seeds and black beans, mashed with brown sugar, and then mixed to make stuffing.

Su: Why do you plan to make scholar pies?

Song: This is the food of Imperial Palace Hospital, which has been handed down from our family. It used to be scholar cake but now I have improved it into a pie and put stuffing in it. At first, only black sesame seeds were fried and mashed with sugar. This time, I added black beans, because in Chinese medicine, water is associated with the potential of new life hidden in the dark ground and is believed to govern the kidney, which makes the kidney tonic more effective. Our family has an old saying, "Respect the past without rigidly adhering to it, innovate without losing the tradition". My father often said, "Even if you make something good, you can't throw away the old ancestors' stuff, but you can add to the original recipe." Which is summarized into four words: "perfect" "consolidate" "enrich" and "improve".

Training 120 Medicinal Diet Chefs

Song: Datong Restaurant is the director unit and vice president unit of the Medicinal Diet Association. It has trained 120 medicinal diet chefs in cooperation with Tong Ren Tang, which is unique in the whole country.

Su: How did you carry out cooperative training?

Song: Classes were held at the University of Traditional Chinese Medicine, Tong Ren Tang Research Institute and Beijing Vocational Research Institute. I took the lead in the training and contributed more than RMB 500,000 in total. In addition to funding, I am also responsible for teaching them how to make medicinal meals.

苏：具体教哪些菜？

宋：我们大通饭庄还有其他单位做的菜都有教，还教他们现场调胶、怎么把胶融入菜里，他们再去各单位做。但原料还是我由提供，熬胶是非物质文化遗产，不外传。我把胶都做成半成品，他们进行最后一道工序。

苏：这些药膳师是您给自己公司培养的吗？

宋：对，但干一段时间后都被其他公司挖走了。可是我很高兴，因为他们跟着我学了药膳，得到了提升。迄今为止，别的地方没有公司培养药膳师。做这个是因为我不光想恢复自己的老字号，还想把它发扬光大。牛膏、羊膏一般回民都不知道，但现在大家全知道了，仙鹿膏、凤凰膏、金牛膏、固元膏、针灸膏……都被我宣传出去了。回族的医药很厉害，以前宫廷里都用他们的药，但很少有人知道，只有当时太医院的人掌握了这些东西，我想让过去皇宫里的东西服务于现在的老百姓。我现在是老字号协会的副会长，我有社会责任，得办实事。

苏：现在国际上很流行的营养师和您培养的药膳师有什么区别呢？

宋：最大区别的是——营养师是指导和监管的，但药膳师是要做菜的。营养师不懂得药膳的配餐，也不懂制作。药膳师和厨师也不是一个概念，但他们可以互通。

苏：现在中国的药膳师已经有了行业标准吗？

宋：有考核标准，但很多都是地方上自己办的，没有质量保证。我们主持培训的讲课老师有国药泰斗金世元、同仁堂研究院院长解素花、原北京中医药大学校长高思华、奥运营养专家王宜教授、健康教育首席专家赵霖教授，还有中日友好医院的两个博士，一共9个人的教师团队。

苏：在培养药膳师的过程中，您扮演什么样的角色？

宋：第一我也要去学习，第二我要把药膳跟团餐结合起来。现在中西餐结合加养生药膳是金丰的一大特点，也是大通饭庄的特色。

苏：您也跟这些专家学习？

宋：当然了，药食同源，遇到不知道的事情我就去问他们。我经常向北京中医药大学校长高思华请教，有时候老师随便一句话就点拨了我。我记得有一个龟鹿二仙膏，他跟我讲，龟和鹿一个是滋阴，一个是壮阳，它俩搁一起是最佳搭档，而且男女通用、强筋健骨，就适合运动员，高校长还亲自在现场拿鹿和龟炖给我们品尝。金世元老先生也给我们讲了四堂课，都是关于药和食物如何搭配、制作、结合的课程。

Su: What dishes have been taught actually?

Song: The dishes made in Datong Restaurant and other our restaurants were taught; also, we taught them how to mix gelatin, how to put gelatin into dishes, then, they went to other units to make it. However, the raw materials were still provided by me, and the gelatin boiling is intangible heritage which is not allowed for public disclosure. I made all the gelatin into semi-finished gelatin, and they went through the final process.

Su: Are these medicinal diet chefs trained by you for your own company?

Song: Yes, but after working for a while, they were all poached by other companies. But I am very happy, because he followed me to learn medicinal food and got promoted. So far, there is no company to train medicinal diet chefs in other places. This is because I not only want to restore my old brand, but also want to carry it forward. Cattle ointment and sheep ointment are generally unknown to Hui people, but now everyone knows them all. Xianlu Ointment, Fenghuang Ointment, Jinniu Ointment, Gelatin Ointment, Acupuncture Ointment... have all been publicized by me. Hui medicine is very powerful, they used to be used in the palace, but few people know about it, only the people of the Imperial Hospital at that time mastered these things, I want to make the things of the past palace to serve the people now. Now I am the Vice President of the Time-honored Association. I have to take social responsibility and do practical things.

Su: What's the difference between the nutritionist who is very popular in the world and the medicinal diet chefs you trained?

Song: The biggest difference is that a nutritionist is a guide and supervisor, but a medicinal diet chef is also a cook. Nutritionists don't know how to prepare or make medicinal food. A medicinal diet chef and a chef are not the same definition, but they are interconnected.

Su: Is there now an industry standard for medicinal diet chefs in China?

Song: There are assessment standards, but many of them are run by own without quality assurance. Our lecturers in charge of the training include Jin Shiyuan, Chinese medicine leader, Xie Suhua, Dean of Tongrentang Research Institute, Gao Sihua, former President of Beijing University of Chinese Medicine, and Wang Yi, Olympic nutrition expert, Zhao Lin, chief expert of health education, and two doctors from China-Japan Friendship Hospital, altogether nine trainers team jointly give classes.

Su: What role do you play in the process of training medicinal diet chefs?

Song: First, I want to study, and second, I want to combine medicinal meals with group meals. Nowadays, the combination of Chinese and Western meals plus health-boosting medicinal meals is a major feature of Jinfeng Catering, and also the specialty of Datong Restaurant.

Su: You also learn from these experts?

Song: Of course, medicine and food are of the same origin, so I will ask them when I meet something I don't know. Gao Sihua, the president of the Beijing University of Chinese Medicine, I always ask him, and sometimes the teacher gives me some advice with just one sentence. I remember there was a Guilu Erxian Ointment, and he told me that turtle and deer were nourishing yin and yang, and they were the best partners when put together. Moreover, they were unisex, strong in muscle and bone, and were suitable for athletes. President Gao also personally took deer and turtle to stew for us to taste at the scene. Mr. Jin Shiyuan also gave us four lectures, all about how to match, make and combine medicine and food.

苏：您也在这个药膳师培训过程中跟着学习吗？

宋：我一堂课都没落下过，这样的顶级大师培训上哪儿去找？这些大师不是我请来的，都是药膳委和国药集团请来的。王凤岐、吴大真都是我的老师，我加入了孟河学派，王凤岐正在完善孟河学派的内容，我也在完善我们家的药膳内容。给学生上课用的国家级药材药典教材能随便添加内容进去吗？如果没有真材实料，给多少钱，人家也不会给你搁的。[1]

药膳行业的发展

宋：我有三个烹饪大师的称号，一个是饭店协会评的，一个是中国烹饪协会评的，一个是药膳协会评的。这次我又被老字号评为非遗传承人大师。

杨：药膳协会的称号是什么时候评的？

宋：应该是奥运会过后，2010年左右在中医药大学考的。2005年、2006年的时候，我加入了北京中医药大学的药膳协会，现在是药膳协会的副会长，还举办过全国第一个药膳比赛“大通杯”。

苏：您能具体讲讲做药膳比赛的故事吗？

宋：当时是中国食品杂志社主编佟老师带着中医药大学校长周文泉找到了我，因为我们家是做药膳的，就想让我支持这个比赛。比赛的筹办方是中医药大学药膳委员会，我当时既是出资方，同时也是参赛选手。

苏：都有哪些人来参加这个药膳比赛？

宋：全国各地的都有，有200多个单位参加，除了专门的餐饮企业，还有一些医药单位、中医药大学组织的团队参加。

苏：您曾经说过，您想推广药膳标准，现在这方面的工作进展如何？

宋：还不成熟。毕竟我一个人的能力有限，加上学做药膳的人又少，我只是有这个想法，想法变成现实还需要一段很长的过程。

苏：您现在的构想是怎样的？

---

1 这里说的是吴大真、王凤岐编《秦伯未谦斋中医学全书》，河南科学技术出版社2020年版。宋子刚撰写的胶药文章以“附篇”的形式收录其中。

Su: Do you also study during the medicinal diet chef training?

Song: I have never missed single one class. Where can I find the top master training? I didn't invite these masters, they were all invited by the Chinese Medicine Committee and Sinopharm Group. Wang Fengqi and Wu Dazhen are both my teachers. I joined Menghe School. He is improving the content of Menghe School, and I am also perfecting the content of our family medicinal diet. Can you add content to the national herbal pharmacopoeia textbook for students' classes? If there is no real talent, no one will allow you to add any content no matter how much you pay. [1]

Development of Medicinal Diet Industry

Song: I have three titles as culinary masters, one was granted by the Hotel Association, one by the Chinese Cuisine Association and one by the Medicinal Food Association. This time, I also was granted with also awarded as an inheritor of national intangible culture.

Yang: When was the title of Medicinal Food Association granted?

Song: After the Olympic Games, I took the exam at the University of Traditional Chinese Medicine around 2010. In 2005 or 2006, I joined the Chinese Medicinal Dishes Association of Beijing University of Traditional Chinese Medicine, and now I am the Vice President of the Chinese Medicinal Dishes Association. I also held the first Chinese Medicinal Diet Competition Datong Cup.

Su: Can you tell me a specific story about hosting the Medicinal Diet Competition?

Song: It was Mr. Tong, editor-in-chief of China Food Magazine, who brought Zhou Wenquan, president of University of Traditional Chinese Medicine to me. Because my family is engaged in medicinal diet, they wanted me to support this competition. The organizer of the competition was the Medicinal Diet Committee of the University of Traditional Chinese Medicine, and I was both a funder and a contestant at that time.

Su: Who are the people coming to this Medicinal Diet Competition?

Song: Participants came from all over the country, with more than 200 units participating. Besides specialized catering enterprises, some medical units and universities of traditional Chinese medicine organized teams to participate.

Su: You once said that you wanted to promote the standard of medicinal diet. How is this work going now?

Song: Not yet mature. After all, my ability alone is limited, and there are few people studying make medicinal diet. I just have this idea, and it will take a long time for the idea to become a reality.

Su: What is your current idea?

1 This is recorded in *Qin Bo Wei Qian Zhai Complete Book of Traditional Chinese Medicine*, edited by Wu Dazhen and Wang Fengqi, Henan Science and Technology Press, 2020. The medicinal gelatin article written by Song Zigang is included in the Appendix.

宋：先把基础打好，药膳的基础就是产品，通过研发更多的药膳来服务大家，经过实践检验、总结积累，然后形成企业标准。

苏：您觉得做药膳最起码得满足什么样的要求？

宋：首先具有做药膳的意愿，其次自身有条件去做药膳，最后还得有资金支持。三个条件缺一不可。

苏：您觉得什么样的菜能被称为药膳呢？

宋：国家有一个药食同源目录，将里面记载的东西与其他食物搭配，通过科学的烹调方法做成菜，就是药膳。我认为药膳还是应该以补益和长寿为主要目的，如果想通过食疗治病，应该在医院的药膳里体现，我做的药膳更倾向于提升身体素质。

苏：您现在总结了哪些药膳标准呢？

宋：我现在有熬膏的标准、选料的标准、制作方法的标准，但不全面，特别是临床应用上有所欠缺，这还需要一个过程。

苏：临床是指什么？

宋：想形成真正的标准就得有一个长期的过程，不是三年五载就能完成的。需要有人在我们餐厅一年四季吃药膳，然后给我们反馈。需要不断地检验这个菜适不适合这个季节，适不适合客人。

苏：您所预想的药膳标准具体细分到哪些方面？

宋：我认为应该有三项：一、药膳的原料标准；二、工艺标准；三、菜品的流程以及它的食品安全、卫生检测和制作标准。

原料标准方面，我去过云南、河北、安徽等各地的药材市场了解药食同源的药材、琢磨怎么跟菜相结合，寻找原料质量最好的产地。

最好的蜂胶是大兴安岭的阿木尔蓝莓蜂胶，对眼睛特别好；芝麻用山东、河北的；大枣用山东、河北、新疆的；枸杞子用河北、宁夏的，这些都是我分别去考察，一个地儿一个地儿看的，一个地儿一个地儿选的，心里有谱。

中国产鹿的地方比较多，我都亲自去考察过。我去过东北大兴安岭加格达奇，吉林辽源、双阳、四平、东丰，辽宁西丰考察梅花鹿。去过新疆伊犁、江苏盐城考察马鹿。还去过湖北、海南考察鹿。

要想考察好东西，必须这样跑。我去大兴安岭阿木尔看蓝莓蜂胶的时候，路不好走，但就算手、腿都被扎破，我也得亲自去看一眼那蜂胶到底啥样。弄出来一看，是黑色的蜂胶，跟别的地儿不一样，是道地药材。只有道地好产品才能做出好药膳。

Song: First, lay a good foundation. The foundation of medicinal diet is products. We will serve everyone by developing more medicinal diets. After practice testing, summing up and accumulating, we will form enterprise standards.

Su: What kind of requirements do you think must be met at least for making medicinal diet?

Song: first with the will to do medicinal diet, followed by their own conditions to do medicinal diet, and finally there must be financial support. All three conditions are indispensable.

Su: How do you think a dish can be called a medicinal diet?

Song Dynasty: China has a national list of homology of medicine and food, which matches the contents with other foods and makes them into dishes by scientific cooking methods, that is, medicinal diet. I think that the main purpose of medicinal diet should be for tonic and longevity purpose. If you want to take dietary therapy to cure diseases, it should be reflected in the hospital's medicinal diet. The medicinal diet I made is more inclined to improve physical fitness.

Su: What medicinal diet standards have you summarized now?

Song: I have the standards for boiling gelatin, material selection and preparation methods, but they are not complete, especially in clinical application, and a process is needed in the future.

Su: What is clinical?

Song: If you want to form a true standard, you must have a long process, which can not be completed in three or five years. We need someone to eat medicinal meals in our restaurant all year round, and then give us feedback. We need to constantly check whether this dish is suitable for this season and guests.

Su: What are the specific subdivisions of your expected standards for medicinal diet?

Song: I think there should be three standards: first, a standard for medicinal diet raw materials. Second, a process standard. Third, a standard for dish process flow, food safety, and hygiene testing and production standards.

As for the standard of raw materials, I have been to Yunnan, Hebei, Anhui and other local medicinal materials markets to learn about the medicinal materials with the same origin as medicine and food, to consider how to combine with food, and to find the place of origin with the best quality of raw materials.

The best propolis is Daxinganling's Amur blueberry propolis, especially good for the eyes; sesame seeds from Shandong, Hebei; jujube from Shandong, Hebei, Xinjiang; Chinese wolfberry from Hebei, Ningxia. I visited these places one by one so that I could have a clear picture in my mind.

There are more places in China where deer are produced, and I have personally visited them all. I have been to Jiagedaqi in the Daxing anling region in Northeast China, Liaoyuan, Shuangyang, Siping and Dongfeng in Jilin, and Xifeng in Liaoning to inspect Sika deer. I have visited red deer in Yili, Xinjiang and Yancheng, Jiangsu. I have also visited deer in Hubei and Hainan.

If you want to inspect things properly, you must do it like this. When I went to Amur in the Daxinganling region to see the blueberry propolis, the road was not good, but even if my hands and legs were punctured, I had to see for myself what the propolis was like. Get out and see, it is black propolis, different from other places, the authentic medicinal material. Only authentic and good products can make good medicinal food.

苏：您去浙江、云南、河北、安徽是考察什么呢？

宋：去浙江考察熬胶用的料酒；去云南考察鲜花、三七、何首乌，我去过云南丽江挨着越南的边界，那儿的甘蔗做糖是最好的，还有菠萝、香蕉、鲜花，如果我要做菠萝馅儿，那里有最好的原料；去河北安国看他们的药材，因为我以前听父亲说过同仁堂就在那儿选药材，同仁堂选完以后，剩下的再拿到市场卖，我就想去看看到底是什么情况；去安徽也是考察药材市场。

苏：这是什么时候去的？

宋：大概十来年了。

苏：您有没有整理过各种原材料最好的产地？

宋：都整理完了。

苏：您为什么要走访这么多的地方？

宋：不把食材搞清楚是不能乱做的。举个例子，某个地区的白蘑，我先在春天的时候过去看，等到夏天、秋天、冬天分别再去看看，第二年我还要去复核，接连去了不下十来趟。把这儿的蘑菇跟其他地方的蘑菇做比较，后来觉得这个白蘑不能用，就把它从我们家素胶菜谱当中替换掉了。因为我发现那地方的环境污染太严重，导致产出的白蘑跟大兴安岭、云南的白蘑差太远。本来那儿的白蘑很香，但因为外在环境导致它内在品质发生了变化，因此我就换成了黑龙江和云南的白蘑，所以不能光照本宣科。

苏：我看到了您这儿的鹿角，是在哪儿采的？

宋：这是新疆的马鹿，梅花鹿的角没这么大。还有一些是从哈萨克斯坦、俄罗斯进口的，我每年买两吨自己熬。

苏：现在这些原料还是您自己去买吗？

宋：当然了，这可不是闹着玩的！上次广交药博会，我特意去看了鱼鳔胶（花胶），各种原料摆着，现场一看就知道好坏。

杨：花胶可贵了。

宋：非常贵，900块钱一公斤。因为出料少，大约五公斤原料才能出一公斤胶，但是它能治胃病、补肾。

杨：您的药膳知识是从家里传承下来的中医理念，但您说到的花青素则完全是西医营养学概念，您是从什么时候开始把它们相结合的呢？

宋：学习营养配餐的时候，经常能听到领导给首长讲养生知识，就像老师念课文，天天念，门口保安都会了。

Su: What do you want to investigate when you went to Zhejiang, Yunnan, Hebei and Anhui?

Song: I went to Zhejiang to inspect the cooking wine for gelatin boiling; I went to Yunnan to see flowers, Panax notoginseng and Polygonum multiflorum Thunb. I have been to Lijiang, Yunnan, near the border of Vietnam, where sugar cane is the best, as well as pineapples, bananas and flowers. If I want to make pineapple stuffing, it is the best raw material. I went to Anguo, Hebei to see their medicinal materials because I heard my father said Tong Ren Tang was there to choose medicinal materials. After the selection of Tong Ren Tang, the rest was sold in the market, so I wanted to see what the situation was. Going to Anhui is also to see their medicinal materials.

Su: When did you go there?

Song: About ten years ago.

Su: Have you sorted out the best producing areas of various raw materials?

Song: It's all sorted out.

Su: Why did you want to visit so many places?

Song: You can't cook without knowing the ingredients clearly. For example, for the white mushrooms in a certain area, I first went to see what spring is like, and then went to see them in summer, autumn and winter. In the second year, I had to check them, and I went to no less than ten times in succession. Comparing his mushrooms with those from other places, I found this white mushroom unusable, so I replaced it in our vegetarian diet. Because I found that the environmental pollution in that place was too serious, the white mushrooms produced were far behind those in Daxinganling and Yunnan. The white mushrooms there are very fragrant, but because of the external environment, its internal quality has changed, so I replaced them with the white mushrooms from Heilongjiang and Yunnan, so I can't just follow the books.

Su: I see some antlers here, where did you purchase the antlers?

Song: This is the red deer in Xinjiang. The horns of sika deer are not so big. And some are imported from Kazakhstan and Russia. I buy two tons every year and cook them by myself.

Su: Are you still going to buy these raw materials yourself?

Song: Of course, this is no joke! Last time, I went to see isinglass (huajiao) specially in Guangzhou International Health Care Industry Exposition, and all kinds of raw materials were placed there. I knew whether it was good or bad when I saw it on the spot.

Yang: Isinglass can be very expensive.

Song: Very expensive, RMB 900 a kilogram. Because the output is less, about 5 kg of raw materials can produce 1 kg isinglass, but it can cure stomach diseases and tonify kidneys.

Yang: Your knowledge of medicinal diet is the traditional Chinese medicine idea inherited from your family, but the anthocyanin you mentioned is entirely western medicine nutrition. When did you start to combine them?

Song: When learning nutrition and catering, you can often hear leaders talking about health knowledge to their senior officers, just like a teacher reading a text every day, and the security guards at the door will know it.

苏：您觉得目前的药膳发展还有什么欠缺呢？

宋：缺乏平台，我需要更大的平台去展示药膳、推广药膳，让大家对药膳有更多的认识。

苏：在推广药膳文化这块儿，您觉得存在什么障碍呢？

宋：还是有部分人群比较排斥药膳，不愿意尝试，他们认为没得病为什么要吃药膳。其实这是错误的理念，药膳讲究的是未病先治，是保养身体。

宋子刚和他的产品

Song Zigang and his products

中国饭店协会会长韩明向获奖的宫廷“御”字牌细八件主理人、非物质文化遗产传承人宋子刚表示祝贺

Han Ming, President of China Hospitality Association, congratulated Song Zigang, the intangible heritage inheritor and maker of Court food “Eight Pieces” who just won an award

Su: What do you think is lacking in the development of medicinal diet at present?

Song: Lack of platforms, I need a bigger platform to display and promote medicinal diet, so that everyone can have a better understanding of medicinal diet.

Su: What obstacles do you think exist in the promotion of medicinal diet culture?

Song: There are still some people who reject medicinal diet and are unwilling to try. They think why they should eat medicinal diet when they are not sick. In fact, this is a wrong idea. Medicinal diet pays attention to treating diseases before they become ill, which is to maintain people's health.

宋子刚考察鱼胶（摄于2015年）

Song Zigang inspected Isinglass (photo taken in 2015)

宋子刚考察鹿角（摄于2016年）

Song Zigang inspected antlers (photo taken in 2016)

北京有127家老字号，大通饭庄是唯一一家做药膳的老字号，其营业执照上写的是养生菜

There are 127 old brands in Beijing, and Datong Restaurant is the only one that makes medicinal food, and its business license states that it produces health-care food

鹿胶膏非遗奖牌

Intangible Heritage Medal for Deerskin Gelatin Ointment

大通饭庄的老字号证书

The Time-honored Certificate of Datong Restaurant

金丰集团获颁“北京餐饮十大品牌”证书

Jinfeng Group was awarded the certificate of “Beijing Top Ten Catering Brands”

宋子刚与烹饪大师王义均、屈浩参观“天下第一黑店”

Song Zigang with master chef Wang Yijun and Qu Hao visit the “world’s No.1 black restaurant”

中国饭店协会会长韩明、北京老字号协会会长姜俊贤亲自为“大通饭庄”主持开业

Han Ming, President of China Hospitality Association, and Jiang Junxian, President of Beijing Time-honored Brand Association, personally presided over the opening of Datong Restaurant

御德堂梅花鹿结构与功效图

鹿胶膏技艺

鹿胶膏制作技艺为宋氏胶药门第六代传人宋玉德、宋天德所创，时逢康熙盛世，战事渐息，社会安定。因鹿全身皆宝，二人发现新疆伊犁马鹿、关东梅花鹿，为制作鹿皮胶的上佳材料，经多年反复试制，遂创出大通古法鹿胶膏，专供皇室。因鹿胶膏在皇室延续子嗣方面的独特贡献，为历代皇宫延续使用至今，并造福百姓。由宋氏胶药门第十六代传人宋子刚继承发扬至今。

鹿胶功效

鹿胶膏制作技艺是中华胶剂制作艺术的瑰宝。

用鹿皮熬炼成胶，早在《神农本草经》就将鹿胶与龙骨、麝香、牛黄、熊脂、阿胶同列为上品六兽，并强调其功效：“为君，主养命以应天，无毒。多服、久服不伤人。欲轻身益气，不老延年者”。

鹿胶膏是以梅花鹿、马鹿皮、筋为原料，辅以黑芝麻、核桃仁、松子、枸杞、人参、灵芝及多种辅料调和而成。鹿皮胶富含多种氨基酸与微量元素，有温补肝肾、益精养血、补气生精、滋阴壮阳、生精髓、续筋骨等营养保健作用。对阳痿滑精、腰膝酸冷、虚劳羸瘦、崩漏下血、便血尿血、阴疽肿痛等病痛有辅助疗效。

鹿的烹调方法：

1. 鹿尾：煲汤、红烧；2. 鹿鞭：煲汤、红烧、干烧；3. 鹿筋：煲汤、红烧、煨炒；4. 鹿腿：烧、烤、炸；5. 鹿排：红烧、烤；6. 鹿里脊：滑炒、熘；

7. 鹿心、鹿肝、鹿肚、鹿肺、鹿肠、鹿肾：卤水、酱、爆炒、煨炒、炝炒、汆锅、烩；8. 鹿腩：红烧、汆丸子、制馅（包子、饺子、馅饼）；

9. 鹿血：蒸、炒、泡酒；10. 鹿皮：熬胶、制冻；11. 鹿脑：炖、火锅、汆锅；12. 鹿头：扒、烧、卤水、酱、制焖子；13. 鹿胎：制膏；14. 鹿骨：熬汤、制粉。

宋子刚整理的鹿结构与食用功效图

Deer structure and edible efficacy map edited by Song Zigang

宋子刚制作的宫廷药膳鹿胶月饼、阿胶月饼被《中国烹饪》杂志选登

Song Zigang's palace dietary specialities, Deerskin Gelatin Moon Cake and Donkey-hide Gelatin Moon Cake, were published on Chinese Cuisine

2016 年，大通鹿胶月饼、阿胶月饼获老字号时尚创意大赛金银铜奖

In 2016, Deerskin Gelatin Moon Cake and Donkey-hide Gelatin Moon cake won Gold, Silver and Bronze Awards in the Time-honored Brand Fashion Creativity Competition

世界中餐业联合会清真餐饮（食品）产业委员会主席、北京烹饪协会会长云程向奥运美食伊德诚固元糕制作者宋子刚表示祝贺并合影留念

Yun Cheng, Halal Industry Committee of World Federation of Chinese Catering Industry and President of the Beijing Culinary Association, congratulates Song Zigang, the maker of the Olympic delicacy Yidecheng Gelatin cake, and takes a group photo

金丰大通中国首届团餐药膳师开班典礼

Opening Ceremony of Jinfeng Datong China 1st Group Meal Medicated Diet Chef Class

北京老字号协会会长陈文向获得“老字号工匠”称号的宋子刚表示祝贺，并合影留念

Chen Wen, President of Beijing Time-honored Brands Association, congratulated Song Zigang, who won the “time-honored craftsman” title, and took a group photo

世界中餐业联合会食药养生委员会主席团合影

Group photo of the Presidium of the Food, Therapy Health Committee of the World Federation of Chinese Catering Industry

中国药膳研究会慢病调养专业委员会成立，合影留念

the Professional Committee of Chronic Diseases Rehabilitation of China Medicinal Diet Research Association was established and took a group photo

宋子刚当选中国药膳研究会慢病调养专业委员会副主任委员

Song Zigang was elected as the Deputy Director of the Professional Committee of Chronic Diseases Rehabilitation of China Medicinal Diet Research Association

北京烹饪协会2020年京华名厨新春团拜会

Beijing Cuisine Association 2020 Jinghua Famous Chefs New Year Reunion

宋子刚展示公司获得的各项荣誉

Song Zigang shows the honors the company has won

宋子刚获颁北京老字号工匠证书

Song Zigang was awarded the Certificate of Beijing Time-honored Craftsman

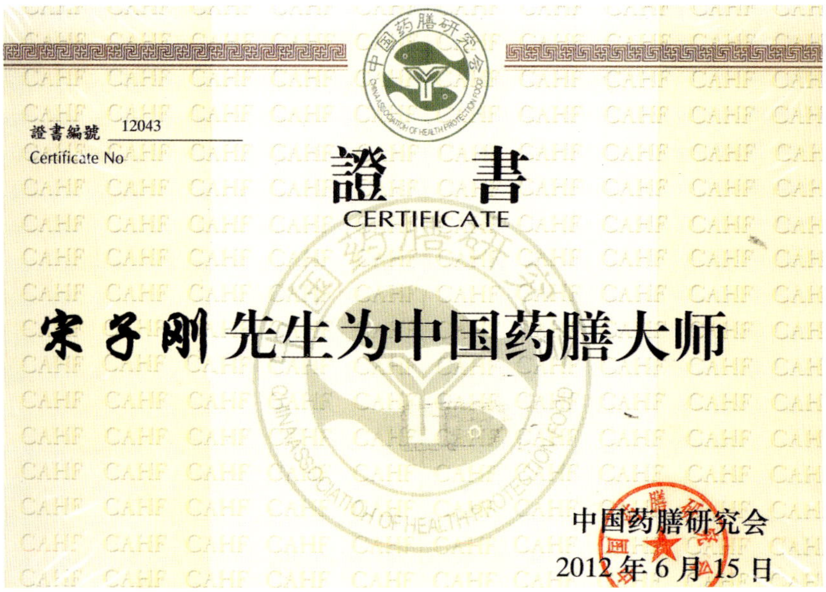

宋子刚获颁中国药膳大师证书

Song Zigang was awarded the Certificate of Chinese Dietary Therapy Master

宋子刚获颁北京市海淀区非物质文化遗产项目，鹿胶膏制作技艺代表性传承人证书

Song Zigang was awarded the representative inheritor certificate of deerskin gelatin production, an Intangible Cultural Heritage Project of Beijing Haidian District

荣譽證書

中国烹饪协会第六届理事会
特邀副会长单位
北京金丰餐饮有限公司
代表人：宋子刚

有效期：2018年5月至2019年11月

北京金丰餐饮有限公司获中国烹饪协会第六届理事会特邀副会长单位

Beijing Jinfeng Catering Co., Ltd., was invited as the vice chairman unit of the 6th Council of China Cuisine Association

荣誉证书

中国餐饮30年功勋人物奖

宋子刚

二〇一七年五月

宋子刚获颁中国餐饮30年功勋人物奖荣誉证书

Song Zigang was awarded the honorary certificate of the Chinese Catering 30 Years Meritorious Figure Award

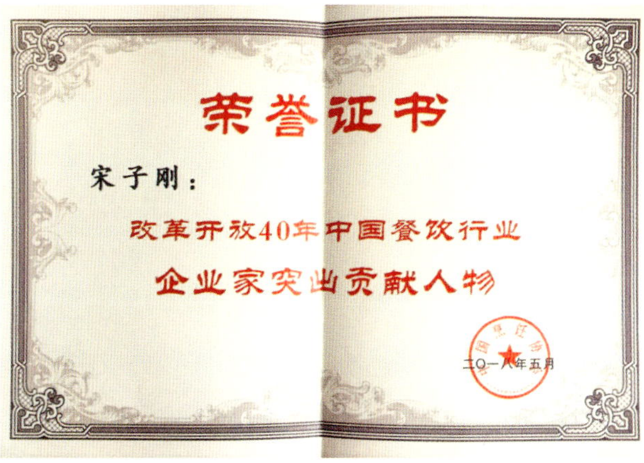

荣誉证书

宋子刚：
改革开放40年中国餐饮行业
企业家突出贡献人物

二〇一八年五月

宋子刚获颁改革开放40年中国餐饮业企业家突出贡献人物荣誉证书

Song Zigang was awarded the Certificate of Honor for Outstanding Personal Contributions to Chinese Catering Industry in the 40 Years of Reform and Opening Up

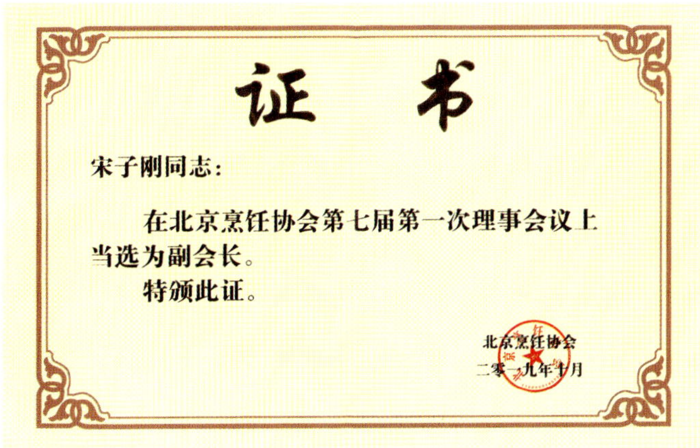

证书

宋子刚同志：
在北京烹饪协会第七届第一次理事会议上当选为副会长。
特颁此证。

北京烹饪协会
二零一九年十月

宋子刚获颁北京烹饪协会副会长证书

Song Zigang was awarded the Vice President Certificate of Beijing Cuisine Association

中华老字号工作委员会原主任安惠民和北京老字号协会原会长刘小虹向获得创意大赛金奖的鹿胶膏制作者宋子刚表示祝贺并合影留念

An Huimin, former President of China Time-honored Brand Association, and Liu Xiaohong, former President of Beijing Time-honored Brand Association, congratulated Song Zigang, the deerskin gelatin ointment maker who won the gold medal in the Creative Competition and took a group photo

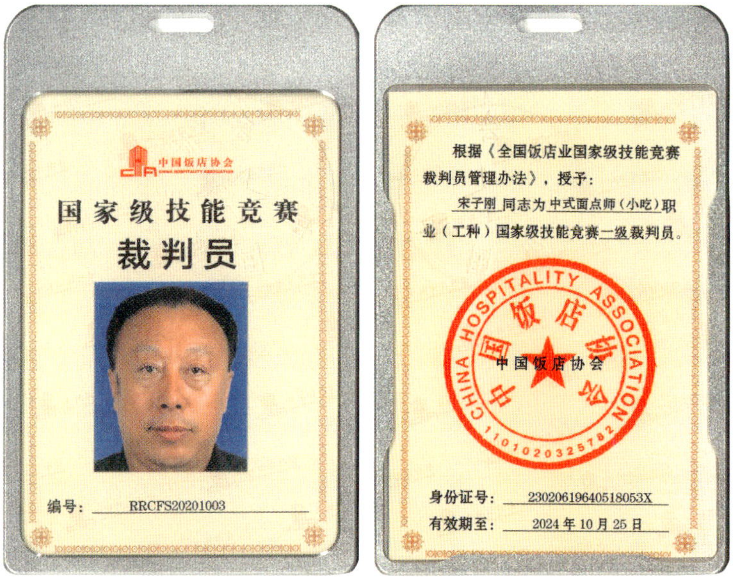

宋子刚获中国饭店协会颁发的国家级技能竞赛裁判员证

Song Zigang was awarded the National Skills Competition Referee Certificate by the China Hospitality Association

宋子刚获颁中国烹饪协会团餐委员会副主席证书

Song Zigang was awarded the Certificate of Vice Chairman of the Group Meal Committee of the China Cuisine Association

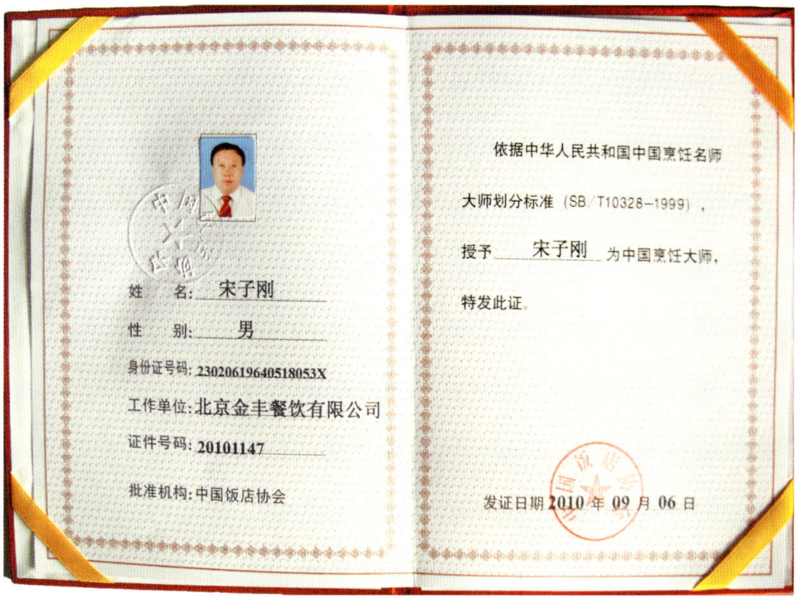

宋子刚获颁中国烹饪大师证书

Song Zigang was awarded the Chinese Cooking Master Certificate

宋子刚编写的宫廷药膳被收录进了吴大真、王凤岐编的《秦伯未谦斋中医学全书》（河南科学技术出版社2020年版）中

The palace medicated diet compiled by Song Zigang is included in *Qin Bo Wei Qian Zhai Complete Book of Traditional Chinese Medicine*, edited by Wu Dazhen and Wang Fengqi, Henan Science and Technology Press, 2020

"飞天"，斩获2020世界奥林匹克烹饪大赛"糖艺雕塑"项目金牌的作品

"Flying", the work that won the gold medal of the "Sugar Sculpture" in the 2020 IKA/Culinary Olympics

中国国家烹饪队斩获2020世界奥林匹克烹饪大赛金、银、铜奖

China National Culinary Team won gold, silver and bronze medals in the 2020 IKA/Culinary Olympics

宋子刚与中国烹饪协会会长姜俊贤在中国国家烹饪队成立仪式上合影

Group photo of Song Zigang and Jiang Junxian, President of the China Cuisine Association, at the launching ceremony of the China National Culinary Team

宋子刚捐赠百万元，奖励获得2017IKA奥林匹克世界烹饪大赛金牌的中国国家烹饪队队员

Song Zigang donated RMB one million yuan to reward the members of the China National Culinary Team who won the Gold Medal of the 2017 IKA/Culinary Olympics

临县高级中学家长监督委员会赠予北京金丰餐饮有限公司锦旗

The Silk Banner from Linxian Senior High School Parents Supervision Committee to Beijing Jinfeng Catering Co., Ltd.

证书

北京金丰餐饮有限公司

2021年度中国团餐服务质量十强

证书编号：TCBQ2021-002

北京金丰餐饮有限公司获颁"2021年度中国团餐服务质量十强"证书

Beijing Jinfeng catering Co., Ltd. was awarded the certificate of "Top 10 Chinese Group Meal Service Quality in 2021"

北京烹饪协会

副会长单位

编号：020　　有效期至2025年1月

金丰集团获颁"北京烹饪协会副会长单位"证书

Jinfeng Group was awarded the certificate of "Vice President Unit of Beijing Cuisine Association"

商务部机关服务局党委书记兼局长宋振光品鉴大通药膳"宫廷细八件"，并给予肯定

Song Zhenguang, secretary of the Party committee of the Ministry of Commerce and director of the organ service bureau, tasted and affirmed the "Eight Pieces" of Datong medicinal meals

2019 年 2 月 25 日，金丰集团美食服务团队全面入驻山西临县高级中学，为全校 6800 多名师生（41%为国家在册贫困生）提供餐饮服务

On February 25, 2019, the food service team of Jinfeng Group settled in Shanxi Linxian Senior High School, providing food and beverage services to more than 6,800 teachers and students (41% of them are nationally registered poor students)

第五章

Chapter 5

全业态转型

Transformation of All Business Forms

【访谈者按】我们对宋先生的访谈主要在他公司一间大约5平方米的会客室进行，进门是一张圆桌，后面是一排书柜，其中有数百本书籍，医案药方类最多，烹饪、清史、北京历史文化等次之，所藏不乏专精生僻之目，并非摆架装潢之流，可以看出确是宋先生个人所好。中间还有一些关于企业管理、组织行为的书籍，很引人注意。在后来的交流中我们了解到，宋先生的好学不倦一以贯之，并且，他还有经营社会网络的天然直觉，不仅一次参加各大商学院的培训。他的公司有整面墙的反馈表格，细致到工作的边边角角，这是他从培训中学来的可视化、表格化管理，给他的公司带来了很多收益。但在重要决策上，过去在军队中接受的训练使他很容易“理论联系实际”，没有生搬硬套外企流行的“立体化管理”，而是“支部建在连上”，管理扁平、直接。我们认为他的企业管理经验很值得研究，因此，在这个部分，我们集中访问了他这几十年积累下来的管理、培训心得，并在最后请他谈了谈对自己的总结和未来的展望。

扁平化管理

苏：您写的这套企业管理的书是2010年出版的？

宋：对，那个时候出的成果比较多。

苏：您公司的组织结构其实非常现代，这也向别人请教过吗？

宋：就是我自己弄的，因为我在清华大学念过EMBA。

苏：当时为什么想要读这个呢？

宋：我想学习经济和管理，结识人脉。

苏：您都去学了些什么呢？

宋：学习现代化的管理，也认识了一些政商两届的人。后面到各省市的分公司出差的时候，就会顺便拜访我的同学们，互相聚聚、拓展业务。

苏：您也去别的城市做食堂服务？

宋：对，不光是北京，全国的食堂服务我都有做。外地最早是在杭州机场干。

杨：在您的这套企业管理书籍里，服务标准写得非常细，是您自己写的吗？

宋：我参加过四次国际标准认证培训，一个是14001环境认证培训，一个

[Interviewer's Note] Our interview with Mr. Song was mainly conducted in a reception room of about 5 square meters in his company, with a round table at the entrance and a row of bookcases at the back. Among them, there were hundreds of books, with the most medical records and prescriptions, followed by cooking, history of Qing Dynasty, Beijing history and culture, etc., and there was no lack of specialization in the collection, not the trend of setting up shelves and decorating. It can be seen that Mr. Song really liked it personally. There are also some books about enterprise management and organizational behavior, which may attract people's attention. In the later exchanges, we learned that Mr. Song's tireless learning is consistent, and he also has the natural intuition of running social networks, and he has participated in the training of major business schools more than once. His company has a whole wall of feedback forms, detailed to all aspects of his work. This is the visual and tabular management he learned from his training, which has brought a lot of benefits to his company. However, in terms of important decision-making, his past training in the military made it easy for him to "link theory with practice", and he did not rigidly apply the "three-dimensional management" popular in foreign companies, but "built the branch on the company", with flat and direct management. We thought his experience in business management was worth studying, so in this section we focused on interviewing his management and training insights accumulated over these decades, and asked him to talk about his summary and future outlook at the end.

Flat Management

Su: This business management book you wrote was published in 2010?

Song: Yes, there were more achievements at that time.

Su: Your company's organizational structure is quite modern. Have you consulted others?

Song: I did it myself, because I studied EMBA at Tsinghua University.

Su: Why did you want to read this at that time?

Song: I want to study economics and management and meet people.

Su: What have you learned?

Song: I studied modern management and also met some people from both the political and business sectors. Then I went to the branch offices in various provinces and cities, so I stopped by to visit my classmates to get together with each other and expand my business.

Su: Do you also go to other cities for running canteen service?

Song: Yes, not just in Beijing, I ran canteen service all over the country. I ran this business first in Hangzhou Airport.

Yang: In your set of business management books, the service standard is very detailed. Did you write these standards by yourself?

Song: I have attended four international standard certification trainings, one is 14001 environmental certification training and one is HACCP food quality training, both of which I was

是HACCP食品质量培训，都是在部队的时候要求我参加的。这本书95%的内容都是我自己写的，我的老师，哈尔滨商业大学校长杨铭铎先生帮我完善了一部分内容，剩下的就是请各个领导、专家审核。

杨：国际认证的服务标准跟您给部队首长服务的标准是不是不一样？

宋：不一样，国际标准是环境认证和质量认证，是在工作中的流程标准和制度规范。给首长服务的标准是提供细致化、个性化的服务，我也是第一个提出在团餐中提供个性化服务的人。

杨：团餐怎么进行个性化服务？

宋：针对北京人，就做北京菜；针对东北人，就做东北菜；针对四川人，就做四川菜。"设计中求全面"就是要把全国各地的东西综合起来，要是在新疆，就以新疆物产和当地风味为主。

苏：您举几个对您影响比较深的人。

宋：一个是我的老师杨铭铎教授，他说，标准是决定成败的关键，标准做好了，就确定了你的地位。另一个是北京市农林科学院研究员李武，他是蔬菜专家、全国政协委员，他教我标准化切制，在果蔬加工方面给予我特别大的指导和支持，比如：怎么切菜、怎么用科学的手法进行保管、需要用什么样的设备等等。还有北京烹饪协会副会长王云，他帮我联系各种专家，起到了桥梁的作用。

杨：他都帮您联系过谁？

宋：马克西姆餐厅总经理贺广银、鸿宾楼做清真菜的佟建国、北京饭店的国宴大师郑秀生，还有中国烹饪大师郑绍武、便宜坊行政总厨孙立新，都是王云老师帮忙联系来参加研讨会的。

苏：您是怎么认识王云的？

宋：王云是我在奥运会期间认识的专家。还有一个人对我的影响也特别大，就是健康教育首席专家赵霖教授，他专门研究团餐的营养配餐。中国农业大学的范志红教授，原中国农业大学副校长李里特教授，还有江南大学食品学院食品安全专家钱和教授，都给予了我直接的指导和帮助。

苏：您都是怎么认识他们的？

宋：都是通过奥运会的专家课题组认识的，他们指导我按照国际化、现代化的理念去做团餐和药膳，对我的帮助很大。但我觉得不能生搬硬套，就改良成了现在的这种方式。因为长时间做食堂的经验告诉我，食堂应该更加直接地扁平化管理，不适合立体化管理。我们在部队学习毛主席理论，"支部建在连上"这样能够直接把服务政令落实到基层，砍掉中间的领导环节。

required to attend when I was in the army. I wrote 95% of the book myself, and my teacher, Mr. Yang Mingduo of Harbin University of Commerce helped me to improve part of the book, and then I asked some leaders and experts to review it.

Yang: Are the standards of service for international certification different from the standards of service you offered to the senior officers in army?

Song: No, the international standards are environmental certification and quality certification, which are process standards and system norms in work. The standards of serving the senior officers are to provide meticulous and personalized services, I was also the first person to propose personalized services in group meals.

Yang: How to provide personalized service for group meals?

Song: For Beijingers, make Beijing cuisine; for the northeast people, make northeast dishes; for Sichuanese, cook Sichuan food. "Seeking comprehensiveness in design" means integrating things from all over the country. If it is in Xinjiang, we will focus on Xinjiang products and local flavor.

Su: Name a few people who have a deep influence on you.

Song: One is my teacher, professor Yang Mingduo. He said that the standard is the key to success. When the standard is well done, your position will be established. The other is Li Wu, a vegetable expert, who is a researcher of Beijing Academy of Agriculture and Forestry Sciences and a mumber of the CPPCC National Committee. He taught me standardized cutting and gave me great guidance and support in fruit and vegetable processing, such as how to cut vegetables, how to keep them in a scientific way, what kind of equipment to use, and so on. Also, Wang Yun, Vice President of the Beijing Cuisine Association, who helped me contact various experts and played a bridge role.

Yang: To whom did he contact for you?

Song: He Guangyin, general manager of Maxim Restaurant, Tong Jianguo specialized in Muslim food from Hongbin Building, Zheng Xiusheng, master of state banquet at Beijing Hotel, Zheng Shaowu, Chinese culinary master, and Sun Lixin, executive chef of Bianyifang were all contacted by Wang Yun to attend the seminar.

Su: How do you know Wang Yun?

Song: Wang Yun was an expert I met during the Olympic Games. Another person who has a great influence on me is Zhao Lin, chief expert of health education, who specializes in nutritional catering for group meals. Professor Fan Zhihong from China Agricultural University , Professor Li Ritter and Former Vice President of China Agricultural University, Professor Qian He of school of food science and technology of Jiangnan University, a food safety expert all gave me direct guidance and help.

Su: How do you know them?

Song: I met them all through the expert research group of the Olympic Games. They guided me to make group meals and medicinal meals according to the concept of internationalization and modernization, which helped me a lot. But I felt that I couldn't copy it, so I improved it to the way it is now. Because the experience of running a canteen for a long time tells me that canteen should be subject to more direct and flat management, which is not suitable for three-dimensional management. We study Chairman Mao's theory in the army, "branch built on the company" so that the service orders can be implemented directly to the grassroots by cutting out the intermediate leadership links.

苏：您还有一个专门的厨师长微信群，所以您现在也是垂直领导？

宋：对，公司现在有上万人，我敢把我的电话给所有人。有的人就说这样光接电话都得累死了，但实际情况是没有人给我打电话。因为我是诚信经营、正规经营，分清全部的职责，各负其责，我怕啥？

苏：您写的第三方监理团又是什么意思？

宋：第三方监理团是我聘请的一些退休人员定期来我们这儿检查，其中包括了12位国家药品监督管理局的领导。

杨：所以得有监管。

宋：我还是最早设立审计部的酒店，一般经营性酒店都没有。还有大客户维护总监，主要针对公共部门和政府。

苏：您的组织架构确实非常先进，您跟国际团餐龙头企业的管理有什么不一样的地方？

宋：我更直接、更简便。很多团餐都是大锅菜，在我这儿不允许，为了做得更精细，我们采取一岗双责制，一件事俩人负责。灶台上分主荤菜、半荤菜、素菜、汤粥、涮炸、蒸菜六套线，每套线俩人，我的人工成本就比别人高，但为了保证好品质，我愿意降低自己的利润。同时因为有了这么大的投入，才有后续的产出，才能突出自己的特点。必须得投入，舍得在教育上投入，舍得在研发菜品上投入。

杨：您这儿管理的表格也很多。

宋：中欧商学院最提倡格式化管理、可视化管理，这些表格化管理就是我在商学院上学的时候学到的。前厅后厨配合衔接，就有一个表格，所有的菜品什么时候出餐、出多少量都写得很清楚。全国我最早提出健康食堂，现在我又提倡明星餐厅。

综合性人才培训

宋：这些光碟都是关于团餐标准、操作规范流程、菜品制作的内容。主要是给员工培训时候用的。我们获得全国首届“中餐科技进步一等奖”以后，《中国食品》杂志花了一年时间才把我们的团餐标准登完，还有饭店协会、烹饪协

Su: You also have a special chef WeChat group, so you are also a vertical leader now?

Song: Yes, the company now has tens of thousands of employees, and I dare to give my phone number to everyone. Some people say that this will be exhausting just to answer the phone, but the reality is that no one is calling me. Because I operate in good faith and in a regular way, I distinguish all my responsibilities and shoulder my responsibilities. What am I afraid of?

Su: What do you mean by the third-party supervision team?

Song: The third-party supervision team is a group of retirees hired by me to come here for regular inspection, including 12 leaders of the National Medical Products Administration.

Yang: So, supervision shall be in place anytime and anywhere.

Song: I was the first person to set up an audit department in a hotel. Generally speaking, hotels do not have an audit department. I also set up a director of key account maintenance, mainly for the public sector and governments.

Su: Your organizational structure is really very advanced. What's the difference between you and the management of leading enterprises in international group meals?

Song: Mine is more direct and simple. Many group meals are big pot dishes, which I don't allow here. In order to make them more delicate, we adopt a system of double responsibility for one post, and two people are responsible for one thing. There are six sets of lines on the stove, including main meat dishes, semi-meat dishes, vegetarian dishes, soup and porridge, hot fried dishes and steamed dishes. Each line has two people, so my labor cost is higher than others, but in order to ensure good quality, I am willing to reduce my profits. In addition, with such a large investment, there will be a follow-up output, in order to highlight our own characteristics. Investment is necessary including investment in education and dish R&D.

Yang: You also have many management forms here.

Song: CEIBS advocates formatted management and visual management, which I learned when I was in business school. A table should be required for the coordination and connection of the front office and kitchen, and it should record clearly when and how much all the dishes will be served. I was the first person in China who proposed health canteen, and now I advocate star restaurant.

Comprehensive Talent Training

Song: These CD-ROMs are all about the standard of group meals, the standardized operation process and the production of dishes. They are mainly used for staff training. After we won the "First Prize of the First National Chinese Catering Science and Technology Progress Award", *China Food* took a year to finish publishing our group meal standard, and the restaurant association and culinary

会都有刊登我们的团餐标准。

苏：您能讲讲创办这个学校的故事吗？

宋：我的初衷是想把企业做大做强。但一个人的能力毕竟有限，我需要找更多的人来配合我，当时没有一所这样的学校，而我认为单一的培训也不行，要有一个长期和全面的打算，于是一直在找机会创办学校。我非常重视培训学习，在部队当过六七年的老师，教酒店管理、酒店服务、酒店的厨师培训和考核，我认为培训也是搭班子、带队伍、带人才的一个基础。

苏：创办学校是什么时候的事？

宋：学校已经有11年的历史了。

苏：现在学校主要培训哪些内容？

宋：主要是分两大块，一个是厨师培训，一个是服务培训。系统的教育体系也能更好地把我的中国团餐标准和药膳传承下去。

苏：都有什么人来学？

宋：面向社会公开招生，他们有的拥有厨师基础，有的没有，完成学习后直接进入我们公司工作。

苏：您大概培养了多少学生？

宋：有证的药膳师120个，没有证的药膳师得有五六千，厨师培养了上万人。我们是一整套中餐、西餐、药膳的学习体系。

苏：您干这行多久后开始考虑开学校的？

宋：我在部队就认为做教育才是企业长久发展的基础。我老写一些企业文化方面的文章，实际金丰有13种文化。

苏：都有什么呢？

宋：红色文化，就是敢为人先的首创精神。最开始团餐是没有标准的，都是我自己一点一点摸索写出来的；我的中英文菜谱也开创了全国首例；同时我也是第一个在《中国烹饪》上发表中英文文章的厨师。

金丰还要做奥运文化，奥运就是勇于争第一、积极参与、更高更强，我的团餐也要更高更强。从金丰走出去的人太多了，我的司机离职后都去别的单位当老总，有的员工跟我搞了几天标书，就去别人那儿当标书总监，我的员工出去当厨师长、经理的遍地都是。这让我既感到自豪也非常欣慰。

杨：您能举一个比较典型的例子吗？

宋：我有一个战友苏喜斌，跟我干了一年多，就去饮食文化研究所当了团

association have published our group meal standard.

Su: Can you tell me the story of founding this school?

Song: My original intention was to make the business bigger and stronger. But one person's ability is limited, I need to find more people to cooperate with me, at that time there is no such school, and I think a single training will not work, to have a long-term and comprehensive plan, so I have been looking for opportunities to start a school. I always attach great importance to training and learning, in the army I was a teacher for six or seven years, teaching hotel management, hotel services, hotel chef training and assessment. I think training is also a basis for building a team, leading a team and talents.

Su: When was the school founded?

Song: The school has a history of 11 years.

Su: What are the main training courses in the school now?

Song: The school is mainly divided into two parts, one is chef training and the other is service training. A systematic education system can also better pass on my Chinese group meal standards and medicinal meals.

Su: Who comes to the school?

Song: The school is open to the public to recruit students. Some of them have a chef's foundation, while others do not. After completing their studies, they will directly work in our company.

Su: How many students have you trained?

Song: We trained 120 certified medicinal diet chefs, and there are 5,000 or 6,000 non-certified medicinal diet chefs, plus trained tens of thousands of chefs. We have a whole learning system of Chinese food, western food and medicinal food.

Su: How long after you started thinking about opening a school?

Song: When I was in the army, I thought that education was the foundation for the long-term development of enterprises. I always write some articles about corporate culture. Actually, Jinfeng catering has 13 kinds of cultures.

Su: What are they?

Song: Red culture is the pioneering spirit of being the first. In the beginning, there was no standard for group meals, so I wrote it out by myself little by little; my Chinese and English recipes were the first of their kind in China; I was also the first one to publish an article in Chinese and English in *Chinese Cuisine*.

Jinfeng Catering also will build the Olympic culture. The Olympic Games is to be brave in striving for the first place, actively participate, be higher and stronger, and my group meal will be higher and stronger. Many people have gone out from Jinfeng Catering, my driver left me then acted as the general manager of other companies; some employees have worked with me on preparing bid documents for a few days, then they acted as a bidding director. There are many chefs and managers in other companies acted by my former employees. This makes me both proud and gratified.

Yang: Can you give a typical example in this regard?

Song: I have a comrade-in-arms, Su Xibin. After working with me for more than a year, he

餐主席。另外一个是兵器大厦的厨师长张俊成，现在在中石油阳光会议中心当餐饮总监。还有我的司机到东贸国际当运营总监，不胜枚举。

杨：人都走了，您这儿缺人怎么办？

宋：我不受影响，我有学校不断地给我培养人才。

工业化生产

苏：您希望药膳文化在社会上推广到什么程度？

宋：全民皆知，因此我准备做御德堂健康科技发展公司。这个想法已经有十年了，落在实处已经有五年了，我为此花了一个多亿，国家已经立项，执照也都批完，厂地就在平谷。

苏：你们有些产品已经走出国门了，都去了哪儿？

宋：德国、阿联酋、日本，还有美国。

苏：具体是什么场合呢？

宋：食品交流、食品展览。

苏：这些展览和交流给您什么样的感受？

宋：非物质文化遗产都是独门绝技，尤其我做的是宫廷食品，我的这些东西他们都没见过，觉得特别兴奋和好奇。

苏：在国际上，您下一步有什么计划吗？

宋：我建立平谷工厂就是走"一带一路"。未来我要把中国食品通过工业化生产、标准化生产带到国外去，宣传中国的传统宫廷饮食文化和药膳文化。我有自己的拳头产品，我想把它们发扬光大。用我的配方做的药叫特医食品，也就是医院里给患者吃的。内科、外科、妇科、儿科，不同的科用不同的养生食品。北京现在没有一家工厂生产这个，都是各医院自己生产的，但那些医院也没有像我做得这么全面。下一步我准备单独做阿胶海参、鹿胶海参，因为熬完的胶可以作为原材料再工业化生产。

杨：您这工业化生产的食品是什么状态？回家还需要再熬吗？

宋：不用熬，是液态状。里面胶的比例不超过3克，一般就放1～2克。这

went to the Institute of Food Culture and became the chairman of the group meal. Zhang Juncheng, the former chef in Weapons Building, is now the director of catering in the Sunshine Conference Center of China National Petroleum Corporation. And, my former driver is the COO of Dongmao International, and such examples cannot be exhausted.

Yang: When talents are gone, what should you do if you are short of talent here?

Song: I am not affected. I have schools that constantly train talents for me.

Industrialized Production

Su: To what extent do you want the medicinal diet culture to be popularized in the society?

Song: Everyone knows it, so I'm going to establish Yudetang Health Technology Development Company. I have had this idea for ten years, and it has been put into practice for five years. I spent more than RMB 100 million on it. This project has been approved by the government, and its business license has been approved. The factory is located just in Pinggu.

Su: Some products have gone abroad. Where have they gone?

Song: Germany, United Arab Emirates, Japan and the United States.

Su: What is the specific occasion?

Song: Culinary exchange and food exhibition.

Su: How do you feel about these exhibitions and exchanges?

Song: Intangible heritages all are unique skills. Especially, I am engaged in court food. They have never seen any of my products. They feel very excited and curious.

Su: Do you have any international plans for the next step?

Song: I set up Pinggu Factory is just a response to "the belt and road initiative". In the future, I will bring Chinese food abroad through industrialized production and standardized production, and publicize Chinese traditional court food culture and medicinal diet culture. I have my own signature products, and I want to carry these products forward. The medicine made with my prescription is called special medicine food, which is eaten in hospitals. For internal medicine, surgery, gynecology, pediatrics, different departments use different health foods. At present, there is no factory in Beijing that produces this product, but all hospitals produce it themselves, but those hospitals are not as comprehensive as I did. Next, I'm going to make donkey-hide gelatin and sea cucumber and deerskin gelatin and sea cucumber separately, because the boiled gelatin can be used as raw material for re-industrial production.

Yang: What's the state of your industrialized food? Is recooking required after back home?

Song: Not necessary, it is still in the liquid state, and gelatin covers less than 3g in it, and

是养生食品，不能放太多。

苏：这两年我身边很多人都吃桃胶。

宋：桃胶是桃树上流出来的胶质，主要成分是胶原蛋白和一些微量元素，一般用来美容养颜，现在南方特别流行吃桃胶。

苏：您认为自己跟其他卖胶的企业相比，有什么竞争优势？

宋：我是一个门派，拥有树胶、鹿胶、阿胶、龟胶……一整套体系，共二十几种胶，一年四季采用不同的食材搭配，而别人可能只有单一的品种，可以说我们更系统、更专业。养生食品随便吃吃起不到什么作用，只有长期食用，才能治标治本，发挥作用。

苏：所以平谷那边也不光是做桃胶？

宋：所有胶药门的东西，包括月饼都是在那儿生产。我现在开发的产品，大部分都是给老百姓吃的。之所以选择在平谷建厂，是因为我要把平谷的桃做成桃泥馅儿。一般传统的馅料有莲蓉、豆沙、枣泥，但没有香蕉馅儿、桃馅儿，因为它们不好保管，而且它的原料水果也不是一年四季都有。把厂建在平谷，开春就能直接收大桃，收完后进行加工制作，这样做出来的桃胶点心非常纯粹，这是我的专利。下一步我准备开店，再通过“一带一路”把中国的胶卖到全世界。

杨：您现在已经有技术可以现场做膏了，是吗？

宋：对，当场做就可以当场吃，要不怎么叫胶药门传人呢。我将传统手工技艺和现代科学工艺相结合，中药西制，现场就能成膏。我研究了不同的系列，像糖尿病、高血压等，根据不同的人，加入不同的粉末，比如山药、苦瓜、何首乌，用水化开搅拌成膏状。这是我特有的，别人弄不了。

杨：这个尝起来没有药味？

宋：养生哪能吃出药味？我做的药膳没有一个有药味。

苏：这个现在开始卖了吗？

宋：现在还没有。我不想去商场卖，想自己开店。因为这都是真材实料，成本昂贵，没办法打折。我都自己在家里试验，再往里面放点蜂胶，味道可好了。

苏：您之前给其他人做过吗？

宋：领导来我这儿吃饭，我就会表演这套功夫。往那儿一坐，衣服一换，摆上五六套罐，旁边写着御德堂非遗美食，现场给大家制作。

苏：这也是您大通饭庄里面的服务吗？当场由您的徒弟来做？

宋：对，我先根据糖尿病、高血压、高血脂、内科、外科等不同的情况配

generally use 1~2g is enough. This is a health food, so you can't put too much.

Su: In the past two years, many people around me have eaten peach gum.

Song: peach gum is the gum flowing from the peach tree, the main component is collagen and some trace elements, generally used for beauty and skin care, and now it is especially popular to eat peach gum in the south.

Su: What competitive advantages do you think you have with other companies selling gelatin products?

Song: I managed a school, including gum, deer-skin gelatin, donkey-hide gelatin, turtle gelatin... a full set of systems and more than twenty gelatin, and different ingredients are used all year round, while others may only have a single variety, so we are more systematic and professional. Eating casually won't do much good, only after long-term use, can we treat both the symptoms and the root causes and play a role.

Su: So Pinggu isn't just making peach gum products?

Song: All gelatin series, including moon cakes, are produced there. Most of the products I develop now are for ordinary people to eat. I chose to build a factory in Pinggu because I want to make peach in Pinggu into peach puree stuffing. Traditional stuffing includes lotus seed paste, red bean paste and jujube paste, but there are no banana fillings and peach fillings, because they are not easy to keep and raw fruits are not available all year round. By building the factory in Pinggu, we can collect the big peaches directly at the beginning of spring, and process and make them afterwards, so that the peach gum snacks made are very pure, which is my patent. Next, I'm going to open outlets, and then I'll sell Chinese gelatin to the whole world through "the belt and road initiative".

Yang: Now you have the technology to make gum ointment on site, right?

Song: Yes, make and eat it on the spot, otherwise, how can you call me the inheritor of gelatin family. I combine traditional craftsmanship with modern science and technology, and Chinese medicine is made in western way, and ointment can be made on the spot. I studied different series, such as ointment for diabetes, hypertension, etc. According to different people, I added different powders, such as Chinese yam, balsam pear and Polygonum multiflorum, and dissolved them with water and stirred them into ointment. This is unique to me, and others cannot do it.

Yang: How about the taste, like eating medicine?

Song: Health food can't taste like medicine. None of the medicinal diets I made have the taste of medicine.

Su: Is this on sale now?

Song: Not yet now. I don't want to sell them in mall, I want to open my own store. Because this is all real material, the cost is expensive, there is no way to give discount. I experimented at home by myself, and put some propolis in it, which was delicious.

Su: Have you done it for others before?

Song: When a leader comes to my place for dinner, I will perform this kungfu. I sit down there, change clothes, and put on five or six sets of cans, next to which is written the intangible heritage food of Yude Restaurant, and I play this kungfu for everyone.

Su: Is this also the service in your Datong Restaurant? Do it by your apprentice on the spot?

Song: Yes, I'll prepare it according to different conditions such as diabetes, hypertension,

好原料，客人来后，店里的厨师就能直接按照我写好的配方为他们制作。举个例子，现代人爱上火，我会在煮普洱茶的过程中加入苦荞。客人来后，我会根据客人的喜好给他们的茶里放胶。

杨：您这些早都批量生产好了？

宋：已经是最后一道工序。我正在从餐饮业转化到食品工业，现在这些东西还是季节性生产，以后我要做到常年生产。这里面没有一点添加剂，都是用蜂蜜、黑糖调的甜味。

苏：这个也需要保密配方的吧？

宋：配方都是对外公布，但都有专利，别人不能进行仿制。

苏：您这些都是在营养配餐里面学的吗？

宋：对。我学的是中国药膳学和营养配餐两种。

苏：您当时学了多长时间？

宋：不到一年。我在医院实习的时候，就在配餐的过程中学习，看人家的低脂、低盐、低糖配餐怎么做。医院不同的科用不同的菜，像糖尿病、高血压、高血脂，我都有不同的单子。学习到这些配比的方法，我做药膳的时候就更细了。

苏：团餐、药膳，包括您现在做的工业化食品，这三者之间对于您来说是一个什么样的关系？

宋：团餐是基础，大通饭庄是升华，三个工厂是跨越式的保障。

苏：什么叫作跨越式保障？

宋：现在都是手工操作，一旦御德堂健康科技发展公司、食品公司，还有伊德诚清真食品厂启动，就能形成标准化、工业化的食品加工模式，实现由餐饮业向食品工业的转化，受众也将从食堂的客户转化为社会上的大众。对此我很有信心，我一定要做中国餐饮和食品的引领者。我的对标企业就是稻香村、好利来，只不过我做的是另外一种类别的食品，就是宫廷里我们家传承的药膳食品、特医食品、养生食品。

苏：您未来有什么样的工作计划？

宋：未来的工作计划就是把“三基工程”做好——储基金、建基地、兴基业，把挣到的95%的钱全部存下来用于基地建设——中国团餐科技孵化园。在我的规划里，园区涵盖了中餐、西餐、标准化、仓储、加工、物流，还有博物馆等跟餐饮相关的全套产业，我要把它做成旅游、教育基地。

hyperlipemia, internal medicine and surgery. After the guests arrive, the chef in the store can prepare it directly according to what I wrote. For example, modern people always suffer from excessive internal heat, and I will add tartary buckwheat in the process of cooking Pu'er tea. When guests come, I will put some gelatin in their tea according to their preferences.

Yang: You have all this mass-produced?

Song: It is the last process. I am converting from the restaurant industry to the food industry, and now these products are still produced seasonally, and in the future I want to make them year-round. There is no additive in it, but it is sweet with honey and brown sugar.

Su: This one also needs a secret recipe, right?

Song: All of them will be disclosed to the public, but all of them are patented, so others are not allowed to copy them.

Su: Did you learn all this in nutrition catering?

Song: Yes. I studied Chinese medicinal diet and nutrition catering.

Su: How long did you study at that time?

Song: Less than one year. When I was an intern in the hospital, I studied in the process of catering, and watched how people made low-fat, low-salt and low-sugar catering. Different departments in the hospital use different dishes, such as dishes for diabetes, hypertension and hyperlipidemia. I have different prescriptions. After learning these catering methods, I will be more careful when I cook medicinal food.

Su: What is the relationship between group meals and medicinal meals, including the industrialized foods you are making now?

Song: The group meal is the foundation, Datong Restaurant is the sublimation, and the three factories are the leap-forward guarantee.

Su: What is the leapfrog guarantee?

Song: Now they are all operated by hand. Once Yudetang Health Technology Development Company, Food Company and Yidecheng Halal Food Factory are started, a standardized and industrialized food processing mode will be formed, and the transformation from catering industry to food industry will be realized, and the service receivers will also be transformed from canteen customers to the general public. I am very confident to this, and I must be the leader of Chinese catering industry. My benchmarking enterprises are Daoxiang Village and Hollyland, but I cook another kind of food, namely, medicinal food, special medical food and health food inherited by our family in the imperial court.

Su: What kind of work plan do you have in the future?

Song: In the future, I will do a good job in the "three basic projects"–fund storage, base construction and industrial development, and save 95% of the money earned for the base construction–China Group Meals Science and Technology Hatchery Park. In my planning, the park will cover Chinese food, Western food, standardization, storage, processing, logistics, museum, as well as a complete set of catering-related industries, and I want to make it a tourism and education base.

苏：准备建在哪儿呢?

宋：我的目标是在全国建6个这样的基地，咱们现在的部队分5大战区，我就以5大战区的布局思路来建设，南京、沈阳、兰州、成都、北京。还有一个建在广州，选择广州是因为它发展快、进出口贸易发达。我还计划在全国建4个做研发培训的学校，分别选址在四川、上海、北京、广州。这些都是早已经在我头脑中成形的想法。

苏：最早是什么时候形成的?

宋：应该是2008年后。三年前我在平谷买了工厂，当年没建设是因为图纸被反复地推翻，总觉得还有不先进、不合理的地方。

苏：您还打算扩张大通饭庄吗?

宋：得找适合的地方，现在北京不好找这种地方。

苏：您认为什么地方合适?

宋：故宫周围。

苏：选地点的时候会考虑哪些因素呢?

宋：主要是具备政府规定的合法手续，最早我就是因为不合法的手续吃了亏。当我有两个亿闲钱的时候，就在景山或故宫前后买套四合院做大通饭庄，主要还是想宣传宫廷传统文化。

苏：我看您写的身份定位，第一个就是“首席服务员”，为什么?

宋：人首先得搞清楚自己的身份，我觉得我就是“首席服务员”。到我这儿来的客人，我一定要把服务做好，在服务的过程当中，推广我们的药膳和团餐。

苏：您还写了一个“中国食品推广使者”。

宋：对，我热衷于推广中国的食品、药膳文化，经常说着说着就说到这上面来了。

苏：“烹饪领导人物”怎么理解呢?

宋：我一定要做中国烹饪的领导者，我要带领大家做一个敢为人先的行业标准，我也确实做到了。做药膳、办比赛、出版书籍……我应该算是烹饪界中能说会练的真把式，上得了课堂，下得了厨房，还能做企业管理。我给那些烹饪大师做出了榜样，如果以后中国的厨师都像我这样，那中国的烹饪就能成为世界之王。现在的烹饪大师很少有能用多种设备做菜的，而我能用五种设备做菜。第一种，小铜锅。第二种，大勺、炒勺。第三种，边锅。第四种，地锅。第五种，万能蒸烤箱。从传统设备一直到智能设备，全套我都会。这里面有两

Su: Where will the park be built?

Song: My goal is to build six such bases all over the country. Nanjing, Shenyang, Lanzhou, Chengdu and Beijing are taken as the major zones for base construction. Another is built in Guangzhou, and the reason why I choose Guangzhou is that it develops fast and import and export trade is developed. I also plan to build four schools for R&D and training in Sichuan, Shanghai, Beijing and Guangzhou. These are ideas that have long been shaped in my mind.

Su: When were they first shaped?

Song: After 2008. I bought the factory in Pinggu three years ago. However, they were not built in that year because the drawings were repeatedly overturned, and I always felt that there was something unadvanced and unreasonable.

Su: Are you still planning to expand Datong Restaurant?

Song: I have to find a suitable place, and it's not easy to find such a place in Beijing right now.

Su: What place do you think is suitable?

Song: Around the Forbidden City.

Su: What factors do you take into consideration when choosing a place?

Song: The main factor is that the place has the legal formalities stipulated by the government, because I suffered losses due to illegal formalities. When I have two hundred million yuan of spare money, I will buy a set of quadrangle courtyard as Datong Restaurant before or after Jingshan or the Forbidden City, and I still wanted to promote the palace traditional culture.

Su: In your identity positioning, the first one is "chief attendant". Why?

Song: The first thing we need to figure out is who we are. I think I am the "chief attendant". I will do a good job in the services for my customers. In the process of service, I will promote our Chinese dietary therapies and group meals.

Su: You also wrote "Chinese Food Spreader".

Song: Yes, I am keen on promoting Chinese food and dietary therapy culture. I always talk about it.

Su: How to understand "Cooking Leader"?

Song: I must be the leader of Chinese cuisine. I want to lead others to be an industry standard that dares to be the first, and I have achieved it. Making dietary therapy, holding contests, publishing books... I can speak and practice in the cooking world. I can give lessons, cook and also conduct business management. I have set an example for cooking masters. If Chinese chefs are like me in the future, then Chinese cuisine can become the king of the world. Few of cooking masters can cook with multiple devices, whereas I can cook with five kinds of devices. First, small copper pot. Second, strockle and round-bottomed frying pan. Third, frying pan. Fourth, ground kettle. Fifth, multifunctional steaming oven. I can operate from traditional devices to smart devices. Usually, cooking masters cannot use two devices. One is the ground kettle that is 1.2 meters long, the other is the multifunctional steaming oven. The ground kettle is generally used for stews, braises, stir-fries. It will be used in group meals and banquets. The Great Hall of the People often uses large

样东西，一般的烹饪大师用不了，一个是一米二的地锅，另一个是万能蒸烤箱。地锅一般用来做炖菜、烧菜、炒菜，团餐中会用到，也可以用于宴请，人民大会堂都是用大锅。万能蒸烤箱的思路跟中国传统烹饪器具不一样，那些年纪大的烹饪大师不会用这些，但我学过西餐，西餐就使用这个。

苏：您的身份很多元，不像一个单纯的厨师。

宋：想要当引领者就得这样。

苏：您怎么看待自己的职业生涯？

宋：我非常热爱餐饮行业，我喜欢烹饪，喜欢服务，喜欢我们家的药膳。直到今天，我一直都把它当成一个事业在做。随着时间的推移，研究的不断深入，我们公司还起到了一个引领行业的作用。这不是说大话，因为我做出了行业的标准。目前为止，中国餐饮业只有我跟全聚德获得过全国首届“中餐科技进步一等奖”。我能持续地为奥运会服务、阅兵式服务、上海世博会服务、园博会服务，为那么多的国家政府机关、部队、大专院校服务，是因为我们踏实做事、认真服务的精神，因为我给社会、国家做出了贡献。这次我又被评为北京市老字号协会副会长，这里面只有我一个人是民营企业，别的全是国企，这就是社会给我的高度认可！

pots. The idea of the multifunctional steaming oven is different from that of the traditional Chinese cooking utensil, which the elderly chefs can't use. It is used in Western food. I have learned Western food.

Su: You have multiple identities instead of a simple cook.

Song: That's what I have to do to be a leader.

Su: What do you think of your career?

Song: I love the catering industry very much. I like cooking, service and our medicinal dishes. To this day, I have been doing it as a career. With time passing by and the deepening of research, our company also plays a leading role in the industry. I am not bragging, because I have made the industry standard. So far, in China's catering industry, only I and Quanjude have won the “First Prize of the First National Chinese Catering Science and Technology Progress Award”. The reason why I can continuously serve the Olympic Games, the military parade, the Shanghai World Expo, and China International Garden Flower Expo, and serve so many national government organs, armed forces, and colleges and universities is the spirit that I work steadfastly and serve earnestly. I have made contributions to society and the country. This time, I was named the vice president of Beijing Time-honored Brands Association. I was the only private enterprise, and the rest were all state-owned enterprises, indicating that I was highly recognized by society!

2009年至2015年，宋子刚受中国航空运输协会、世界中国烹饪联合会、中华人民共和国农业部委托到美国、德国、法国、日本、瑞士、瑞典、荷兰、英国等国家及地区交流传播中国药膳及团餐

From 2009 to 2015, entrusted by the China Air Transport Association, World Association of Chinese Cuisine, Ministry of Agriculture of the PRC, Song Zigang visited the United States, Germany, France, Japan, Switzerland, Sweden, the Netherlands, the United Kingdom and other countries and regions to communicate and spread Chinese medicinal meals and group meals

2019年春节，金丰集团参与“雄安新区嘉年华”活动，为雄安新区提供餐饮保障

In the Spring Festival of 2019, Jinfeng Group participated in the “xiong’an New Area Carnival”, and provide catering support for xiong’an New Area

2021年7月1日，金丰集团举行纪念中国共产党建党100周年主题学习活动

On July 1, 2021, Jinfeng Group held a theme learning activity to commemorate the 100th anniversary of the founding of the Communist Party of China

宋子刚在公司企业文化墙前展示药膳产品仙鹿膏

Song Zigang displayed the medicinal diet product Xianlu Ointment in front of the corporate culture wall of the company

宋子刚在杭州展示药膳产品仙鹿膏、凤凰膏、鹿茅酒、阿胶酒、宫廷普洱茶、阿胶月饼、鹿胶月饼、桃胶粽子、蜂胶元宵

Song Zigang displayed medicinal diet products such as Xianlu Ointment, Fenghuang Ointment, Lumao Wine, Donkey-hide Gelatin Wine, Court Pu’er Tea, Donkey-hide Gelatin Moon Cake, Deerskin Gelatin Moon Cake, Peach Gum Zongzi and Sweet Propolis Dumplings

2019年，金丰集团成立十五周年，宋子刚专程去上海表彰奖励7名功勋员工

In 2019, on the 15th anniversary of the founding of Jinfeng Group, Song Zigang made a special trip to Shanghai to commend and reward 7 meritorious employees

非物质文化遗产代表性传承人宋子刚在为北京老字号协会原会长刘小虹、原副会长马宇泰演示素胶膏制作技艺

Song Zigang, the representative inheritor of intangible cultural heritage, was demonstrating the making techniques of Vegetarian Gum for Liu Xiaohong, former President of Beijing Time-honored Brands Association, and Ma Yutai, former Vice President of Beijing Time-honored Brands Association.

宋子刚在川菜大会展示药膳龟鹿二仙膏、牛胶固元膏的制作方法

Song Zigang showed the preparation method of Guilu Erxian Ointment and Bovine-hide Gelatin Ointment on Sichuan Cuisine Conference

宋子刚与法国驻中华人民共和国大使黎想合影

Song Zigang took a Photo with Jean-Maurice Ripert, ambassador of France to the People's Republic of China

向抗疫英雄捐赠鹿胶、阿胶

Donate deerskin gelatin and donkey-hide gelatin to anti-epidemic heroes

丹江口市慈善总会赠予北京大通饭庄、北京金丰餐饮有限公司奖牌

Citation from Danjiangkou Charity Federation to Beijing Datong Restaurant and Beijing Jinfeng Catering Co., Ltd.

黄冈市红十字会颁发捐赠证书

Donation Certificate Issued by Red Cross Society of China Huanggang

向抗疫英雄捐赠宫廷普洱茶

Donate Court Pu’er Tea to anti-epidemic heroes

第六章

Chapter 6

经典菜品

Classic Dishes

大通鹿胶海参

Stewed Datong Donkey-hide Gelatin with Sea Cucumber

原料：海参5根，阿胶100克，青椒半个，胡萝卜半根，小葱1根，芹菜少许，蒜头3瓣，油适量，盐1茶匙，醋1汤匙，料酒1汤匙，生抽2汤匙，白糖1茶匙，清水适量。

Ingredients: 5 sea cucumbers, 100 grams of donkey-hide gelatin, half a green pepper, and half a carrot, 1 shallot, a little celery, 3 cloves of garlic, appropriate amount of oil, 1 spoon of salt 1 spoon of vinegar, 1 spoon of cooking wine, 2 spoons of light soy sauce, 1 spoon of sugar, and appropriate amount of water.

制作方法 Steps

1. 准备好所有食材，海参（冰冻海参）、青椒、胡萝卜、蒜头、小葱、芹菜；
2. 冰冻海参用饮用水解冻并泡发，海参是之前就处理好冷藏在冰柜的；
3. 将海参改刀，切成半指宽的细丝，再浸泡在纯净水中。没有处理干净的内脏和砂囊记得去掉；
4. 青椒、胡萝卜切丝，小葱、蒜头切末，芹菜取叶；
5. 用酱油、醋、料酒、白糖、盐、清水调制成一碗酱汁；
6. 起油锅，放入葱末、蒜末爆香；
7. 将海参倒入锅中，滑炒均匀；
8. 炒至海参上油后，将调制好的酱汁及阿胶倒入锅中；
9. 翻炒使海参均匀吸收酱汁；
10. 小火慢慢煮至锅中汤汁收汁一半；
11. 加入青椒和胡萝卜丝翻炒均匀；
12. 炒至断生即可出锅；
13. 装盘，撒上芹菜叶做装饰。

1. After having all the ingredients prepared, including sea cucumber (frozen sea cucumber), green peppers, carrots, garlic, shallots, and celery;
2. Get the frozen sea cucumbers thawed and soaked with drinking water. The sea cucumbers are processed and refrigerated in the freezer before;
3. Cut the sea cucumber into half-finger-wide filaments and soak them in clean water. Remember to remove internal organs and sandbags that have not been cleaned;
4. Shred green peppers and carrots, mince shallots and garlic, and celery leaves;
5. Prepare a bowl of sauce with soy sauce, vinegar, cooking wine, sugar, salt, and water;
6. Get frying pan ready to put in minced shallots and minced garlic;
7. Pour the sea cucumber into the pot and stir-fry evenly;
8. After the sea cucumbers are fired and soaked with food oil, pour the prepared sauce and donkey-hide gelatin into the wok;
9. Quick fry to make the sea cucumber absorb the sauce evenly;
10. Slowly simmer the sea cucumber until the soup in the wok is concentrated with a half of the sauce;
11. Add green pepper and carrot shreds and stir-fry evenly;
12. After green pepper and carrot shreds have fully cooked, then it can be out of the wok;
13. Serve it on a plate and sprinkle with celery leaves for decoration.

菜品特点：海参无味，所以需要吸收具有特殊香味的食材的味道，才能成就它的美味，于是在这道菜中加入了青椒和芹菜，并用生抽提鲜。

Features: Sea cucumber is tasteless, so it needs to absorb the taste of the ingredients with special fragrance to highlight its deliciousness, thus green pepper and celery are added to this dish and light soy sauce is used for extracting its freshness.

发明专利证书

大通海水豆腐

Datong Seawater-flavored Tofu

原料：卤水豆腐、葱、盐、黄酒、白胡椒粉各适量。
蘸料：拌饭酱少许。

Ingredients: brine tofu, shallot, salt, yellow wine, white pepper.
Condiment: bibimbap sauce.

制作方法
Steps

1. 卤水豆腐冲洗干净，用手掰成较大的块；
2. 起锅坐油，爆香葱花后加入开水，加少许黄酒；
3. 大火烧开后放入豆腐，加少许盐，转小火炖煮约2分钟；
4. 撒上白胡椒粉，关火。吃的时候蘸拌饭酱。

1. Rinse the brine tofu and break it into larger pieces by hand;
2. Heat the wok with oil up, saute shallots and add boiling water and a bit of yellow wine;
3. Put the tofu into wok on high heat with a little salt before turning to low heat and simmering for about 2 minutes;
4. Put some white pepper and turn off the heat. Add it with some bibimbap sauce while having it.

菜品特点：大通海水豆腐不但美味，营养也有保证，就是对豆腐的要求很高，一定要用卤水豆腐，色微黄，口感绵韧，豆香味浓。蘸料可以自己调制。

Features: It is not only delicious, but also nutritious as it requires high-quality tofu which must be brine tofu in slightly yellow color and soft taste and strong bean flavor. Condiment can be made as per your own taste.

大通牛胶萝卜

Datong Stewed Beef Gelatin with Radish

原料：白萝卜1根，牛胶100克，葱10克，生抽1汤匙，盐少许。

Ingredients: 1 white radish, 100 grams of beef gelatin, 10 grams of shallots, 1 spoon of light soy sauce, and a little salt.

制作方法
Steps

1. 白萝卜洗净去皮，切厚片（约1.5厘米）待用；
2. 锅内放油，微热后倒入萝卜略微翻炒；
3. 倒入适量清水大火煮开；
4. 加入牛胶、生抽和盐，转小火慢炖；
5. 炖至萝卜熟透，呈半透明晶莹状；
6. 装盘，撒上葱花即可。

1. Clean and peel off the white radish and cut into thick slices (about 1.5 cm);
2. Put oil and the radish in the wok and stir fry slightly after heating up;
3. Pour in an appropriate amount of water and boil on high heat;
4. Add beef gelatin, light soy sauce and salt, turn to low heat and simmer slowly;
5. Stew until the radish is fully cooked in translucent and crystal clear color;
6. Put on a plate with chopped shallots.

菜品特点：牛胶炖萝卜是一道营养美食，属于主菜类，其味道鲜美，营养丰富，是适合家庭制作的美食。

Features: Stewed beef gelatin with radish is a nutritious delicacy. As a main course, it is delicious and nutrient-rich dish, suitable for home meal.

大通蜂胶元宵

Datong Propolis Sweet Dumplings

原料：干核桃仁150克，蜂胶100克，江米50克，江米面150克，麻仁100克，小枣50克，面粉、桂花少许、白糖适量。

Ingredients: 150 grams of dried walnut kernels, 100 grams of propolis, 50 grams of rice, 150 grams of rice flour, 100 grams of hemp kernels, 50 grams of jujube, a little flour and a little osmanthus, appropriate amount of sugar.

制作方法
Steps

1. 将白糖放入碗内，加桂花、麻仁、面粉少许，再加开水少许拌匀；
2. 将拌匀的料放在案上，用刀先拍成1.5厘米的厚片，再改切成1.5厘米的丁，做成元宵馅；
3. 将江米面放入簸箕里。元宵馅放在漏勺里，用凉水浸过，倒入簸箕内，双手摇动使汤圆馅沾满江米面，连续3次，即成元宵；
4. 下入锅内煮10分钟左右，漂起即熟；
5. 核桃仁用开水冲两次，剥去外皮剁碎。小枣洗净，用凉水浸泡12小时；
6. 把江米、核桃仁、小枣肉放入碗中，加清水200克拌匀，用小磨磨成细浆；
7. 净勺放开水，下入白糖，上火见开，撇去浮沫，迅速将核桃仁浆和蜂胶下入，搅匀成粥状，熟后盛于碗内，将煮熟元宵捞入即成。

1. Put white sugar in a bowl and add it with osmanthus, hemp kernels, a little flour and a little boiled water before mixing;
2. Put the well-mixed ingredients on the table, use a knife to slice them into 1.5 cm thick slices before cutting into 1.5cm dices to make stuffing;
3. Put rice flour in a pan. Put the stuffing in a colander, soak it in cold water before pouring it into the pan, then shake it with both hands for three times to make the dumpling stuffing cover the rice flour;
4. Put it into wok and cook for about 10 minutes, and it is deemed as fully cooked when it floats;
5. Rinse the walnuts twice with boiling water, peel off the skin and chop them. Rinse the jujube and soak in cold water for 12 hours;
6. Put the rice, walnuts, and jujube in a bowl, add 200 grams of water and mix them well before grinding into a fine slurry with a small grinder;
7. Pour in boiled water and add the sugar, and skim the foams away when it is boiling, then quickly pour in the walnut pulp and propolis, stir evenly until it is in a porridge state, and place it in a bowl after it is cooked, add the cooked sweet dumplings.

菜品特点：元宵是中国汉族传统节日食品之一。北方“滚”元宵，南方“包”汤圆，这是两种做法和口感都不同的食品。

Features: Sweet dumplings is one of the traditional festival foods of the Han people in China. "Rolling" sweet dumplings in the north and "Bao" sweet dumplings in the south are two similar foods with different cooking methods and tastes.

大通桃胶粽子

Datong Peach Gum Zongzi

原料：中粽叶、糯米、猪肉、桃胶、豆沙、味精、白糖、酒、盐、生抽各适量。

Ingredients: reed leaves, sticky rice, pork, peach gum, bean paste, monosodium glutamate, sugar, wine, salt, and light soy sauce.

制作方法
Steps

1. 先将新鲜的猪肉、桃胶、豆沙用少许味精、白糖、酒、盐、生抽拌匀，反复揉擦至调味品渗入猪肉。
2. 用粽叶将糯米和粽馅捆扎好。
   粽子的捆扎：豆沙粽不宜捆得太紧，防止米粒挤进豆沙中，如果煮不透会出现夹生现象。咸肉粽如果用肥猪肉不宜扎紧，松紧适度即可。如果用瘦猪肉就要扎紧，因为瘦肉熟了以后会收缩，粽馅的肥汁会漏入水中，不能保持粽子的肥糯。
   粽子的烹煮：煮粽子一定要水滚以后才落粽子，水要浸过粽面，待重新滚起以后再用旺火煮3个小时左右即可。在煮的过程中不要添生水。要注意，枧水粽不能和其他粽子一同煮。煮好以后趁热取出，吃时打开粽叶，粽香喷鼻，入口油而不腻，糯而不黏，咸甜适中，香嫩鲜美是为上品。

1. Firstly, fresh pork, peach gum and bean paste are to be mixed with a little monosodium glutamate, sugar, wine, salt and light soy sauce until the seasoning has been absorbed into the pork.
2. Bundling sticky rice and stuffing use the reed leaf.
   Bundling of Zongzi: Zongzi should not be tied too tightly to prevent the rice from squeezing into the bean paste. If it is not cooked thoroughly, it will be tasted like half-cooked. If pork fat is used as stuffing, the Zongzi should not be tied tightly; just keep it moderate would be enough. If it is lean pork, then it must be tied tightly, because the lean meat will shrink when it is cooked, and the fat juice from stuffing will leak into the water, which can't maintain the succulent taste of Zongzi.
   Cooking technique: Zongzi can only be put into water when the water is boiling. Zongzi shall be soaked into water entirely, and it shall be kept boiling for another 3 hours after it floats above water surface. Do not add additional water during the cooking process. It should be noted that Zongzi covered with sugarcane leaves shall be cooked separately from other Zongzi. After it is cooked, take it out while it is hot. Open the leaves, and you will smell the fragrance of the leaves and taste the juicy and glutinous meat.

菜品特点：粽子由来久远，最初是用来祭祀祖先神灵的贡品。由于各地饮食习惯的不同，粽子形成了南北风味。从口味上分，粽子有咸粽和甜粽两大类。

Features: Zongzi with a long history in China was originally a tribute to ancestors and gods. Due to the different dietary habits across the country, the Zongzi has two different main flavors prevailing in the south and north receptively. In terms of taste, it can be either salty and sweet.

宫廷细八件——御字牌仙鹿膏（糕）

Court food “Eight Pieces”——Xianlu Ointment

简介：自先祖宋扬室开始，医门宋氏主要为皇家提供医疗服务和专供道地药材。仙鹿膏为宋氏家族第一代传人宋继仁所创，以鹿鞭为主药，加入灵芝、大芸、枸杞子、雄蚕蛾、牡蛎、核桃、黑芝麻、党参、黄芪、鹿角、鹿皮、鹿尾、鹿筋等名贵中药材，增加其补肾益精的功效。特别是在宋氏医门第六代传人宋玉德、宋天德将制胶技艺与之融合后，不仅为皇室宫廷所喜用，且为广大老百姓传宗接代的佳品。

Introduction: Since Song Yangshi, the Songs, a family of doctors, have been providing provides medical services and authentic medicinal herbs for royalty. The Xianlu Ointment was created by Song Jiren, the first-generation heir of the Songs, using deer penis as the main ingredient and incorporating precious Chinese medicines such as Ganoderma lucidum, Cistanche deserticola, Chinese wolfberries, male silkworm, oyster, walnuts, black sesame, Codonopsis pilosula, Astragalus membranaceus, deer antler, deer skin, deer tail and deer tendon to increase its efficacy in nourishing the kidneys and strengthening the essence. Especially after Song Yude and Song Tiande, the sixth-generation heirs of the Songs, applied their gelatin-making technique to the production, the ointment became not only popular among royals, but also useful for the general public in treating infertility.

宫廷细八件——御字牌凤凰膏（糕）

Court food "Eight Pieces"——Fenghuang Ointment

简介：凤凰膏为宋氏家族第一代传人宋继仁所创，以德州乌驴皮熬制的东阿纯黑驴皮九昼夜阿胶为主要原料，加以当归、黄芪、党参、山药、熟地、大枣、黑芝麻等中药材，对症女性宫寒不孕、气血两亏、月经不调等。因此，受到广大皇室女眷们的欢迎，名震宫廷，历经明清两代而不衰，流传至今。

Introduction: The Fenghuang Ointment was created by Song Jiren, the first-generation heir of the Songs, using black donkey hide from Dezhou, Shandong, as the main ingredient and incorporating Chinese herbs such as Angelica sinensis, Astragalus membranaceus, Codonopsis pilosula, Chinese yam, Rehmannia glutinosa, Chinese dates and black sesame. It is used for women with cold uterus and infertility, deficiency of qi and blood, and menstrual disorders. Therefore, it was popular among women of the royal family and became famous at the court, and has been handed down through the Ming and Qing dynasties.

宫廷细八件——御字牌八仙糕（膏）

Court food “Eight Pieces”——Eight Immortals Cake

简介：八仙糕（膏）为宋氏家族第八代传人宋广生所创，在八珍糕的基础上改良而成，由人参、茯苓、莲子、苡仁、山药等八种药材加工制成。诸药配伍，药性中和，无偏寒偏热之弊，对于脾胃虚弱，心肾不足之症，更为相宜。

Introduction: The Eight Immortals Cake was created by Song Guangsheng, the eighth-generation heir of the Songs, on the basis of the Eight-Dainty Cake. It is made from eight kinds of herbs, including ginseng, Wolfiporia extensa, lotus seeds, Chinese pearl barley and Chinese yam. The combination of the herbs is neutral in nature, devoid of cold and heat, making it more suitable for those with weak spleen and stomach and deficiency of heart and kidneys.

宫廷细八件——御字牌八珍糕（膏）

Court food "Eight Pieces"——Eight-Dainty Cake

简介：八珍糕（膏）为宋氏家族第八代传人宋广生所创。宋广生在宋氏先祖宋杨室所创制的八珍膏（糕）基础上，加入茯苓、莲子、芡实、扁豆、苡仁、藕粉等材料，烹制成月饼状的小点心。因其药食同源的特点，深受皇室贵胄、王公大臣们的喜爱。

Introduction: The Eight-Dainty Cake was created by Song Guangsheng, the eighth-generation heir of the Songs. Song Guangsheng added Wolfiporia extensa, lotus seeds, prickly waterlily seeds, lentils, Chinese pearl barley, lotus root powder and other ingredients to the cake created by Song Yangshi, Song's ancestor, and made them into mooncake-shaped snacks. Thanks to the theory of the homology of medicine and food, the cake was loved by the royal family, imperial officials and ministers.

宫廷细八件——定胜糕（膏）/鹿胶月饼

Court food “Eight Pieces”——Victory Cake/Deerskin Gelatin Moon Cake

简介：鹿胶是以鹿皮为主要原料而制成的滋补、补血上品。大通鹿胶月饼，具有药疗、食疗的双补作用，是世界上第一款药膳月饼，获国家专利（专利号：ZL2014 1 0183235.9），由鹿胶膏制作技艺第四代传承人、中国烹饪大师、中国烹饪协会特邀副会长、北京烹饪协会副会长宋子刚先生亲自料理，具有补气补血、健脑补肾、安神的作用。

Introduction: Deerskin gelatin is an excellent blood tonic made from deer skin as the main ingredient. Datong Deerskin Gelatin Moon Cake, with the dual tonic effect of pharmacotherapy and dietary therapy, is the world’s first medicinal moon cake. It was awarded the national patent (Patent No. ZL2014 1 0183235.9) and is personally made by Mr. Song Zigang, the fourth-generation inheritor of the production technique of deerskin gelatin ointment, a Chinese culinary master, a guest vice president of the China Cuisine Association, and vice president of the Beijing Cuisine Association. It has the efficacy of nourishing qi and blood, strengthening the brain and kidneys, and calming the mind.

宫廷细八件——定升糕（膏）/阿胶月饼

Court food "Eight Pieces"——Promotion Cake/Donkey-hide Gelatin Moon Cake

简介：阿胶是以驴皮为主要原料而制成的滋补、补血上品。大通阿胶月饼始创于1667年，具有药疗、食疗的双补作用，经宋子刚改良后，获国家专利（专利号：ZL2014 1 0183235.9），由中国阿胶第十六代御德堂传人、中国烹饪大师、北京烹饪协会副会长宋子刚先生亲自料理。具有补气补血、健脑补肾、安神的作用。大通阿胶月饼，于2016年获国家中华老字号时尚创意大赛金奖；2017年，由北京老字号协会推荐，参加在德国科隆举行的国际美食节，受到国际友人的称赞。

Introduction: Donkey-hide gelatin is an excellent blood tonic made from donkey hide as the main ingredient. Created in 1667, Datong Donkey-hide Gelatin Moon Cake has the dual tonic effect of pharmacotherapy and dietary therapy. It was awarded the national patent (Patent No. ZL2014 1 0183235.9) and personally made by Mr. Song Zigang, the sixteenth-generation heir of Chinese donkey-hide gelatin brand Yudetang, a Chinese culinary master and vice president of the Beijing Cuisine Association. It has the efficacy of nourishing qi and blood, strengthening the brain and kidneys, and calming the mind. The moon cake won the gold medal in the National Creative Competition of Chinese Time-honored Brands in 2016. Recommended by the Beijing Time-honored Brands Association, it was brought to an international food festival in Cologne, Germany in 2017, and was well received by guests from around the world.

宫廷细八件——状元糕

Court food “Eight Pieces”——Scholar Cake

简介：状元糕为宋氏家族第九代传人宋茂盛所创，具有补肾壮阳、益气补血、健脑、添精、益髓之功效。

Introduction: The Scholar Cake was created by Song Maosheng, the ninth-generation heir of the Songs, and has the efficacy of tonifying the kidneys, strengthening the yang, benefiting the qi, replenishing the blood, and strengthening the brain, enhancing the vitality and nourishing the marrow.

宫廷细八件——千叟糕

Court food "Eight Pieces"——Qian Sou Cake

简介：千叟糕为宋氏家族第五代传人宋济生所创，能提高脑力和体力劳动的效率，增强人体免疫功能，具有补气养血、滋补肝肾、养心安神、强筋健骨、健脾开胃之功效。

Introduction: The Qian Sou Cake was created by Song Jisheng, the fifth-generation heir of the Songs. It can improve the efficiency of mental and physical work, and enhance the immunity of the human body. It has the efficacy of nourishing qi and blood, tonifying the liver and kidneys, strengthening the heart, calming the mind, strengthening the muscles and bones, and invigorating the spleen and appetite.

清宫代茶饮

Tea substitutes

简介：清宫代茶饮，可分为清热代茶饮、回乳代茶饮、加味参莲代茶饮、元参麦冬汤代茶饮、清肝和胃代茶饮等。用途十分广泛，虽然不是什么偏方，但贵在用药简单、搭配合理、配制方便。在无茶时期，作为茶叶的代替品。

Introduction: Tea substitutes in the Qing Dynasty can be divided into heat-clearing tea substitute, back milk tea substitute, flavored dangshen & lotus seed tea substitute, Scrophularia & Ophiopogon japonicus decoction tea substitute, liver-clearing and stomach-harmonizing tea substitute, etc, which have a wide range of uses. Although it is not a traditional remedy, it is simple in medication, reasonable in combination, and convenient in preparation. In the period of no tea, it is used as a substitute for tea.

清宫代茶饮（春）

Tea substitutes in the Qing Dynasty（Spring）

清宫代茶饮（夏）

Tea substitutes in the Qing Dynasty（Summer）

清宫代茶饮（秋）

Tea substitutes in the Qing Dynasty（Autumn）

清宫代茶饮（冬）

Tea substitutes in the Qing Dynasty（Winter）

宫廷普洱茶

Court Pu'er tea

宫廷龙井茶

Court Longjing green tea

宫廷贡菊茶

Court Gongju tea

宫廷茉莉花茶

Court Jasmine Tea

附录

Appendix

宋子刚个人年表

Personal Chronology of Song Zigang

1964年5月18日，出生于山东省德州市武城县。

1967年，随父亲宋泽清、母亲王桂兰迁居至内蒙古自治区呼伦贝尔市扎赉诺尔矿区，三年后转至富拉尔基。

1979年11月4日，参军入伍；次年被调往北京，开始在各个饮食保障单位观摩学习烹饪与服务知识。

1984年5月，前往黑龙江商学院旅游烹饪系学习。

1985年—1998年，先后在沈阳军区陆军总院、大连陆军总院营养部、中央党校学习，任大连棒棰岛、京西宾馆、中央军委经营局协理员，其间随军调动变换工作地点。

1998年，从部队转业，在全易达等单位担任厨师长、技术总监工作。

1999年，任原信息产业部赛迪集团赛迪会议中心餐饮部总经理，开始负责运营集团旗下的酒店、会议中心和餐厅。

2003年，在“非典”期间出色地保障了餐厅的公共安全，发明了3块毛巾保洁法和餐具2次消毒法。

2005年8月1日，组建北京金丰餐饮有限公司，任董事长。

2006年，参与科技部“十一五”发展规划课题组，开始筹备奥运服务；成为科技部“十一五”大城市营养配餐科技带头人，主持中国团餐标准制定，并在中国商业出版社出版发行《团餐管理》《团餐食品质量与安全》《团餐中英文菜谱》。

2008年，为北京奥运会总指挥部及部分场地提供餐饮服务；公司荣获“北京市海淀区十佳税收企业”。

2009年，参加国庆大阅兵餐饮保障服务，被通令嘉奖。

2010年，为上海世博会提供餐饮服务，被通令嘉奖；获得中国烹饪协会认定的中式烹调工种全国餐饮业二级评委资格。

2011年，注册成立成都金丰餐饮管理有限公司。

On May 18, 1964, he was born in Wucheng County of Dezhou City, Shandong Province.

In 1967, he moved with his father, Song Zeqing and his mother, Wang Guillan, to the Zalainuoer mining area in Hulun Buir City, Inner Mongolia Autonomous Region, and then to Hulan Ergi three years later.

On November 4, 1979, he joined the army; in the next year, he was transferred to Beijing and began to learn cooking and service knowledge in various food guarantee units.

In May 1984, he went to the Department of Tourism and Cuisine of Heilongjiang Business School.

From 1985 to 1998, he successively studied in the Army General Academy of Shenyang Military Region, the Nutrition Department of the Army General Academy of Dalian and the Party School of the CPC Central Committee, and served as Assistant to Dalian Bangchui Island, Jingxi Hotel and the Management Bureau of the Central Military Commission. During the period, he was transferred with the army and changed his workplace.

In 1998, he retired from the army to work as a chef and technical manager in Quanyida.

In 1999, he served as General Manager of Sadi Group of The former Ministry of Industry and Information Technology, and began to be responsible for the operation of the group's hotels, conference centers and restaurants.

In 2003, during the period of "SARS", he ensured the public safety of the restaurant excellently, and invented the cleaning method of three towels and the disinfection method of tableware for twice.

On August 1, 2005, he established Beijing Jinfeng Catering Co., Ltd. and served as the Chairman of the Board of Directors.

In 2006, he participated in the "Eleventh Five-Year Plan" project group of the Ministry of Science and Technology of China, and began to prepare services for Olympic Games; became the scientific leader of nutrition catering in big cities during the "Eleventh Five-Year Plan" of the Ministry of Science and Technology of China, and presided over the formulation of Chinese group meal standards. And published "*Group Meal*" "*Quality and safety of group food*" "*Menu of group meal in Chinese and English*" in China Commercial Publishing House.

In 2008, he provided catering services for the headquarters of Beijing Olympic Games and some venues, and won the title of "Top 10 Taxation Enterprises in Haidian District, Beijing".

In 2009, he participated in the National Day Parade and received a commendation award for catering services.

In 2010, he provided catering services for the Shanghai World Expo, and was received a commendation award; and was recognized by the Chinese Cuisine Association as the second-level judge of Chinese food in the national catering industry.

In 2011, he registered and established Chengdu Jinfeng Catering Management Co., Ltd.

2012年，注册成立北京郎悦大通餐饮有限公司；获得全国首届“中餐科技进步一等奖”。

2013年，注册成立北京郎悦大通物流有限公司、天津金丰餐饮管理有限公司；公司获得“中餐科技进步唯一创新型企业特等奖”；率领金丰团队连续八年成为中华人民共和国全国人民代表大会和中国人民政治协商会议的荣誉服务商；率领金丰团队成为北京园博会荣誉服务商。

2014年，所创制的鹿胶月饼、阿胶月饼获国家专利；大通饭庄获得“北京老字号”认证。

2015年，注册成立金丰（上海）餐饮管理有限公司。

2016年，注册成立北京海赋国际酒店管理有限公司、北京海龙物业管理有限公司、北京金丰大通有机农业有限公司、重庆金丰餐饮有限公司。

2017年，作为中国老字号的代表之一参加在德国科隆举行的国际美食展。

2018年，所持有的“鹿胶膏制作技艺”被授予北京市海淀区非物质文化遗产名号。

2019年，获得“改革开放40年中国餐饮业·企业家突出贡献人物”“北京餐饮十大企业家”“中国烹饪协会特邀副会长单位代表人”等荣誉称号；北京金丰餐饮有限公司获得“全国饮食类非物质文化遗产保护与传承示范单位”荣誉称号；宋子刚向中国烹饪协会第25届世界奥林匹克烹饪大赛捐款100万，成立宋子刚金丰厨艺基金用于奖励为国争光成绩突出者。

2020年，任中国烹饪协会第七次会员代表大会主席团副主席；获北京市商务局、北京市人才工作局、北京市人力资源和社会保障局、北京市文化和旅游局、北京老字号协会联合认定的“北京老字号工匠”称号；获中国饭店协会认证的中式面点师（小吃）职业（工种）国家级技能竞赛一级裁判员资格；宋子刚向武汉抗疫英雄捐赠6吨鹿胶、阿胶，价值155万元，捐赠100箱宫廷普洱茶，价值46.5万元，荣获“大爱无疆”“慈善之星”荣誉称号。

In 2012, he registered and established Beijing Langyue Datong Catering Co., Ltd., and won the "First Prize of the First National Chinese Catering Science and Technology Progress Award".

In 2013, he registered and established Beijing Langyue Datong Logistics Co., Ltd. and Tianjin Jinfeng Catering Management Co., Ltd.; the Company won the "Special Prize of the Only Innovative Enterprise in Chinese Catering Science and Technology Progress"; he led Jinfeng team to become the honorary service provider of the National People's Congress and the Chinese Political Consultative Conference for eight consecutive years; and led Jingeng team to become the honorary service provider of China International Garden Flower Expo.

In 2014, moon cakes stuffed with deerskin gelatin and donkey-hide gelatin obtained national patents, and Datong Restaurant was granted the certification of "Beijing Time-honored Brand".

In 2015, he registered and established Jinfeng (Shanghai) Catering Management Co., Ltd.

In 2016, he registered and established Beijing Haifu International Hotel Management Co., Ltd., Beijing Hailong Property Management Co., Ltd., Beijing Jinfeng Datong Organic Agriculture Co., Ltd., and Chongqing Jinfeng Catering Co., Ltd.

In 2017, he participated in the International Food Expo in Cologne, Germany as one of the representatives of Chinese time-honored brands.

In 2018, the "skill of making deerskin gelatin ointment" was awarded the intangible cultural heritage of Haidian District, Beijing.

In 2019, he was awarded the honorary titles of "Outstanding Contributor to Entrepreneurs in China's Catering Industry in the Past 40 Years of Reform and Opening-up", "Top Ten Entrepreneurs in Beijing Catering Industry" and "Representative of Special Vice-President Unit of Chinese Cuisine Association"; Beijing Jinfeng Catering Co., Ltd. was awarded the title of "National Demonstration Unit for the Protection and Inheritance of Intangible Cultural Heritage of Diet"; Song Zigang donated RMB 1 million to the 25th IKA Culinary Olympics of the Chinese Cuisine Association to set up the Songzigang Jinfeng Cooking Skill Fund to reward those who have made outstanding achievements in winning honors for the country.

In 2020, he served as Vice Chairman of the Presidium of the Seventh Congress of the Chinese Cuisine Association; was awarded the title of "Beijing Time-honored Craftsman" jointly by Beijing Municipal Commerce Bureau, Beijing Municipal Bureau of Talents, Beijing Municipal Human Resources and Social Security Bureau, Beijing Municipal Bureau of Culture and Tourism and Beijing Time-honored Brands Association; he was certified by the China Hotel Association as the first-class judge of the National Skill Competition for Chinese-style pastry chefs (snacks); Song Zigang donated 6 tons of deerskin gelatin and donkey-hide gelatin to heroes in Wuhan combating COVID-19, worth RMB 1.55 million and donated 100 boxes of Court Pu'er, worth RMB 465,000 , and won the honorary titles of "Great Love Without Borders" and "Star of Charity".

奥运情缘

冯丽丽

去年12月20日，我们团队由李红强率队，正式入驻国家体育总局训练局运动员餐厅，负责为备战奥运会的运动员提供营养膳食的服务和保障。

由于运动员膳食要求比较特殊，既要吃得好，又不能吃后增加体重。为此，我们的烹调技师每餐都精心设计，用心制作，确保了餐品色、香、味俱全，营养搭配合理均衡，同时努力做到餐餐有新品，让运动员们吃得可口舒心。跳水队、游泳队、体操队、花游队、田径队，女排、女篮等各队队员，都对菜品给予高度评价及赞美。餐厅负责人对项目团队精湛的业务技能、专业的服务态度也非常满意，专门写了一封感谢信。特别令人自豪的是，国家体育总局训练局局长刘大庆亲自向宋董事长赠送一面题有“助力奥运、厨技精湛”的锦旗，以表达对金丰集团的赞扬。

和国家队运动员朝夕相处，我们和他们也结下了深厚的情谊。在运动员们出征奥运之际，面点总监曹大师特意为队员们准备一个“决战东京，为中国加油”的大蛋糕，中国女排教练郎平亲手切分蛋糕，预祝中国健儿取得好成绩。中国女排、中国女篮分别送给金丰团队带有队员亲笔签名一个排球和一个篮球。各队队员还将合影照片送给我们留作纪念。

我们收获最大的，是从运动员身上学到了很多东西。他们立志为国争光的崇高信念，他们对体育事业的热爱和坚持，他们的团结协作和乐观自信，他们在训练过程中不怕苦、不怕累的顽强拼搏精神，这些都深深影响和激励着我们。金丰愿景是成为最具国际竞争力的领先团餐集团，我们一定要以国家队运动员为榜样，在宋董的带领下，坚定信心，埋头实干，把金丰做得更大、更优、更强，为中华美食走向世界增光添彩！

河南突发严重灾情 集团慰问员工家人

7月中下旬，河南遭受暴雨突袭，多地水灾严重。根据宋子刚董事长的指示，集团工会迅速组织落实，向在京的100多位豫籍员工的家人，紧急发放抗洪救灾慰问金。以此表达集团对员工的关心厚爱及对其灾区家人的深深关切。

金丰关爱 员工暖心

赵继东

2021年一场特大洪灾袭击河南：

7月19日，郑州、巩义、登封等地出现暴雨，局地大暴雨；

7月20日郑州、新乡两地区和洛阳、开封部分地区降水量100毫米以上；

7月20日，全省13座大中型水库超汛限水位，部分山区河道已发生山洪灾害；

7月20日，河南省气象局将重要气象灾害（暴雨）应急响应状态提升至二级……

河南多地遭遇极端强降雨，造成重大人员伤亡和财产损失。突如其来的灾情牵动着金丰董事长、总经理的心，金丰工会立即启动慰问程序，向100多位在京豫籍员工的家人发放慰问金，展现了中华民族“一方有难、八方支援”的传统美德和血浓于水的大爱。

很快，远在河南的父母收到了金丰集团汇出的抗洪救灾慰问金，父母非常意外、开心、感动：身处灾区，收到来自于北京子女所在公司的慰问及关爱。

父母感谢金丰，身为金丰员工的我们也感谢金丰，不仅是因为金丰慰问了我们的家人，更是因为金丰平台的大爱让我们感恩并为之自豪：

2020湖北爆发疫情，在武汉最危难的时刻，中国团餐业第一个慰问疫区的品牌是金丰：“心系湖北 · 金丰大爱 · 抗疫救灾 · 金丰同在”。

2021河南洪灾，在郑州最危难的时刻，中国团餐业第一个慰问灾区的品牌是金丰：“心系河南 · 金丰大爱 · 抗洪救灾 · 金丰同在”。

面对大灾大难，金丰彰显大爱，心系国家，关爱员工。金丰不愧为中国团餐行业的龙头企业，不愧为中国的团餐功夫，祝愿金丰越做越强！

建党百年庆典气象保障顺利 北京市气象局致函表达谢意

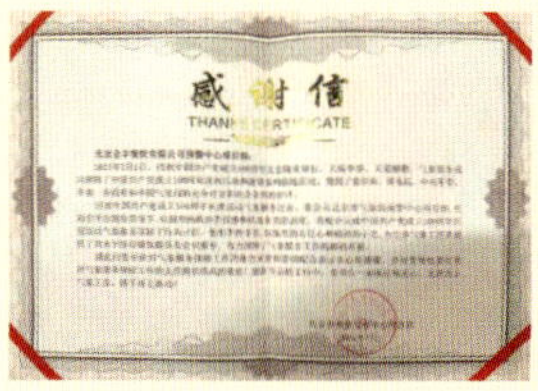

精细化 专业化 标准化 重庆市水利局职工充分认可

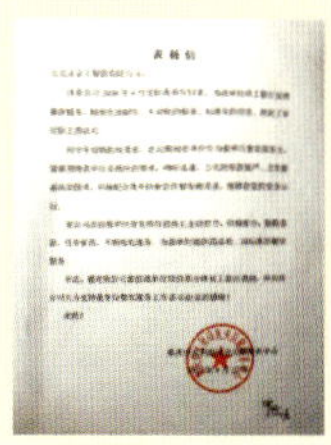

金豐集团报

金丰集团 Beijing Olympic Club
北京奥林匹克俱乐部理事单位

北京金丰餐饮有限公司·北京郎悦大通餐饮有限公司主办 400-007-6986 www.kingjinfeng.com 2021年08月第07期

董事長視界

山高人为峰 海阔心无界

——宋子刚董事长谈金丰16年奋进历程

自2005年8月1日成立至今，北京金丰餐饮有限公司已经走过了16年发展历程。金丰的愿景，是成为具有国际竞争力的中国团餐领军品牌，安全运营、品牌影响在全球团餐业拥有强劲竞争力。为此，金丰公司始终坚持品质、发展两手抓，一手紧抓安全服务质量，一手紧握企业总体发展战略。时刻不忘初心，不断夯实企业发展和项目建设，坚持为客户打造品质项目、坚持为员工谋福利、坚持将员工发展纳入企业整体发展战略。

16年来，金丰公司不断提升企业综合实力、提升核心竞争力。提升资质水平、掌握行业领先技术、创新管理模式。紧跟时代潮流，用新思维、新视角、新理念、谋新发展。采用准军事化管理，服务于中央党政机关、国有大型企业、部队、银行、学校、养老院、幼儿园、外资总部、星级酒店、写字楼、工厂、大型活动等组织机构。提供中西团餐与集体配送等全天候应急保障服务。经营食堂早餐、中餐、晚餐、茶歇、客饭接待餐、大型活动国宴餐、宫廷药膳、咖啡厅及食堂超市等各种餐饮业态。

16年来，公司不断完善发展机制、坚持多方合作，放眼全国深入开展业务交流，加强共同创业合作发展，坚持合作共赢。如今，金丰业务已经全面拓展，公司业务范围已由北京扩展至全国，公司所辖项目遍及京津冀、上海、广州、四川、云南等大部分地区，与多个企事业单位、院校团体建立了良好的合作关系，在时代的浪潮中，携手合作，共创辉煌。

16年来，金丰集团先后成为奥运会荣誉服务商、上海世博会荣誉服务商、连续十一年保障两会荣誉服务商，获得中国团餐十大品牌、中国团膳十大领军品牌、国际团膳最具影响力品牌、全国团膳双十佳品牌，且连续八年荣获“信用中国”国家纳税双A级先进单位、脱贫攻坚突出贡献单位、扶贫工作先进单位等殊荣。

16年来，金丰全体员工凝心聚力，精耕细作、不忘初心。铭记金丰使命：安全第一，质量第一。弘扬中华饮食文化、中医养生文化，延长生命时间。始终坚守金丰核心价值观：客户为本，员工为先，卓越温馨的服务是金丰生存的唯一理由。企业与员工共同进步，做客户信赖的长期合作伙伴。我们不断总结经验，完善机制，规范管理，提升服务信誉度。精抓项目质量，细察客户需求。公司的经营理念、服务质量，受到了新老客户的一致认可，并赢得了广大客户相扶相携。

我们真诚地感谢所有客户，感谢所有金丰员工及家属，感谢大家在金丰经营发展之路上，与金丰风雨同舟，不离不弃，戮力同行。

今年是金丰发展的关键之年，立足当下，面对金丰承接的国家重点团餐项目，机会与挑战并存。金丰在成长中，还存在着很多不足，我们必须脚踏实地，不断学习，为金丰发展赋能，绝不能辜负党和国家对我们的信任与厚望。

长风破浪正当时！我们生逢伟大时代，肩负复兴使命。我相信，在全体员工的不懈努力下，我们一定能圆满完成任务，实现金丰梦想，不断为中国团餐事业谱写新的辉煌篇章！

助力中华美食登上世界舞台 金丰奖励奥烹大赛获奖选手

7月27日，中国烹饪协会对参加第25届世界奥林匹克烹饪大赛的中国国家烹饪队予以表彰。傅龙成会长颁发了荣誉证书；宋子刚董事长代表金丰集团为金牌获得者发放了奖金。

2020年2月，由中国烹饪协会组建的中国国家烹饪队克服新冠疫情的不利影响和重重困难，参加了在德国斯图加特举办的第25届世界奥林匹克烹饪大赛，取得了团体糖艺展示金牌、热厨房银牌、厨师餐桌项目铜牌以及个人现场果蔬雕刻项目金牌的优异成绩，展现了当代中国厨师的精湛烹饪技艺和良好精神风貌。

为了激励中国国家烹饪队员奋力拼搏，2019年5月，宋子刚董事长向中国烹饪协会捐赠一百万元，建立双方公管账户，设立世界奥林匹克烹饪大赛奖励基金，以实际行动为弘扬中华美食文化贡献力量。

金豐团餐赛道的奥运冠军

安全
VERY SAFE

金丰环境目标

ENVIRONMENTAL OBJECTIVES

安全事故为零
THE SAFETY ACCIDENT RATE IS 0

就餐用具消毒率达100%
THE DISINFECTION RATE OF TABLEWARE IS 100%

油烟净化器合格率达100%
THE QUALIFIED RATE OF LAMPBLACK PURIFIER IS 100%

环境卫生保洁率达100%
THE ENVIRONMENTAL SANITATION CLEANING RATE IS 100%

员工体检合格率达100%
THE RATE OF PHYSICAL EXAMINATION FOR EMPLOYEES IS 100%

员工健康证持有率达100%
EMPLOYEE HEALTH CERTIFICATE HOLDING RATE OF 100%

食品留样48小时合格率达100%
FOOD SAMPLE RETENTION FOR 48 HOURS PASSING RATE OF 100%

原材料采购出入库台账合格率达100%
RAW MATERIALS PURCHASING AND WAREHOUSING LEDGER PASS RATE OF 100%

全年食品检测公示12次且合格率达100%
TEN ANNUAL FOOD INSPECTION PUBLICITY 12 TIMES AND PASS RATE OF 100%

金豐集团报　　2021年08月第07期　3

奥运健儿为国争光
金丰餐饮全力保障

赠
北京金丰餐饮有限公司
厨技精湛
助力奥运
国家体育总局训练局膳食处
二〇二一年七月

2020年12月，金丰餐饮正式进入国家体育总局训练局，负责为十四支国家队运动员和教练员提供备战奥运膳食服务。

为确保科学饮食，烹调技师每餐都精心设计，用心制作，确保了餐品色香味型俱全，营养搭配合理均衡，同时力求花样翻新，做到餐餐有新品。在中国体育代表团出征之际，项目团队还特意制作一个"决战东京，为中国加油"的大型蛋糕，为奥运健儿鼓劲壮行。

金丰餐饮服务保障得到了运动员和教练员的一致好评；餐厅负责人对项目团队的精湛业务技能、专业服务态度非常满意，特别写了一封感谢信；训练局局长及相关领导亲自向宋子刚董事长赠送锦旗。

宋子刚厨艺良师益友名录

宋泽清 赵荣光 王旭东 侯瑞轩 王云
潘喜发 阎喜霜 陈松如 佟建国 李耀云
金喜升 朱福根 王锡田 胡桃生
杨福成 王胜果 黄子云 李春祥
汪荣 熊四智 康辉 王义均
杨铭铎 彭铭泉 张文海 屈浩

Song Zigang's list of good cooking teachers and friends

Song Zeqing　Zhao Rongguang　Wang Xudong　Hou Ruixuan　Wang Yun
Pan Xifa　Yan Xishuang　Chen Songru　Tong Jianguo　Li Yaoyun
Jin Xisheng　Zhu Fugen　Wang Xitian　Hu Taosheng
Yang Fucheng　Wang Shengguo　Huang Ziyun　Li Chunxiang
Wang Rong　Xiong Sizhi　Kang Hui　Wang Yijun
Yang Mingduo　Peng Mingquan　Zhang Wenhai　Qu Hao

宋子刚药膳良师益友名录

王贵兰 李武 钱和 周文泉 吴大真
秦伯未 许勇 胡晓松 邵刚 王宜
陈可冀 郑淑芳 范志红 金世元 高思华
赵霖 宋署芳 吴继红 王凤岐 谢素花

Song Zigang's list of good teachers and friends of medicinal meals

Wang Guilan　Li Wu　Qian He　Zhou Wenquan　Wu Dazhen
Qin Bowei　Xu Yong　Hu Xiaosong　Shao Gang　Wang Yi
Chen Keji　Zheng Shufang　Fan Zhihong　Jin Shiyuan　Gao Sihua
Zhao Lin　Song Shufang　Wu Jihong　Wang Fengqi　Xie Suhua

宋子刚西餐良师益友名录

李胜清 何仁贵 王蜜妮 支振通
腾文元 王宝安 邹志源 栾桂成

Song Zigang's list of good teachers and friends of western food

Li Shengqing　He Rengui　Wang Mini　Zhi Zhentong
Teng Wenyuan　Wang Baoan　Zou Zhiyuan　Luan Guicheng